More Praise for *Impact & Excellence*

"Sheri is the BEST when it comes to measuring outcomes! You can't manage what you don't measure, and if you're not measuring, you can't communicate your nonprofit's impact. Her book *Impact & Excellence* is a must-read for today's executive leaders who want everyone to know the good work their nonprofit is doing."

—**Sandy Rees**, CFRE, nonprofit coach and founder, Get Fully Funded

"As someone who serves as a facilitator, grant writer, and strategist with nonprofit organizations, I know that fresh, relevant data and a strategic measurement process are critical for decision-making. Sheri Chaney Jones has written a practical, easy-to-follow guide for any organization that is ready to take the next step toward excellence. This is a must-read for every nonprofit and government agency leader who is ready to chart their course toward proven, long-term success."

—**Christy Farnbauch**, community engagement strategist, Strategic Links, LLC

"*Impact & Excellence* offers two unique insights not found in other performance management books. In addition to the theoretical, 'What you should do,' Sheri Chaney Jones presents very practical recommendations on how to implement performance management practices. *Impact & Excellence* also provides case studies highlighting how organizations have overcome the unique challenges found in the nonprofit and government sectors to succeed."

—**David Childs**, PhD, City of El Paso Texas tax assessor; author of *Fit for Service*

"Stories matter—they are often the emotional bridge between a donor and the meaningful work of a social sector organization—but stories with data excel. *Impact & Excellence* provides an articulate and compelling rationale for why creating a high-performance culture is necessary for long-term and sustainable success. Using data in the way that Sheri Chaney Jones outlines is powerful. It strengthens the connection between donor and organization and gives practitioners clear guidance to make programmatic decisions that will ultimately change lives."

—**Kerri Laubenthal Mollard**, owner and principal, Mollard Consulting

What is your organization's Measurement Culture Score?

The Measurement Culture Survey helps organizations achieve high-performance measurement cultures. What should your organization be doing differently to increase its impact and excellence? How do you compare to other organizations in using data-driven management strategies to achieve desired results?

Find out your measurement culture score by taking the Measurement Culture Survey. Visit www.impactandexcellence.com and take the survey.

Enter the code below to access the survey and receive a free customized benchmarking report.

Access code: 10152010

IMPACT & EXCELLENCE

Data-Driven Strategies for Aligning Mission, Culture, and Performance in Nonprofit and Government Organizations

SHERI CHANEY JONES

JB JOSSEY-BASS™
A Wiley Brand

Cover design by Wiley

Published by Jossey-Bass
A Wiley Brand

One Montgomery Street, Suite 1200, San Francisco, CA 94104-4594—www.josseybass.com

Jossey-Bass books and products are available through most bookstores. To contact Jossey-Bass directly call our Customer Care Department within the U.S. at 800-956-7739, outside the U.S. at 317-572-3986, or fax 317-572-4002.

Wiley publishes in a variety of print and electronic formats and by print-on-demand. Some material included with standard print versions of this book may not be included in e-books or in print-on-demand. If this book refers to media such as a CD or DVD that is not included in the version you purchased, you may download this material at http://booksupport.wiley.com. For more information about Wiley products, visit www.wiley.com.

Library of Congress Cataloging-in-Publication Data

Jones, Sheri Chaney, 1978-

Impact & excellence : data-driven strategies for aligning mission, culture, and performance in nonprofit and government organizations / Sheri Chaney Jones.

1 online resource.

Includes bibliographical references and index.

Description based on print version record and CIP data provided by publisher; resource not viewed.

ISBN 978-1-118-91119-8 (pdf) — ISBN 978-1-118-91097-9 (epub) —
ISBN 978-1-118-91111-2 (cloth)

1. Nonprofit organizations — Management. 2. Public administration. 3. Leadership. I. Title.

HD62.6
658.4'012—dc23

2014017143

Printed in the United States of America

FIRST EDITION

HB Printing 10 9 8 7 6 5 4 3 2 1

Contents

Foreword

I have had the privilege of working with Sheri Chaney Jones, and I am honored to have been asked to provide a foreword for her book *Impact & Excellence.* Jones worked with me at the Ohio Department of Aging and was instrumental in developing our ability to give Ohio's seniors an opportunity to remain in their own homes, where they prefer to be, even when receiving long-term care. In fact, her use of data allowed our state agency to persuade lawmakers that giving older adults the option to stay home and receive their care there was a significant step in curtailing the unsustainable growth of Ohio's Medicaid budget. I only wish she had been with me throughout my career, as I believe her approach to leadership and agency operations would have resulted in improved outcomes for all those we served and in savings for Ohio's taxpayers.

During my tenure working with nonprofit and government organizations, I often wished for a manual that laid down a path to success in the social service sector. Jones has done that and so much more. In fact, it is tempting to lay out here a summary of the key provisions captured in *Impact & Excellence,* just in case you were to decide to read no further than this. But please read on, as this is one book that every nonprofit and government leader should take in and act on. It is a practical guide to making your way through the maze of change that social-sector agencies now face. Now is the time to apply a more organized, data-driven approach to making decisions about what we do, how we do it, why we do it, and at what cost. We cannot cling to the status quo. In fact, I would posit that there is no status quo today; rather, change is a constant—and if you do not figure out how to achieve excellence as outlined here, you or your organization may not be here tomorrow.

Jones makes a strong case for how a high-performance measurement culture can work for you. She uses a workbook approach that provides an evidence-based formula for change. Her work targets the nonprofit and government social sectors and refutes the assumption that if the social sector acted more like a business we all would be more successful. She doesn't denigrate either nonprofit or government leaders; instead, she emphasizes the societal good that both sectors can produce, if they adapt. Adapting in the twenty-first century requires that you meet the expectations of funders, decision makers, taxpayers, and the general public, all of whom expect you to produce measureable outcomes that concretely contribute to the good of society. She clearly differentiates between the social sector and the business sector, and she lays out what it means to be mission driven rather than profit driven.

Included here are a formula for change and explicit guidelines that can position you and your organization to succeed. The journey to success begins with dissatisfaction with the current state, moves you forward to articulating your vision for the future state, and creates the model for taking the concrete steps necessary to get there. All of this builds on the foundation of collecting, analyzing, and using the right data derived by identifying your desired outcomes and knowing whom you need to persuade. Each chapter in *Impact & Excellence* reads like a workbook, making good use of case studies, citing available online tools, and posing end-of-chapter questions that will make you think and take action. Pay special attention to her chapters on what Jones calls the 5 C's, as those will lead you from what you do to why you do it—the essential building block for success.

My experience with social sector organizations taught me the value of the five C's, but that involved many years, and I believe this book may help you avoid some of the traps and pitfalls I encountered along the way. Jones believes that the hope and promise of a vital social sector begins with becoming clear on your organization's *culture and leadership*, followed by being able to articulate and *clarify your agency mission* and link it to what is important to those you serve. Remember, you serve not just the consumers of your direct service, but also the funders, the decision makers, the general public, and the staff who work with you and share your vision. Next, you must *capture the impact* and link the collected data to the agency mission in order to measure your impact on what you set out to achieve. This data must measure not only the outputs but also the outcomes of your work, and the process does not end with data collection, or even data analysis, but puts the data to use in making decisions about what you will continue to do, what you will change, and what you may choose to abandon.

In presenting her case for data measurement, Jones takes into consideration how you will use that data externally as well as internally. She emphasizes the need to *communicate* what you learn. Tell others why what you do is important, set forth the positive impact your data shows you can have, and share what needs to occur for you to broaden and improve on those outcomes. Finally, the C continuum concludes with *change*—using the data analysis to determine what needs to be done differently to move you closer to excellence. Remember, you chose to read this book because you are unsatisfied with the status quo, you aim for excellence, and you want improvement; all of that equals change, change that you must embrace and sell. And, if you have followed Chaney Jones's outline for excellence, you will find yourself ready to *celebrate* your organization's high performance, borne of creating a new performance model based on data-driven decision making.

I believe *Impact & Excellence* can have a profound positive impact on the societal good you can bring about as an organization, and on your ability to lead your organization to excellence.

Barbara E. Riley
public policy consultant
former director of the Ohio Department of Aging and the Ohio Department of Job and Family Services
Columbus, Ohio

Preface

In God we trust; all others must bring data.
—W. EDWARDS DEMING

Whether we recognize it or not, W. Edwards Deming changed the world when he spoke the words in our opening epigraph. The American statistician and scholar was the first to provide both a philosophy for continual improvement and a method that allowed individuals and organizations to plan for improvement. His work removes blame, redefining mistakes as opportunities for improvement. Deming first helped the world understand the power of data.

Impact & Excellence is my gift to government and nonprofit leaders, who, like Deming, want to change the world in their specific way. This book is for leaders with big dreams, those who fully embrace a mission to solve complex and challenging problems, locally and globally. It is for those who know the status quo is not sustainable and for those who are looking for practical strategies that create more effective and sustainable organizations.

Impact & Excellence is written especially for those leaders who desire to strive for excellence, those who will not stop until they have achieved the greatest degree of impact possible for the constituents and communities they serve. It is the book I wished I had more than ten years ago when I began my career as the deputy director of performance evaluation for a local government organization.

A decade into my career, I had fallen in love with the mission of the social sector. It was a privilege to use my analytical and organizational development skills to help strengthen organizations that were providing services for the greater good. I saw firsthand the good that organizations could do when they adopted cultures built on data, information, and learning.

During this time, I held two separate positions that allowed me to lead the transformation of organizations, helping them to be more impactful by incorporating data-driven strategies. I observed firsthand so many nonprofit and government organizations struggling with how to stay alive financially and obtain the necessary funding. Many were competing for the same coveted grants and missing the power of using data and outcome measurement practices to transform their organizations. *Impact & Excellence* was born from a desire to make a difference for these organizations.

It was in many ways an exercise of courage that would motivate me to leave my stable, responsible government job to start my evaluation and research firm, Measurement Resources, and make an even greater difference. Instead of being of service to just one organization at a time, I desired to serve as many as possible and help social sector organizations to recognize and implement the data-driven strategies I saw having such a clear impact. I wanted then and still want to play some part in transforming the sector into one that is thriving and providing positive, amazing results for communities across our nations and throughout the world.

I knew the power of data and wanted solid data to back up what I had observed firsthand. I decided to launch the Measurement Culture Survey project to gather the data and information that would illustrate clearly what data nonprofit and government organizations were collecting and how those organizations were using the data they collected. My initial motivation was to determine if there was a sufficient need in my immediate community to launch my business and to gather evidence I could share in communicating with prospective clients.

Within six months, I had gathered more than thirty surveys from a variety of nonprofit and government organizations. The survey results were a clear and powerful demonstration of the need; they brought tears to my eyes. I found a strong positive correlation between high measurement cultures and important and critical organizational outcomes. Sitting on these results was not an option.

My next step was further investigation to determine if these relationships would hold up with a larger and even more diverse sample. Four years and two hundred surveys later, the relationship between a high measurement culture and the achievement of desired results within the social sector is striking. If leaders of social sector organizations want what they say they want—increased revenues, increased impact, and increased excellence—then adopting high-performance measurement cultures is the natural, proven path to success.

What really surprised and also saddened me was the low percentage of social sector organizations that had reached a level of high performance and were actively using data to achieve better organizational outcomes. The vast majority of these organizations were missing a huge opportunity to increase the results they achieved for those they served. My research also uncovered the fact that although nonprofit and government leaders knew measures were important, they rarely felt they had the expertise, time, and resources to move forward to implement these measures.

I had a personal framework that allowed me to understand this perception, as both government positions I held were a result of the respective agency directors seeking out this very expertise. My former employers had recognized that to increase their agency's impact they needed to evaluate programs and use program evaluation data to improve program and operational efficiency; yet they did not have the knowledge to do so within the organization.

I was new to the social sector when I took the first position, and unsure of how, specifically, I would apply what I knew to institute a data-driven approach. I had a solid grasp of research methods and organizational development strategies, but the concept of program evaluation and applying data-driven strategies in the social sector was a new challenge. I accepted the challenge, conducting thorough research from as many sources as possible, using what I learned, and tweaking what did not work.

After ten years, I realized I had found the perfect combination of strategies for predictable success. Most of the strategies I have used are not new. Rather, they are borrowed from multiple fields—business, nonprofit, marketing, psychology, public performance, and management, to name a few.

My desire was to share all I had learned with nonprofit and government leaders. My goal was to share not only the theoretical evidence that demonstrated why using data mattered but also to provide resources that offered a path to developing successful, high-performance measurement cultures. I wanted to alleviate the continual searching for a solution in academic books and obscure sources. I saw the clear need for a book written specifically for the nonprofit and government practitioner seeking to master the strategies that would put their organizations on the path of greater impact and excellence.

My intention is that the reader will learn a few key strategies that will strengthen social sector organizations and ultimately drive these organizations toward greater performance. The overarching goal is to improve on how today's nonprofit and government organizations change lives and circumstances by identifying clear steps that make your work more meaningful, more impactful, and more efficient—as well as more fun! And as you do, I believe you will change the world in your own way.

Introduction

Planning for uncertainty asks, "What has already happened that will create the future?"
—PETER DRUCKER

Change is inevitable. It is how people, organizations, and systems adapt to predictable change that determines the degree of success achieved. Successful leaders and managers must do what Peter Drucker (1992) recommends; they must constantly scan the environment and ask one critical question, "What has happened that is likely to create your future?" Major changes are brewing for nonprofit and government organizations. How well social sector organizations respond to the changes at play will directly impact the long-term strength and vitality of the communities they serve.

The economic struggles following the Great Recession of 2008–2009 have resulted in deep repercussions that have had a ripple effect throughout our society. Social sector organizations have been impacted significantly. Charitable giving fell 15 percent during the height of the recession. Although philanthropic giving is coming back slowly, as of 2013 it remained 8 percent below giving levels prior to the recession (Hrywna, 2013). Deep and lasting budget cuts have led to the suspension of vital programs and the marginalization of needed services. Such diluted impact is not only undesirable, it is unsustainable. Without radical intervention, local communities and individuals will pay the ultimate price.

In addition to a decline in corporate philanthropy and government grant making, several other changes have occurred.

Even as social sector leaders seek to address the situation and funders justify drastic budget cuts, philanthropic leaders are urging nonprofits and even government organizations to become more entrepreneurial and strive to be more business-minded. At the local level, there are conversations about the importance of social entrepreneurship.

Meanwhile, grant makers are urging nonprofit organizations to consider how they can move away from a dependency on public funds and grants and develop for-profit arms that channel money into these organizations. One well-known organization using this model is Goodwill. The organization operates thrift stores and auto auctions in communities across the country. These profit centers support their social programs, which are designed to increase employment for several disadvantaged populations served by the organization.

A tendency to cling to the status quo has led to the closure of many nonprofits. Budget constraints, political pressures, shifting corporate priorities, undesirable media attention, and technological challenges are among the present-day challenges that will continue to impact the future for this sector. As of the writing of this book, the national debt hovers around seventeen trillion dollars. The question of how we will reduce this debt for future generations looms large. Intense public debate rages from all sides. Regardless of who is elected to public office, government officials will need to make difficult funding reduction decisions.

Mario Morino's observations in *Leap of Reason* (2011) highlight the situation: "The cold reality is that in our present era of unsustainable debts and deficits, our nation simple will not be able to justify huge subsidies for social sector activities and entities without more assurance that they're on track to realize results . . . Funders will have to make the difficult choices about what to fund and what to cut."

The mass media's frequent focus on the purported ineffectiveness of various charitable and government functions and their influence on the public's perception of the social sector continues to fuel this new reality. Recent examples range from media coverage of battles over public workers' rights nationwide to collective bargaining in Ohio and Wisconsin. The movie *Waiting for Superman* highlighted the alleged ineffectiveness of U.S. public schools.

The 2009 ACORN scandal and the debate over the effectiveness of Head Start programs have further eroded public confidence in the social sector. News coverage related to each of these has negatively influenced public debate and sentiments.

A recent conversation about this book underscores the influence of media on public perception. When I shared an early working title for this book, which included the term "social sector," a friend expressed serious concern. "Why do you want to write a book for the social sector?" she asked. "Don't you know that sector is ineffective and wasting my taxpayer dollars?" When I probed further, I found she had formed such strong opinions based on negative press reports during recent political debates. Regardless of whether one agrees with her assessment, my friend's perception is one shared by many in our society. Yet she and many others are the very individuals nonprofit and government organizations rely on to fund and support their organizations.

To remain viable, today's social sector organizations must find a way to rise above declining public confidence and stand strong on their own merits. Despite the stark reality, the future is not necessarily bleak for organizations that remain dedicated to filling the gaps where for-profit companies cannot. For communities to thrive, we must address issues such as housing, health care, education, public safety, arts, and culture.

An exciting new world awaits leaders who dare to think differently. Those organizational leaders who are willing to adapt to rapidly unfolding changes and strive for increased excellence and impact are making our world a better place. They refuse to wait on either the public or the media to make the case for funding. Such successful leaders are becoming more strategic and thoughtful as they demonstrate and communicate their unarguable value.

Even in today's volatile economic climate, change *is* possible. One example: while most government and nonprofit organizations were cutting programs and services, leaders of the Ohio Department of Aging invested in and vigorously pursued excellence and impact. The organization successfully transitioned from the typical system of managing revenues and activities to a high-performance measurement culture that focused on constituents' needs and outcomes.

As a result of this transformation, the state agency restored program funding after it was cut following an unprecedented, statewide budget crisis. The Ohio Department of Aging simultaneously held administrative overhead to less than 3 percent of its total budget and provided high-quality services that diverted seniors from nursing homes and allowed them to continue living in their own homes. These actions saved the state approximately $250 million dollars over the course of a year (Jones, 2010).

Why does this matter on a national and global scale? Imagine a world where government and nonprofit organizations are fully realizing their respective missions—eradicating disease, minimizing personal and societal hardships, and strengthening communities. What if, as a result of effectiveness throughout the social sector, the public's tax burden decreased and our individual quality of life increased? Such a world *can* exist. It begins with the embrace of a culture of excellence supported by data-driven outcomes measurement within every nonprofit and government organization.

Contrary to public opinion, the answer does not begin with social sector organizations adopting the operating procedures of private enterprise. As we have seen on a massive scale in recent years, the private sector does not have it all figured out.

What is the answer? How can nonprofits and government organizations move forward? For too long our society has chosen to invest in nonprofits with our hearts instead of our heads. The secret of social sector success can be found in allowing our heads to lead us where our hearts want to go.

Data-driven outcomes measurement in the context of a high-performance measurement culture lays the foundation for repeatable, achievable results within individual organizations and rolls out a red carpet for radical transformation throughout the social sector as a whole.

As greater numbers of mission-driven organizations implement a measurement culture, our nation and our world will see the impact and excellence in an ever-increasing number of changed lives and communities. To succeed and sustain success in this time of economic and social upheaval, social sector organizations must operate more efficiently, measuring and communicating unique impact. They must become more entrepreneurial, more collaborative, and, ultimately, more strategic.

Impact and Excellence: Data-Driven Strategies for Aligning Mission, Culture, and Performance in Nonprofit and Government Organizations examines the current landscape and provides a roadmap for nonprofit and government organizations that recognize the necessity of adopting a high-performance measurement culture now so that they may ensure their continued survival and success. This book presents the case for change infused at every level of the organization, beginning internally with executive leadership and externally with the funding community that enables an organization to sustain its mission and vitality. Without consistent attention to the strategies outlined in this book, business-as-usual nonprofit organizations will become extinct, the impact gap will widen, and society will suffer.

Through the citation of statistical evidence and compelling case studies, this book lays out a clear path for the way forward, providing a roadmap for increasing efficiency in social sector organizations. Drawing on my own experience of working side by side with government and nonprofit organizations, most recently in my role as president of Measurement Resources, this book culls research gathered from a four-year study and distills the surprising findings into easy-to-digest, actionable success strategies for the leaders of today's government and nonprofit organizations.

Despite waning public perception and real challenges, success is possible for every social sector organization. Furthermore, in stark contrast to the link between money and market success seen in the for-profit sector, there is no correlation between successful high-performance measurement cultures and budget size in nonprofit and government organizations.

Currently, a scant 23 percent of government and nonprofit organizations are fully engaged in the proven practices that lead to an increase in revenues, positive press, and improved efficiency, leaving significant room for improvement at the remaining 77 percent of social sector organizations. This book is intended to equip committed public and social sector leaders with critical information and knowledge that will allow the organizations they serve to thrive in the twenty-first century and beyond.

When leaders implement the same critical elements used by the Ohio Department of Aging and other high-performing social sector organizations outlined in this book, the result is nothing short of the transformation of our culture. Leaders no longer need to guess what to do first. *Impact & Excellence* provides a proven step-by-step plan for organizations to make such a transition.

The remainder of this book combines the technical elements of outcomes management, strategic planning principles, change theory, and real-world research written from the perspective of the public servant and nonprofit leader. Through data-driven conclusions and clear strategies for rapid organizational improvement, *Impact & Excellence* is a contributor to the shift that is imperative to the very survival of today's social sector organizations, providing proven practices that organizational leaders can implement immediately.

Overview

Chapter One of this book examines the call to be more strategic and presents the case for embracing change, not from a place of fear but rather with a spirit of opportunity. The funders of today and tomorrow will require organizations both to demonstrate impact and outcomes and to detail precise plans for the evaluation of efficient use of those funds. This chapter provides case studies of both government and nonprofit organizations and highlights how the new reality affords an opportunity for increased impact and excellence within, through, and among those organizations committed to the full embrace of a high-performance measurement culture.

The next two chapters draw on original research conducted with over two hundred nonprofit and government organizations. These chapters underscore the clear differences between social sector organizations content with "good enough" and those dedicated to excellence, demonstrating by the numbers that embracing an organizational culture built around performance and outcomes measurement is the defining differential between mediocre and thriving organizations.

Organizations with a high-performance measurement culture report success in terms of increased revenues, a boost in morale and efficiency, positive press, and overall impact at a much higher rate than those that have not yet embraced such cultures. Despite these remarkable findings, only 23 percent of social-sector organizations surveyed are fully implementing the easy and impactful steps to embrace a measurement culture.

Chapters Four and Five address the similarities and differences between nonprofit organizations and government organizations that opt to develop high-performance measurement cultures. The Measurement Culture Survey research suggests that these two types of social sector organizations are more similar than different when it comes to establishing high-performance measurement cultures. However, when we consider what data to use and how to use that data, each type of organization has its own specific strengths and challenges. These chapters will discuss the different audiences for the data of government and nonprofit organizations and the types of actions that organizations need to take with data.

Chapter Six provides an overview of the exact plan any organization can follow to become a high-performance measurement culture. We will review the Five C's of Easy and Effective Impact and Excellence and lay the foundation for greater success throughout the social sector. Chapter Six speaks directly to social sector readers' current reality, acknowledging the real and significant barriers to developing a measurement culture, specifically those limitations related to time, resources, trained staff, and expertise within the organization. Although such limitations do exist, they can be overcome. This chapter introduces real-world success stories to inspire readers to rise above excuses and take decisive action.

The remaining six chapters, Chapters Seven through Twelve, provide detail about each of the five essential C's, which are the elements of success and reveal the specific strategies required to catapult the social sector from one that is merely sufficient to one that is efficient and has remarkable, far-reaching influence. These are the precise strategies that can and should be implemented by every government and nonprofit agency to ensure a successful future. These proven and practical steps go beyond other "call to action" books on outcomes and performance measures. The ideas and strategies in this book are categorized into the "Five C's": Culture and Leadership; Clarify Mission; Capture Impact; Communicate Value; and Change and Celebrate. These substantive chapters introduce actionable, easy-to-implement solutions that often lead to sweeping change within organizations and the communities they serve.

The final chapter invites organizational leaders to develop a unique action plan tailored to their organization's particular circumstance, based on a proven planning framework. Readers are encouraged to work through a series of experiences and templates to identify first steps toward predictable success, impact, and excellence.

Impact & Excellence contains the specific leadership, organizational culture, and outcomes measurement secrets that will help any organization excel in this challenging new environment. From the all-volunteer organization to those that manage federal programs of $50 million dollars or more, organizational leaders will discover that not only is greater impact and excellence possible in today's challenging social sector environment, but it is predictable when data-driven strategies are applied. By applying focus and determination to the process of moving toward high-performance measurement cultures, government and nonprofit organizations can and will be transformed. In turn, a thriving social sector will potentially transform whole communities and perhaps, in time, our nation.

IMPACT
& EXCELLENCE

1

Social-Sector Impact and Excellence

The Call to Be More Strategic

Ask not what your country can do for you; ask what you can do for your country.
—JOHN F. KENNEDY

OVER FIFTY YEARS AGO, American citizens took President John F. Kennedy's ringing words to heart. In the years since, the number of registered tax-exempt organizations working to solve our country's most serious problems has grown by an astonishing 600 percent—from 200,000 organizations in the 1960s (Hall and Burke, 2002) to over 1.4 million in 2013 (National Center for Charitable Statistics, 2013).

In recent years, these organizations have faced much higher scrutiny of their value and societal impact than ever before. National, state, and local governments can no longer afford to fund initiatives simply because they propose a viable solution. Today, both public and nonprofit organizations are being asked to articulate, justify, and defend what they are doing for the country beyond consuming valuable resources. Funders expect organizations to clearly demonstrate how programs and services are making an impact. Effective measurement and communication of outcomes are essential components of future funding success across the social sector.

What quantifiable and socially desirable changes have occurred as a result of a particular programmatic or organizational effort? How was behavior changed, knowledge increased, the community strengthened, and quality of life enhanced? In other words, did the organization and its programmatic effort fulfill its stated mission? And to what degree were the anticipated results achieved? These are the central questions that must be raised about today's social sector organizations.

The Imperative of Managing to Outcomes

Funders are rapidly modifying grant application processes to include program outcomes along with a plan for the measurement and evaluation of those outcomes. Such expectations extend beyond government grants. Large corporate foundations are shifting requirements as well. One example: while many online grant applications had begun to shrink the physical space allowed for organizations to present the case for funding, Chase Bank now allows applicants approximately ten pages to capture the programmatic impact of previous grants and demonstrate a clear return on investment.

Some funders are providing substantial, unrestricted funding to those nonprofit organizations that align with the funder's mission and can demonstrate clearly how programs are achieving desired results. The Edna McConnell Clark Foundation provides an example. The foundation chooses and structures its investments largely on the basis of empirical evidence that a potential grantee's programs helps economically disadvantaged young people get an education, hold a job, or avoid risky behaviors (Edna McConnell Clark Foundation, 2013).

In order for a nonprofit to be considered for a multiyear investment designed for significant capital growth, it must demonstrate that the organization systematically collects data and verifies, on the basis of this internal data, that young people are benefiting from a particular program. Grantees must show the potential to produce a higher level of evidence through ongoing measurement, such as conducting an independent evaluation of the program's effectiveness within the designated investment period.

Social-sector organizations that are thriving in this new reality are communicating impact and value in a clear and compelling fashion. These government and nonprofit organizations frequently turn to numbers to make the case for the investment of both public and private funding. Those serving in key roles at such leading-edge organizations are willing to engage in difficult conversations rooted in the facts.

Demonstrating value requires more than gathering client testimonials that speak to the effective delivery of a needed service. This type of data works well for communication materials, but it does not ensure immunity to funding cuts. For an illustration of this reality, we can examine what has happened in recent years to those organizations focused on arts education.

In general, people enjoy the arts and share the view that students increase their artistic skill in such programs. Yet these organizations have suffered significant program budget cuts. Why? Funding has decreased because many of these organizations have failed to offer solid data or proof about how programs and services solve community problems or address priorities identified by funders. The lack of concrete evidence makes it easier for funders to justify the elimination of funding support to these organizations.

This reality extends to all social-sector organizations. Successful organizations remain ahead of the curve in measuring and communicating outcomes. They adopt systems that align performance measures with both the organization's mission and the funder's priorities. Successful government agencies and nonprofit organizations share success stories that use a combination of facts and anecdotes.

The case study that follows traces the story of how a strong Medicaid-funded organization might make the case for funding and offers one example of a success story. By focusing on relevant and important outcomes, this hypothetical organization will significantly improve its chances of obtaining adequate funding. Notice the use of hard data and numbers in this example.

Making the Funding Case: A Case Study

Our program serves ten thousand seniors, providing nursing-home level as well as long-term care services and supports to patients in their own home. Without these services, 60 percent of our clients would require care in nursing homes. The remaining 40 percent would require a child or family member to quit a job or make significant economic sacrifices were they to continue to provide care.

Our programs are provided at one-third the cost of nursing home care, saving an estimated $180 million annually in state Medicaid spending. We achieve this by keeping approximately six thousand seniors out of nursing homes. With federal and state Medicaid dollars received, we employ one hundred people and reinvest more than $3.5 million back into our communities through salaries. In addition, we contract with nine local home care agencies, which collectively employ more than 270 direct care workers who provide critical care to the seniors in our communities.

These relationships result in the infusion of an additional $6.7 million back into our local community in the form of salaries. Because employees no longer need to take off from work to provide care for their loved ones, employers save an additional $40 million in annual turnover and absenteeism costs. In addition, our programs reduce the length of hospital stays and readmits for those served by a full 30 percent compared to those who do not receive our services, saving an additional $50 million annually in Medicare spending.

A Closer Look. This case statement clearly demonstrates this program's unarguable impact. A cut to this program could result in more than 370 individuals becoming unemployed and consequently result in the likely tapping of unemployment resources. Ten local businesses would face significant economic trouble should funding be discontinued. Cutting funding to this organization would also result in an increase of over $180 million dollars in state Medicaid spending for nursing home care and a possible additional $50 million in Medicaid spending due to extended hospital stays.

Furthermore, without the continuation of funds, approximately six thousand seniors would be forced to leave their homes and move into nursing homes. Approximately four thousand families would suddenly need to cope with the stress of determining how to manage and afford care for their loved ones, resulting in a potential $40 million burden on local employers.

This organization brings indisputable value to many stakeholders—area employers, aging seniors, individuals caring for loved ones, policy makers, politicians, and employees. The organization has successfully demonstrated its program's benefit to the community with numbers that correspond to issues of primary concern to funders. These numbers also track back to the specific problems the funder wishes to solve and are tied to the specific communities the funder desires to serve. Crafting this type of narrative may not make an organization immune to funding cuts, but it will ensure that decision makers and taxpayers alike understand the true consequences of their investment decisions.

Embracing a Measurement Culture

While the preceding illustration is inspiring and provides a goal for today's social-sector organizations to strive for, it is important to avoid being fooled by the simplicity of the result. Creating an organizational culture that consistently measures and communicates impact and value is far more complex than simply hiring an evaluator or analyst to consolidate and crunch numbers. To truly achieve and sustain impact, organizations must shift the underlying organizational culture and make deep, systemic changes.

Change is difficult for all involved. But the sweetness of sustained success often more than compensates for the temporary inconvenience of embracing such change. The research and evidence needed for today's social-sector leaders to take the first step toward a new future is available now. The chapters that follow provide a step-by-step, strategic plan for those government and nonprofit organizations that seek to attract the investment of time and dollars and lead the sector to a higher level of impact and excellence.

Three Critical Components of Sustained Change

The motivation to create and sustain real change is a function of three factors. The first of these is *dissatisfaction with the current state.* This is followed by the *articulation of a clear vision* that includes a statement of what is possible. Finally, an organization must take the first concrete steps toward *achieving the stated vision* (Beckhard, 1969). All three factors must be present in order for an organization to overcome its natural resistance to change.

If we are to realize the vision of a thriving social sector composed of highly effective, efficient, and impactful government and nonprofit organizations, executives, program leaders, and staff must work in concert to adopt high-performance measurement cultures. High-performing social-sector organizations not only measure and communicate outcomes but also effectively use collected data to retain employees, attract donors, win grants, and secure positive press. They expand services and operations. The work these new and improved social-sector organizations do will change lives and strengthen communities in an unprecedented and unparalleled ways. Results not yet seen within the sector will soon be realized when high-performance measurement cultures become the norm rather than the exception.

The journey to impact and excellence requires more than a set of metrics and spreadsheets. Specific leadership skills and strategies will ensure that the ideal measures and tactics empower organizations to become more effective and efficient. However, rushing to action without a full understanding of the situation at hand could prove detrimental. Before adopting a plan to move from the current state to the desired state—one where impacts are clearly communicated and social-sector organizations are richly rewarded for achieving such impacts—crucial elements must be put in place.

The Next Step

Social-sector organizations must first understand where they currently stand in terms of reaching their desired goal of impact and excellence. The next two chapters take an in-depth look at the desired future state and the current reality of many government and nonprofit organizations and in the social sector as a whole. Chapter Two includes a thorough examination of the barriers that keep organizations from the success they desire and demonstrates how it is possible for organizations to overcome common barriers to success.

Impact & Excellence

Chapter One Discussion Questions

1. What changes in your organization's environment have already occurred and are likely to impact your organization's future? Consider the following areas:
   a. Funding changes
   b. Emerging "best practices"
   c. Federal and state policy changes
   d. Public interests and opinion
   e. Population shifts
   f. Other changes
2. What is the public's current perception of your organization's effectiveness? Do individuals in your community have an awareness and opinion of your organization? If given an opportunity to do so, can you prove, defend, or debunk the prevailing attitude or perception?
3. What is your organization's inarguable value? What would happen if your organization closed its doors tomorrow? Who would be impacted? What absence would be felt? What gap might be experienced? Would anyone care or notice?

2

The Imperative Future State

High-Performance Measurement Cultures

Culture is one of the most precious things a company has, so you must work harder on it than anything else.
—HERB KELLEHER, FOUNDER, SOUTHWEST AIRLINES

SIGNIFICANT CHANGE IN THE SOCIAL SECTOR will occur only as each individual organization embraces a culture of excellence. What are the potential rewards of high-performance measurement cultures throughout the sector? The creation of more jobs. Quality-of-life improvements at every level of society. Children, families, and communities thriving as organizational programs and services meet their stated goals. This is the promise of the desired future state of our nation's social sector fulfilled.

The economic impact is equally significant. As more organizations implement the operational standards of high-performance measurement cultures, reliance on government funds will decrease. Social service organizations funded by government dollars will effectively address the problems that are most on the hearts and minds of taxpayers. As organizations adopt the principles of a high-performance measurement culture, they will naturally divert participants from costly programs and services to more desirable, more effective, and more affordable services.

Similarly, nonprofits will easily attract private, corporate, and government funding as a result of the proven impact of high-quality programming. Churches, civic groups, and volunteers will gladly support and assist these vital organizations in communities nationwide. Newspapers, television stations, and social media channels will consistently highlight successful organizations as positive forces for good in their respective communities. Similar organizations will look to increasingly effective programs as models to be emulated, and elected officials will be more inclined to invest public dollars in support of these programs.

As more and more organizations navigate the shift toward a high-performance measurement culture, the limitation of resources and struggles with staff morale that plague so many nonprofit organizations and government agencies will begin to dissipate. Likewise, when organizations embrace measurement cultures, quality staff will flock to them, recognizing these government and nonprofit organizations as places of real change and impact. The vital contributors to the organization will be thrilled to apply their individual and collective talents and skills to make a difference. Perhaps most important, the resulting motivated social-sector workforce will attain the consistent levels of excellence, quality, and innovation that will drive individual organizations to provide even greater value on a streamlined budget.

The Path Forward: Toward the Desired Future State

The realization of this larger vision depends upon individual organizations. Changes within those organizations originate from leaders equipped to articulate a clear vision and common course for the future. Today's social-sector organizations can find a new way forward as they engage in dialogue and conversation focused on two critical questions:

What does it mean for our organization to embrace a culture of impact and excellence?

What will happen when we achieve a culture of impact and excellence?

Before any organization can implement change, it must articulate and embrace a shared understanding of mission and future goals. The organization's stakeholders must rally around a compelling vision for the future. Later chapters lay out a step-by-step plan for embracing a data-driven approach, exploring The Five C's of Easy and Effective Impact and Excellence:

1. Culture and leadership
2. Clarify mission
3. Capture impact
4. Communicate value
5. Change and celebrate

Before we turn to these specific strategies, we will lay a firm foundation for a high-performance measurement culture.

Skeptics often dismiss the vision just described as nothing more than a pipe dream. Despite their disbelief, success is possible. Throughout the book, we will examine organizations of every scope and size that have successfully navigated the transition to a high-performance measurement culture. The following case study illustrates that such radical change is, in fact, achievable.

Dallas County Tax Office: A Case Study

Like many social-sector organizations in the past decade, the Dallas County Tax Office saw the demand for their agency's services triple during a short time frame in recent years. In spite of this dramatic increase of work, the organization found ways to operate with a smaller staff, improve morale, and control budget growth, all while substantially increasing customer satisfaction. By adopting a high-performance measurement culture, this government organization was able to reach impressive milestones. The number of staff was reduced from 234 to 230 and the annual budget growth held steady at 3.3 percent, less than inflation with the standard cost-of-living adjustment. In contrast, two other county departments experienced an average growth of 10.93 percent and 11.47 percent respectively during the same time frame (Childs, 2010).

While similar organizations experienced even more dramatic staff reductions, the Dallas County Tax Office minimized the effect of staff cuts as it simultaneously increased both morale and productivity. As administrator Dr. David Childs focused his team on providing quality services, staff attendance jumped from just over 90 percent to 97 percent, and the number of staff exceeding exemplary performance standards increased from just five staff members in 2003 to seventy-eight four years later in 2007.

Customer satisfaction also increased substantially. Average customer wait time dropped from more than eight minutes to just over three minutes. Personal complaints decreased from an average of five per day to a single complaint per week. Unsolicited written compliments from the public were up from 24 in 1998 to 221 in 2006, an unprecedented 820-percent increase.

A Closer Look. The Dallas County Tax Office case study offers proof that organizations can rise above the stereotypical stressed-out, overworked, underpaid, and underappreciated social-sector model. Government agencies do not have to be inefficient bureaucracies with low morale and poor service. If success is possible for one organization, it is possible for any organization willing to invest in its future and make the necessary shifts. The inevitable response to what philanthropist and social-sector advocate Mario Morino (2011) has called the "era of scarcity" does not have to involve program shutdowns and staff layoffs.

The Secret to Success

What did Dr. Childs' team and the leaders of similar organizations do differently to achieve success? The success of these organizations corresponds to an internal culture shift. These organizations established high-performance measurement cultures marked by innovation, strategic thinking, and consistent management to outcomes.

Organizational culture constitutes the shared values that guide an organization's decisions and actions. Culture is composed of and influenced by an organization's rituals and rewards along with its stories and legends. Together, these provide staff and stakeholders with clear—though often unspoken—guidelines on what behaviors are acceptable and unacceptable for the organization as a whole and for individual contributors to the organization.

Why does culture matter? In high-performance measurement cultures, shared assumptions, actions, and decisions revolve around consistently striving for greater success and quantifiable improvement. There is a belief that the quickest path to greater impact comes through seeking objective performance data and using that data to effect change. There is a "doing whatever it takes to achieve our mission" attitude among organizational leaders and staff.

In successful social-sector organizations, the culture is consciously planned to align every process, system, and resource to maximize effectiveness. The success of high-performance measurement cultures is often built on a desire on the part of leaders and staff members to exceed expectations and obtain remarkable results. Mediocrity is unacceptable in organizations that embrace a high-performance measurement culture. Instead, a shared culture of excellence drives members to higher and higher standards of performance.

Revenues and Expenditures

In the private, for-profit sector, higher standards of performance are typically equated with reducing costs and increasing sales. Systems and structures typically are built to achieve outcomes that lead to higher profits. By contrast, high performance is not measured by sales and profits in nonprofit and government organizations that have truly adopted cultures that lead to greater impact for clients and communities.

How nonprofit organizations define "high performance" greatly influences the results the social sector will obtain. Because many nonprofit boards are composed of successful for-profit executives, social-sector organizations often attempt to run the nonprofit like a corporation and manage to higher profits. This is often a fatal mistake.

Taxpayers and funders support social-sector organizations for specific reasons. Almost always, funders are investing in desirable social change. When a social-sector organization focuses solely on increasing revenues and decreasing expenditures, it often fails to focus on the core of its mission, such as the provision of services to an aging population, children, addicts, and individuals in local communities. Decisions to maximize revenues often adversely affect the very populations that organizational leaders seek to serve. When nonprofit organizations revert to for-profit thinking models, they often fail to successfully deliver on their mission, and they quickly lose support from their donor base.

Instead of seeing the desired end result, revenues are merely inputs adopted to achieve the organization's mission. Instead of managing only to revenues, social-sector leaders with successful high-performance cultures establish measures linked to organizational outcomes. Those outcomes are defined by the organization's unique impact and value to society. Success measures are discussed more thoroughly later in this book.

Components of Outcomes Management

High-performance cultures and outcomes management go hand in hand in the social sector. Funders require outcomes and strategies aligned to those outcomes, and high-performance measurement cultures built on a solid strategic foundation require outcomes measurement to increase performance. Too many leaders believe that managing to outcomes is simply a matter of establishing performance metrics and running reports. While these activities are a vital part of the solution, embracing a successful culture requires more than surface changes.

When the measures aligned to the organization's unique mission are combined with the right culture, organizations begin to realize drastically different results from those achieved by peer organizations—even those with the almost identical resources and workforces. Driven and supported by organizational leaders, the value of such measures are communicated clearly and embraced at every level of the successful social-sector organization.

High-performance organizations go a step further, leveraging data and information to influence employee decisions and invite actions consistent with organizational expectations. Measurement systems bring together staff and stakeholders and make each contributor feel part of the organizational experience. Leaders use such systems to help employees and stakeholders to both track what happens in an organization and also evaluate why things happen.

In addition, a robust measurement culture includes an adaptive culture that has its finger on the pulse of both internal and external factors. An organization with a robust and high-performance measurement culture will continuously refine its approach based on new information and changing conditions.

Individual Performance Standards

As highlighted earlier in this chapter, the Dallas County Tax Collector's Office achieved a high-performance measurement culture by implementing a straightforward and cost-effective performance measurement system. After identifying the right measures for the organization as a whole, the leadership team created timely, positive, and motivational performance measures to assess individual performance on a monthly basis. When individual performance measures were achieved, staff members received monthly performance bonuses funded through resources that had previously been allocated for a vacant position. Targets were reasonably set at the desired level of performance, and organizational leaders communicated a clear desire for each employee to meet these goals and receive the bonuses.

The staff was motivated to achieve higher levels of success. Employees valued the bonuses and understood they were providing high-quality services and helping citizens as a part of targeted outcomes. They received monthly feedback on how they were achieving these goals relative to the organization's mission. They also could review comparison data in relation to peer performance. This motivated them to work harder and achieve even greater success (Childs, 2010).

The Dallas County Tax Collector's Office's performance measurement system proved successful precisely because it was used for positive reinforcement. The focus was on improvement. Employees were not punished for unmet targets. Rather, small and predictable rewards came to those who reached identified targets.

As potential employees learned about departments that rewarded employees for their efforts and performance, more highly qualified applicants began to apply for positions. Dallas County departments attracted and retained self-motivated, conscientious employees. This cycle of improvement led to greater success, improved cohesion, and increased efficiencies for agencies countywide.

Preparing for Lasting Success

What has worked for one organization does not always equate to success for all organizations. Chasing the latest management fad can prove to be an unwise practice. As a general rule, it is unadvisable for leaders to change course and invest in new practices based solely on the perceptions of another organization's success, as systemic change is both difficult and expensive. One organization's experience does not provide enough evidence to guarantee universal success. Success is often specific to the particular conditions in the organization that achieved a desired result.

Throughout my career, I had worked closely with several forward-thinking government and social-sector leaders who had adopted high-performance measurement cultures based on the foundation of strong measurement. These organizations were implementing systemic and meaningful data systems to catapult their success. Although strikingly different in terms of mission and activities (for one organization, a focus on public safety, juvenile justice, child abuse, and divorce; for the other organization, on increasing choice, independence, and quality of life for seniors), the results achieved by two of the organizations were quite similar. In the case study that follows, we examine this in greater detail.

Two Organizations Embrace a Measurement Culture: A Case Study

At the outset of their respective projects, both organizations had few management practices for performance improvement that used measures and outcomes well. There was no clear process for collecting and using data. Like many other organizations, both of these had access to databases that contained information on clients and services. Yet each lacked a system to analyze and use the collected data.

In the course of working with leadership and program staff to identify the best data to collect and analyze, we needed to confront what author Jim Collins (2001) has called "the brutal facts." As the respective leadership teams acknowledged the less-than-desirable existing situations and began to embrace a culture of change, both experienced significant results and improvement. As a result of instituting a data-driven approach, one organization identified which of its programs were achieving outcomes and which were not. Leaders began to highlight successes, then asked for and received increased grant funding for programs that were working well. They successfully implemented changes to improve those programs that were not functioning to the highest level.

Through these efforts, the organization discovered that a program that released youth early from juvenile confinement and provided intensive wrap-around services to youth and family members was having tremendous success in decreasing recidivism and costs. Evaluation data was used to lobby for another staff person, thereby expanding capacity and allowing the organization and its staff to serve an even greater number of at-risk children while at the same time reducing government expenditures that flowed to the organization's programs and services.

In a few cases, evaluation data revealed that, even after significant changes, a program was not an effective solution for the identified problem. When leaders were unable to make the appropriate changes and yield quantifiable results, they made the difficult decision to discontinue underperforming programs. Although painful, such decisions allowed the organization to reinvest an ineffective $240,000 into programs that achieved far greater success and met identified outcomes.

In another case, evaluation data revealed that one program was unintentionally harming the very children it sought to serve. The program introduced lower-risk juveniles to negative peers whom these first-time offenders might not otherwise have encountered. Shockingly, program leaders discovered that this court-ordered program was actually doing damage rather than improving the situation. These findings allowed appropriate changes to be made. Lives were improved and, in some cases, potentially saved.

Within a government agency focused on an aging population, data and outcomes were quickly becoming the norm due to the director's strong leadership capacity. Data was evaluated and acted upon, resulting in significant savings to the state's Medicaid program. Thanks to the strong leadership and the adoption of a high-performance measurement culture, this department was able to progress beyond only reporting on activities performed.

As department leaders shifted their focus to outcomes, they were able to calculate their positive impact on the citizens, using data to demonstrate how these programs saved taxpayer dollars. In just a few years, the results of data-driven efforts led to increased positive press and a boost in confidence and pride in the significant impact of their work. This created space for the free flow of information needed to establish successful, collaborative partnerships.

A Closer Look. The positive experiences of these two organizations seemed atypical to the leaders of similar agencies and organizations. In reality, these organizations had made a shift and were taking action in a manner different from that of the organizations around them. As a result, they experienced more favorable results. Their success called attention to the struggles shared by similar organizations. The majority of nonprofit organizations and government agencies implement strategies without ever examining the data, so they cannot communicate clear outcomes. In some cases, the decisions of organizational leaders negatively impacted their organization's success.

As I witnessed the cycles being perpetuated in the other organizations, I began to consider how I might help more nonprofit and government organizations realize what was missing and determine the blocks to the achievement of greater success. The skeptics' questions lingered. Was it truly the transformation to a data-driven culture that made the most significant difference for social-sector organizations seeking greater impact and excellence? Would it have been possible for these two organizations that I served to have received new funding, improved their productivity, increased staff satisfaction, and demonstrated significant taxpayer savings without performance measures and clear evaluation systems?

I set out on a quest to validate my life's work and to disprove both my internal skeptic and the many external voices claiming that a turnaround for the social sector was not only improbable but impossible. I did what every good organizational researcher does. I conducted a study.

A Journey to Truth: Collecting the Data on Data-Driven Cultures

The Measurement Culture Survey Project arose from a desire to statistically demonstrate that high-performance measurement cultures were more than just the latest fad. After more than a decade of experience assisting nonprofit and government agencies as they incorporated a data-driven approach and used the information they collected to improve services and operations, Measurement Resources set out to verify that measurement cultures were the determining factor correlated to social-sector success.

The survey project was designed to examine the extent to which government and nonprofit organizations were currently embracing a measurement culture and to discover how such a culture impacted organizational outcomes. Some evidence already suggested an important link between a strong measurement culture and programmatic success. Before designing a survey instrument, Measurement Resources Company turned to the literature.

In his research for the best-selling *Good to Great*, Jim Collins (2001) found that great organizations "gather and use the brutal facts" in their decision-making process. Collins' assertion seemed to support my theory that the organizations with which I had been working were realizing different outcomes due to their embrace of a measurement culture. When compared to other organizations that were not engaged in fact gathering and analysis, these organizations certainly stood out as exemplary. Their effectiveness or "greatness" was directly linked to efforts that created a culture in which decisions were based on specific and ongoing outcome measures and evaluations.

A successful culture does more than collect data, however; it also adopts a system for synthesizing, using, and communicating the collected data. This second step is a crucial differentiator. Two published articles influenced the design of the questions that would appear on the final Measurement Culture Survey. The first was an important study conducted by Jo An Zimmerman and Bonnie Stevens (2006). Funded by the W.K. Kellogg Foundation, this study examined the use of performance measurement in South Carolina nonprofit organizations. A second study, conducted by Joanne Carman and Kimberly Fredericks (2010), examined the evaluation capacity of nonprofit organizations. Questions gleaned from the results of these two studies informed the creation of Measurement Resources' Measurement Culture Survey.

The Measurement Culture Survey sought to measure the type of data organizations collected, determine how often they conducted evaluations, and identify how they used collected data to effect change within the organization. These three factors defined the strength of an organization's measurement culture. The survey also assessed the relationship between having a high-performance measurement culture and important organizational outcomes. Questions focused on the following organizational results:

- Increased revenues
- Implementation of organizational change
- Improvement in internal relationships
- Improvement in staff morale
- Improvement in external relationships
- Improvement in positive press
- Increased operational efficiency
- Strengthening of organizational culture

The survey captured the demographics of the organizations, including size, budget, and growth rate over a two-year period as well as projected growth in next two years. The survey also collected information on the type of organization as well as data on the organization's focus and mission.

The Measurement Culture Survey was offered on the Measurement Resources website (www.measurementresouresco.com) over a two-year period and was shared with various online groups serving social-sector organizations. Each respondent who provided and validated an organizational name, title, and e-mail address received a complimentary Benchmark Report. To date, data has been collected from more than two hundred organizations across the Unites States and Canada.

The Survey Says

Examples similar to the case study presented earlier were replicated again and again in the Measurement Culture Survey research. The bottom-line determination of this seminal study was this: *Success is possible for every social-sector organization, and that success is directly correlated to the full embrace of a high-performance measurement culture.*

Data-driven organizations find success with greater speed and efficiency than those organizations that fail to collect data and accurately respond to it. The following results make this much clear: government and nonprofit leaders no longer have an excuse to resist the investment in time and resources required to transform their organizations to high-performance measurement cultures.

The survey grouped organizations into three categories: high, medium, and low measurement cultures.

High-Performance Measurement Culture Organizations

About a quarter of the organizations surveyed (23 percent) were categorized as having a high-performance measurement culture. These organizations had established performance measures and evaluation processes throughout their organizations. In addition, these organizations had adopted a system for using this data regularly in a majority of management activities.

Moderate-Measurement Culture Organizations

The majority of the social-sector organizations surveyed (64 percent) fell into the moderate-measurement category, suggesting that they had instituted some formalized evaluation and performance measurement practices and also used data for some management activities.

Low-Measurement Culture Organizations

The remaining 13 percent were categorized as low-measurement cultures. These organizations rarely implemented established performance measures and evaluation systems. Organizations with a low-measurement culture were not using data regularly for key management decisions.

The comparisons between organizations with high-, moderate-, and low-performance measurement cultures revealed interesting differences. The more frequently and consistently an organization's leadership team used performance measures in their management decisions, the more effective they were at increasing revenues ($r = .63$, $p < .01$), improving external relations ($r = .61$, $p = .01$), improving internal relations ($r = .63$, $p < .01$), increasing organizational efficiencies ($r = .59$, $p < .01$), strengthening organizational culture ($r = .57$, $p < .01$), and implementing organizational change ($r = .60$, $p < .01$).

High-performance measurement culture organizations provide an example of the desired future state for a thriving social sector outlined at the beginning of this chapter. Table 2.1 displays the variances in the percentages of each group reporting levels of success achieved in various organizational outcomes.

Successful organizations viewed program evaluation and outcomes measurement as more than just an external requirement. Rather, measurement efforts became the very lifeblood of high-performance organizations. Many types of data were gathered and used in organizations with a high-performance measurement culture, including process, outcomes, and customer satisfaction measures. In addition, excelling organizations incorporated measurement and evaluation into everyday practices.

Table 2.1. Comparison of Frequent Users and Infrequent Users of Performance Measures and Evaluation in Operational Decision-Making Organizations and Effective Accomplishment of Organizational Outcomes

Organizational Outcomes	***High-Performance Measurement Culture***	***Moderate-Performance Measurement Culture***	***Low-Performance Measurement Culture***
Organizational Efficiencies	88%	50%	18%
External Relations	82%	48%	7%
Internal Relations	76%	23%	7%
Increased Revenues	66%	18%	4%
Strengthening Organizational Culture	98%	55%	26%
Successful Organizational Change	**72%**	**26%**	**11%**

Source: Measurement Resources Company Measurement Culture Survey.

Well-crafted performance measurement and evaluation systems were used to make decisions that improved staff and program performance.

Excelling organizations also used data to communicate with staff and remain accountable to stakeholders. Collected data was evaluated, interpreted, and applied to manage operations, prepare budgets, and establish critical contracts. High-performing organizations turned to the data to ensure compliance through quality assurance programs. They benchmarked performance against the results of other high-performing organizations. Lastly, data was used as an essential ingredient of long-term strategic planning.

Performance management and evaluation systems were also linked to broader management systems. Survey results indicated that the boards of directors of excelling organizations were regular consumers of performance measurement and evaluation, using these regularly to make budget and other strategic decisions within their organizations. Results achieved were used to promote the organization to external stakeholders, create quality annual reports, and write grant applications.

The data was clear: organizations that created high-performance measurement cultures were the most likely to excel and thrive in this new era of managing to outcomes. What sets an organization that has embraced a high-performance measurement culture apart from similar organizations? What qualities do these organizations have in common? Contrary to a frequent assumption in the social sector, size does not determine success.

Size Doesn't Matter

Surprisingly, the Measurement Culture Survey results showed no significant correlation between organizational size and budget and success achieved. This stands in marked contrast to a common excuse cited by many social-sector leaders as to why they cannot move towards data-driven cultures: lack of access to monetary resources and limitations due to the organization's size. Greater access to money and larger size were not the key ingredients of high-performance measurement culture. The extent to which organizations used measurement and evaluation was the only key differentiator between excelling and average organizations.

The budgets of successful organizations ranged from under $100,000 to greater than $5 million (the maximum category). Results showed that 41 percent of successful organizations had a budget less than $2 million. Similarly, the size of organizations that self-reported success ranged between those with single employee to organizations with more than forty-one thousand full-time staff members. A complete summary of the Measurement Culture Survey results can be found in Appendix A.

Hidden Success Factors

Until the social sector chooses to invest in high-performance measurement cultures, government and nonprofit organizations will continue to struggle to obtain funding, achieve organizational health, and be perceived positively by the general public. Board members, organizational leaders, and stakeholders must begin to have critical conversations around culture and outcomes management. Such discussions impact every area of success, from capacity building and fundraising to decisions related to technology, policies, and procedures.

A thorough and honest review of organizational culture paves the way for strategic and tactical plans that engage all stakeholders in systemic and cultural changes. Only then can underlying problems begin to self-correct. Until more organizations adopt the practices of high-performance measurement cultures, the social sector will continue to miss the mark. Currently, many nonprofit organizations and government agencies are overlooking the hidden success factors that can help them fully realize their missions, achieve success, and thrive in a challenging future.

The Next Step

Now that we have outlined a desired future state, we will assess the current state of the social sector. We will examine common practices and see what the data shows.

Impact & Excellence

Chapter Two Discussion Questions

1. What is your organization's ideal future vision?
2. What does success look like in terms of effectiveness, efficiency, staff morale, stakeholder relations, and client impact?
3. What outcomes could your organization achieve if it had more money, resources, and volunteers?
4. How is your organization currently using data and information? What difference is this making?

3

The Reality: We Are Not as Good as We Think We Are

If we could first know where we are, and whither we are tending, we could then better judge what to do, and how to do it.
—ABRAHAM LINCOLN

IT IS DIFFICULT TO GET to where you want to go if you do not first know where you are. I was reminded of this truism on a recent short road trip from Columbus, Ohio, to Millersburg, Ohio. I had been traveling the route for years to visit my parents. A bad storm had closed the main road, and a highway patrol officer had diverted traffic off the highway and onto a side road. I knew where I wanted to go, but I had no idea where I was.

Without my car's global positioning system (GPS) mapping device, I could have driven around for hours getting no closer to my intended destination—not because I did not know where I wanted to go, but because I did not know where I was. Thankfully, my GPS let me know exactly where I was. It led me down narrow, winding roads, which I carefully navigated in the dark. Eventually, I was returned to the main route and arrived at my destination.

Many leaders of social-sector organizations find themselves traveling down a similar road, winding their way in the dark. They strive to reach their destination of a high-performance measurement culture, but their efforts are hampered because they are unsure about where they are starting from, even when they know where they want to go. Nor are they clear on the best route to take to reach their desired destination.

Many leaders believe they are closer to their desired goal than they actually are, especially in terms of performance and outcomes measurement. They believe that because they *collect* data, have invested in an expensive case management system, and run some reports, that they have achieved success. But high-performance measurement cultures require more than just collecting data. Success hinges on how an organization incorporates outcomes measures into organizational assumptions, values, communications, and actions that create impact and excellence.

I am often asked to speak at conferences and association meetings on the topic of managing to outcomes. Occasionally the organizer will share that those in attendance will include "well-established, advanced organizations," which they indicate requires an intermediate or advanced presentation. This perception has been developed because these organizations attract large grants, are steeped in history, and have access to significant sums of money, which they frequently invest in information technology.

This is a dangerous perception to have. In fact, such perceptions may limit the progress of these organizations, which at first appear to be thriving. The data shows that size, history, and budget are neither accurate predictors of a high-performance measurement culture nor indicative of the success that comes with it. Leaders who believe their organizations are close to reaching their goals without an accompanying internal exploration of how they are using data are most at risk of being left behind. They think they are where they need to be but in fact are entirely missing the ultimate destination of success.

Common Practice

Many leaders believe they are stepping into the twenty-first century, embracing the move toward performance and outcomes measures, and moving closer to a high-performance measurement culture. In reality, they have created a mere mirage of success. These organizations can be compared to the teenager who thinks he is grown up but discovers years later that his choices and limited knowledge of the world have, in fact, impeded his success. Upon review of existing measures and measurement systems, many organizations discover they have been condoning behaviors and practices that have actually blocked their success.

Let's examine a typical conversation about outcome measures.

Leader:	"Our main funder is requiring us to start measuring our mission and impact to the community as part of this grant."
Team Member 1:	"We cannot measure that. Our services are intangible, and we cannot afford that type of evaluation. Our staff can barely keep up with the current workload. We cannot ask them to do any more."
Team Member 2:	"Even if we do go forward with measuring our impact, what happens if we don't reach our goals?"
Team Member 3:	"We can't have that data in our files. What if our funders, board members, and the media find out?"
Leader:	"We have to do something to satisfy this requirement. Let's start with the low-hanging fruit. I'd like everyone to give me a list of easily measured things by tomorrow."

This kind of conversation typically occurs when organizations are asked to measure their impact and value by their funders. The Measurement Culture Survey research indicates that 41 percent of organizations first began to implement outcomes and performance measures in order to comply with funding requirements. Over time, these external funding requirements became the basis for all performance and outcome measurement activity, leading organizational leaders, staff, and stakeholders to believe they have moved toward managing to outcomes.

In such cases, leaders never stretched their teams to consider how these measures aligned with the organization's mission and values. Nor did they consider how certain measures might help the organization to increase efficiency or effectiveness. Leaders failed to determine how they would use the measures that were adopted to motivate stakeholders and funders. In contrast, organizations with strong measurement cultures asked and answered such questions before implementing measures.

The Measurement GPS

One of the aims for the Measurement Culture Survey was to identify the number of social-sector organizations currently gathering and using data in organizational decision making. The results gathered provide new insights into critical first steps for organizations that want to identify where they are and then determine how far they are from realizing their vision of excellence and greater impact. This is an opportune time for social-sector organizations. It is easier now than at any time in the past for organizations of any size to establish effective and powerful performance and outcome measurement systems. Information is easy to find and relatively inexpensive to gather.

Still, success demands more than the ability to measure performance; rather, it is built on foundational measurement activities. These activities themselves, alongside the data an organization has collected, inspire action and motivate staff within government and nonprofit organizations that desire to change, improve, and evolve.

The strength of the social sector is in its ability to gather and apply data. An abundance of performance measures and information is currently available and accessible to nonprofit and government organizations. As shown in Figure 3.1, a full 78 percent of those organizations surveyed reported having evaluation or performance measures in place for at least half of existing programs and services, with 42 percent of organizations reporting measures established for all existing programs and services.

The data shows measurement is in place in a majority of social-sector organizations; 86 percent of organizations reported having measures in place for at least half of their programs. This is good news, and it raises a critical question. If the sector is so saturated with measures, why are only a quarter of today's organizations seeing the full positive organizational shifts caused by data in the areas of increased revenue, improved staff morale, and positive press, among other improvements?

Figure 3.1. The Extent to Which Organizations Use Performance and Evaluation Measures

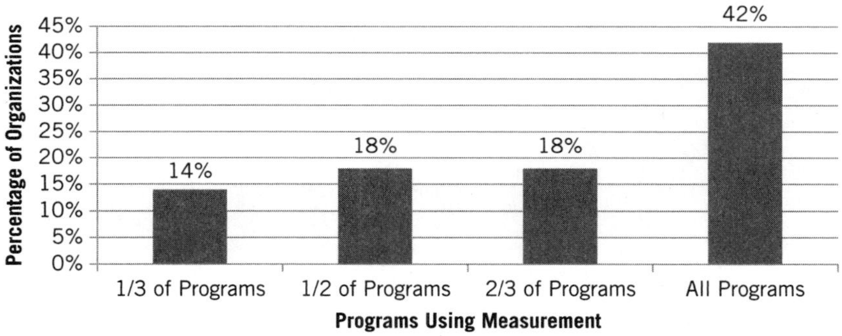

The difference between the passable nonprofit or government agency and one that excels lies in how collected data are used to bring about change. Great organizations go beyond simply gathering data. They analyze it, interpret it, and use it in everyday decision making. The social sector has significant room for improvement in how data is used in organizations.

As displayed in Figure 3.2, a majority of organizations across the sector report using data for assessing programs and communicating how well a program is accomplishing its identified aims to staff, clients, and funders. However, organizations appear to be missing the powerful operational and management tools at their disposal in these measures. Surprisingly, slightly more than half of the organizations surveyed reported using measures for performance improvement, program planning, managing operations, and strategic planning.

In addition, nearly half of all organizations currently using performance measures are viewing these measures as simply an external requirement rather than taking the critical next step and using the information to strengthen the organization and its programming. In the majority of cases, organizations are merely investing in the measures required by funding partners. They do not appear to be strategically examining which measures should be put in place in order to best manage their operations and programs for maximum success.

Figure 3.2. Percentage of Participants Reporting Using Measurement Often or Almost Always in These Decisions

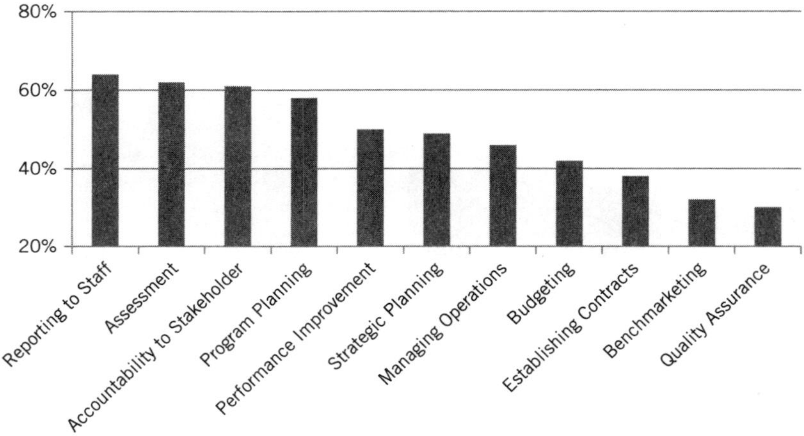

Less than half of organizations surveyed are using measures to make financial decisions. The majority of survey respondents indicated they did not use measures to manage contracts and make budget decisions. Even fewer used measurement to benchmark their organization's performance, measure it against results achieved by organizations with a similar mission, or inform quality assurance decisions.

Great organizations reached their goals with confidence precisely because their measures provided quality information aligned to management objectives. The data collected by such organizations helped guide management decisions. Likewise, poor strategic use of measurement leads organizations to conclude that outcomes measurement is a waste of time.

Organizations need to continually assess what information and inputs they are using to make management decisions. They also need to examine how they are using current measures to strengthen the link between those measures and management activities. Successful organizations have well-crafted performance outcome metrics that align with the following management activities:

- Performance improvement
- Program planning

- Communicating to staff
- Managing operations
- Budgeting
- Accountability to clients and stakeholders
- Strategic planning
- Quality assurance
- Establishing contracts
- Benchmarking

The Data Management Approach

The approach management takes to communicating and using data may be more important than the measures themselves. Organizations that have implemented meaningful measures typically take one of three approaches when it comes to their use of performance measures. The impact achieved varies greatly and is directly tied to the chosen approach to data utilization.

We will examine the three most common categories of data management:

1. Dust Collectors and Recyclers
2. Compliance Officer and Ruler Whackers
3. Coaches and Motivators

The Dust Collectors and Recyclers

Most organizations fall into this category. These organizations have full access to the latest internet technology (IT) systems, data collection efforts, and report analysis tools. They routinely distribute costly performance reports to key stakeholders. The collected data may even be presented at monthly or quarterly meetings. After an initial review, however, this vital information is filed away and forgotten until the next performance report is distributed.

On the surface, these organizations appear to be quite sophisticated in their performance measurement approach. However, they rarely experience significant change or improvement. Measurement efforts by Dust Collectors and Recyclers are not perceived to be part of everyday business. Often employees remain unaware that such reports are even available to them. Their companies' organizational outcomes differ only slightly, if at all, from those of similar organizations with no performance measures in place. The conclusion is clear: success comes from using data, not simply collecting it.

Employees at government and nonprofit organizations that fall into the Dust Collector and Recycler category have been socialized not to place a high emphasis on evaluation and performance data. When organizations are not communicating fully and actively using the information they have gathered, they send the message to staff that measurement activities are not vital to the organization's success. As a result, staff members view measurement activities as busy work and often move this critical component of building a successful and thriving organization to the back burner.

Several years ago, I was providing evaluation training to a group that fell into this category. Leaders came to me because they were having problems with data quality and wanted to retrain staff on data compliance. The first question I asked this organization's leadership team was whether they had ever shared outcomes with staff. The organization had not done so.

Prior to the training, I created individual reports for each employee that showed the aggregated outcomes for their individual clients and how those outcomes compared to those achieved by their peers. This information fascinated employees. Many were surprised that this type of analysis was even possible, and most wanted to receive such reports regularly. For these employees, simply seeing their results and understanding how this information could improve their individual performance naturally increased data compliance.

The Compliance Officers and Ruler Whackers

The second data management approach is found in approximately 20 percent of organizations that have established performance measurement systems. Their use of performance measures and outcomes is frequently more damaging to an organization than not having measures in place at all. Like teachers who use the ruler to discipline misbehaving children, leaders in these organizations use performance reports in a punitive manner. The staff begins to view measurement initiatives as a way to "get them" or ensure that employees "toe the line."

There can be improvements at organizations that fall into this category. However, those improvements are typically realized at the cost of employee morale and trust. Employees who work in these organizations often begin to focus on ways to improve their numbers, regardless of the organizational mission or desired outcomes. In some cases, staff members engage in counterproductive behaviors, all in an effort to improve the numbers. They may also refuse to deal with certain cases that might result in an undesirable change in the numbers.

Measures create distrust throughout these organizations, because employees are fearful of what will happen if they fail to reach a performance goal. We often hear about these cases in the media. In Ohio, for example, several large school districts were found guilty of fixing attendance and test score data in order to achieve higher rankings in the statewide performance system, thereby receiving increased resources. In this case, school workers withdrew students they knew to be still enrolled, deleted their absences, and then reenrolled them. Districts are accused of choosing children with many absences or low test scores (Yost, 2013). By withdrawing and reenrolling students, employees can break a student's string of "continuous enrollment." Only the test scores of students who have been enrolled nonstop from October through the time they take state tests in the spring are counted in a school's overall test-passing rate.

This practice resulted created an illusion that performance was higher than it actually was. Unfortunately, the deceptive practices of a few schools resulted in a pervasive public distrust of all schools output and performance data, making it more difficult for other nonprofit and government organizations to highlight their successes with data and numbers.

The Coaches and Motivators

The 30 percent of organizations that scored as high measurement cultures and experienced the highest level of organizational success typically followed the third approach to data management leadership. Coaches and motivators view organizational measures as a positive management tool. Leaders use the information they gather to tell the organization's story and to consistently communicate the value of these measures to staff.

In such environments, high achievement and outcomes were applauded, poor performance was carefully examined, and numbers were then analyzed and used to improve outcomes. Employees experienced full confidence that these measures would not be used for punitive purposes. Together, staff and leadership identified the reasons for performance issues and sought innovative ways to address existing problems. Coaches experienced the fastest improvements and the highest return on their investment in performance measurement efforts. The case study highlighting the Dallas County Tax Collector's Office shared in the previous chapter provides an excellent example of this type of organization.

As demonstrated by these three distinct approaches, performance measures alone do not create excellence. Prior to developing and establishing performance measurement systems, organizations must plan how and for what purpose data will be used. When management is unwilling or unable to commit to using such measures as positive, vital management tools that are seamlessly integrated with decision making, organizations are better served by delaying the implementation of a performance measures path until such a commitment is firmly in place.

Jazz Academy: A Case Study

Like many nonprofit organizations, a jazz academy in the Midwest understood the value of outcomes measures and assessment but needed help with the "how" of performance measures. "We understood the need for data around outcomes and assessment, but we didn't understand the most effective way to gather these data," said the managing director of the academy. "We needed to dedicate the time, find the right tools, and determine if we had the right skills."

This jazz academy first identified five overall organizational benchmarks related to the organization's mission, suitability, and stakeholder interests:

- Increased participant creativity
- Economic impact
- Cost per participant
- Participant engagement
- Overall satisfaction

A Closer Look. In this case study, all specific program measures captured key components related to the five most important measures the jazz academy had identified. The organization also incorporated additional program-specific measures. Data collection and analysis efforts were designed to fit the organization's culture and were performed internally by organizational staff. A benefit of increasing the evaluation, according to the managing director, was "to have the tools to report and communicate program outcomes consistently and with confidence."

The jazz academy began by including the outcomes of existing programs, along with evaluation plans for future programs, in every grant application. Shortly after adopting this practice, the academy was awarded a grant with more funding than they had received the previous year. The managing director believed that reporting outcomes played a significant part in this success. While the organization has faced challenges in allocating the time and personnel needed to gather some observational measures, the staff is currently exploring ways to use interns and other staff to ease this burden.

The new measurement and evaluation procedures implemented by this jazz academy not only helped with fundraising activities but also allowed the organization's staff to embrace data collection and analysis as an internal management tool. After the first year of collecting the data, benchmarks were established for each of the five measures. The organization uses the data annually to strategically improve program operations.

"We now have conversations about how we are going to measure success related to our five organizational measures when we are developing new programs," said the managing director. This jazz academy's efforts highlight that implementing a system of measurement and increasing an organization's evaluation capacity not only is manageable but also can lead to immediate positive outcomes that have a lasting impact.

Identifying Gaps

When social-sector organizations expect and settle for mediocrity, much is at stake. Mediocre organizations frequently fail donors, taxpayers, and the communities they serve. The majority of government and nonprofit organizations currently waste precious resources on activities and data management systems that do not deliver the highest-caliber results.

Giving up on these efforts is not an option, because they are the key to excellence. Improvement is the only solution to success. There is no doubt that excellence should be the standard that all government and nonprofit organizations strive to achieve. To reach this high standard, nonprofit organizations and government agencies must identify gaps in existing measurement systems.

Successful social-sector organizations have discovered how to overcome excuses and invest in quality performance measures directly tied to important management activities. Organizations that adopt a measurement culture implement performance measures and evaluation practices that positively impact the communities they serve. They continuously reach for and realize goals that stretch them beyond standards that are merely acceptable and expected.

The Next Step

Success is achievable across the social sector, yet decisive action is required. The following chapters outline a clear path to move government and nonprofit organizations from mediocrity to excellence and provide a step-by-step plan proven to create high-performance measurement cultures. To begin, we will examine the differing needs in the nonprofit and government sectors.

Impact & Excellence

Chapter Three Discussion Questions

1. Complete the online *Measurement Culture Survey* at www.impactandexcellence.com. How does your organization score? Does this score surprise you?
2. How are you currently using data to inform the following management activities?
   - Performance improvement
   - Program planning
   - Communication to staff

- Managing operations
- Budgeting
- Accountability to clients and stakeholders
- Strategic planning
- Quality assurance
- Establishing contracts
- Benchmarking

3. Which category best describes your organization's use of data: Dust Collector, Compliance Officer, or Coach? Why did you place your organization in this category? What would your organization need to do differently to move closer to the Coach model?

4

Nonprofits and Measurement Cultures

Give the world the best you have and it may never be enough. Give your best anyway.
—MOTHER TERESA

THE SOCIAL SECTOR IS COMPOSED OF both government and nonprofit entities with missions focused on changed lives and changed circumstances. These social-sector organizations receive monetary donations or tax dollars that support the delivery of programs or services that enable them to achieve their respective missions. These organizations are formed from the desire to make local communities, states, nations, or the world safer, healthier, and happier as well as more creative, productive, and prosperous.

The concepts and strategies presented in this book can be applied successfully in all types of government and nonprofit organizations. Yet there are distinct differences between these two types of organizations, and these differences should inform how leaders approach the strategies and action items shared in the chapters that follow. Understanding the unique characteristics of nonprofit and government organizations related to measurement cultures will enhance both the implementation and the practice of the five keys to embracing a high-performance measurement culture.

Particular characteristics and motivating factors drive each of these two types of social-sector organization to adopt a measurement culture. In addition, various forces may support or hinder the successful adoption of high-performance measurement cultures within both types of organization. The likely consumers of the data collected by government bodies are also distinct from those that will consume data collected by nonprofit organizations. The next two chapters examine the specific issues related to establishing measurement cultures within each type of social-sector organization in greater detail, beginning with a closer look at the circumstances particular to nonprofit organizations within the social sector.

Nonprofit Structures

A nonprofit organization is a recognized legal entity that uses surplus revenue to achieve its mission rather than distributing those revenues to owners or shareholders as profit or dividends. Founders typically set up a nonprofit organization when their primary reason for being in business is to serve a charitable, educational, or civic purpose. With the nonprofit designation or status, organizations are able to solicit donations from the general public as well as apply for grants specifically designated to nonprofit entities. Such grants may come from corporate, private, and public foundations or be supported by government programs or funding. The general public and corporations receive tax benefits when donating to recognized nonprofit organizations.

Nonprofit organizations are diverse in size, structure, and programming, ranging from multimillion-dollar hospitals known nationwide, such as St. Jude Children's Research Hospital, to local, all-volunteer community theaters. Regardless of the organization's budget or size, a nonprofit is typically structured according to three primary functions: governance, administration, and programs.

Governance

All nonprofits are required to have a board of directors that assumes responsibility for the nonprofit's mission and operations. The board determines the nonprofit's mission and governs by deciding how that mission should be accomplished. Directors are responsible for internal policies, such as human resources and codes of conduct. These governing bodies hold the ultimate decision-making power within the organization.

Administration

The second function of nonprofit structure is administration. Administration includes the nonprofit's executive director or president, who reports to the board. In larger nonprofits the administration is composed of paid employees, which may include individuals overseeing program and service delivery as well as internal and external communication. The administration ensures that common resources are used to support program development and operation.

Depending on the size a nonprofit administration and the organization's resources, specific staff members may be responsible for finance, marketing, development, technology, and human resources. However, it should be noted that paid staff are not found in all nonprofit organizations. In many small nonprofits, the executive director may be the sole staff member. In such organizations, administrative and program functions may be fulfilled by board members and volunteers.

Programs

Programs are the third element that may determine the structure of nonprofit organizations. Programs include the activities and services a nonprofit organization provides as it meets a need, thereby fulfilling its mission. Nonprofit programs vary widely. Some provide advocacy for specific causes, such as breast cancer awareness or childhood obesity. Others may provide direct services to consumers, such as mental health counseling or job training courses. Some organizations focus on enrichment and entertainment activities, such as artistic performances or museums, while other nonprofits are designed to equip, support, and inspire a group of people, such as associations and business incubators.

Measurement Cultures: Foundational to Nonprofit Success

The creation of high-performance measurement cultures in all nonprofit organizations is necessary for optimal success. Just as nonprofits are diverse, the look and feel of the measurement cultures within them is diverse. While the organization's stated mission as well as its size, budget, and structure may change the strategies and tools selected to develop a high measurement culture, every nonprofit can improve organizational impact and value through data collection and evaluation.

To use a comparable situation as a point of illustration, every nonprofit organization must use communication tools—such as e-mail, telephone, and social media—though the manner in which these tools are used may vary greatly. Larger nonprofits might have highly sophisticated websites and internal phone systems. Smaller groups may use free and low-cost tools, such as web-based mail like Gmail and similar communication systems, conference call services, and social networks, such as Facebook and Twitter. Given all of these different options, any nonprofit organization should be able to find communication solutions that fit their budgets to successfully achieve their mission. It would be irresponsible and a detriment to the organization if a leader failed to invest in communication. The same should be true for establishing a high-performance measurement culture.

The main reason all nonprofit leaders should demand a high-performance measurement culture is the fact that such a culture leads to increased impact and increased revenue. Nonprofit organizations thrive as they seek the specific data and information that will allow the organization to better communicate and measure its true impact and value.

Measurement Cultures: The Global Perspective

According to the National Center for Charitable Statistics (Roeger, Blackwood, and Pettijohn, 2012) there are approximately 1.6 million nonprofit organizations that receive $1.51 trillion in annual revenues. This money comes from private donors, corporate donations, government grants, foundations, and fees received for the delivery of programs and services. Despite an abundance of both financial resources and human capital devoted to solving problems in communities throughout the United States, many national and local social indicators have remained stagnant or have steadily declined in recent years.

For example, there are over eighty-two thousand nonprofit organizations dedicated to health-related causes in the United States. Yet adult obesity rates have doubled since 1980, from 15 to 30 percent, while childhood obesity rates have more than tripled (Levi et al., 2013). As obesity rates rise in both children and adults, so too does the incidence of more than thirty diseases, including diabetes and heart disease.

This unfortunate reality impacts not only the individual's quality of life but also the business community in the form of rising health care costs. This is further evidenced by the fact that the average number of days individuals report having poor physical and mental health has also increased significantly over the past twenty years (National Center for Chronic Disease Prevention and Health Promotion, 2012). Despite all the education and resources devoted to healthy eating, the quality of children's diets is considerably below recommended levels (Federal Interagency Forum on Child and Family Statistics, 2013). Without intervention and a change in approach, these and many other concerning trends will continue in spite of the funding being poured into nonprofits focused on health-related issues.

Another large segment of nonprofit organizations is dedicated to serving those who live in extreme poverty. These organizations seek to improve the economic condition of the poorest Americans. Yet national social indicators in recent years are underwhelming in terms of desired social change. The overall level of homelessness remained essentially the same from 2011 to 2012, with the number of homeless individuals falling slightly and the number of homeless families increasing slightly (Lowery, 2012). According to the Census Bureau, the poverty rate has climbed for four out of the past five years. It is now 22 percent higher than it was just five years ago.

Declining or stagnant outcomes should not be mistaken for the nonprofit sector's lack of trying or commitment. The sector is filled with devoted and caring people working very hard to change the status quo of these and many other community outcomes. Yet if the nonprofit community's collective efforts are not changing lives and circumstances for the better, what is the impact of that $1.59 trillion in invested resources?

The Measurement Resources Measurement Culture Survey project suggests that only a very few organizations really understand the impact they are achieving. A scant 27 percent are collecting and reviewing the precise data required to make improvements. The majority of nonprofit organizations remain unaware of whether they are simply maintaining the status quo or realizing desired results and therefore are part of the solution.

Taking the necessary steps to move toward a high-performance measurement culture will allow more nonprofit leaders to understand their unique impact and use these data to improve effective programming. Lack of funding may be an issue, but until the sector can demonstrate its collective impact with those that they purport to serve, it will remain difficult to ask donors and funders to continue to invest in programs.

Nonprofits and Measurement Cultures: The Internal Picture

Although it would be ideal if nonprofit leaders were exclusively focused on and motivated by the changed lives and changed circumstance brought about because of their programs and services, this is not a practical reality. As with any endeavor, achieving change and success requires resources. Nonprofits are no different from other organizations in this regard. They require money to support the organization's infrastructure and to recruit quality employees who carry out the programs and services that lead to a desired change. Nonprofit leaders must be concerned with the organization's survival, and this includes a focus on strategies that ensure the organization's sustainability.

Fundraisers and grant writers understand that outlining specific outcomes measures makes their jobs easier. In a survey of nonprofit development professionals, 50 percent report that the lack of outcome measures is one of the most significant challenges preventing the organization from achieving optimal success

(Jones, 2013). This was the second most common answer after lack of funding, which 83 percent of respondents reported as one of the greatest challenges faced by their organizations. Measuring outcomes was perceived as a greater issue than hiring quality people, building outside partnerships, improving intra-agency communication, or maintaining positive board relations.

While at one time nonprofit leaders may have seen evaluation and performance measurement activities as a luxury, the Measurement Culture Project has proved that this is no longer the case. We now understand that a high-performance measurement culture is correlated with an organization's ability to increase revenues and impact. In the past, it may have been sufficient for nonprofits to simply share compelling stories and pull on the heartstrings of potential donors in order to receive big checks. Today's most successful nonprofits are not content to rest on their laurels and keep relying on this timeworn approach.

Rather, thriving nonprofit organizations also use data to back up their compelling messages. This data allows them to clearly communicate the distinct impact their organization is making and clarify how they stand apart from other nonprofit organizations competing for dollars. The media takes notice of the organization that provides evidence of its success. Grant makers are more likely to select these organizations for highly coveted grants because they can clearly see how their investment will make an impact.

Whether the motivation to establish outcomes and performance measures stems from a desire to improve fundraising efforts and increase revenues or from a drive to track true social change, nonprofit leaders who take the steps to move toward the development of a high-performance measurement culture see many benefits and reap greater rewards. When organizations choose impact and excellence, they open up the possibility of greater fulfillment of their stated mission and the support of that mission by the community.

In the end, measurement cultures provide the foundation for success within nonprofit organizations and increase the potential that the organization's efforts will effect great change. As Mother Teresa said, "Give the world the best you have and it may never be enough. Give your best anyway." Without making the effort to use data to become more efficient and effective, a nonprofit organization will fail to implement a high-performance measurement culture and will never know whether its best is good enough, because they have yet to give it.

Audiences for Data

Nonprofit organizations that embrace a high-performance measurement culture are more successful because they gather successful data, stories, and information about successful initiatives that motivate and inspire the organization's stakeholders. Before implementing a measurement system, leaders of organizations with high-performance measurement cultures consider the audience for the data. They consider what they want the data they collect to inspire stakeholders to do.

The group of stakeholders and the interests of that group will vary depending on the size and mission of a nonprofit organization, as will the specific measures collected and desired outcomes. Guidelines for determining which performance outcomes to measure are discussed in Chapter Nine. Prior to making any decisions on what specific information to collect, an organization's leaders need to get clear on who cares about the data and why these individuals and groups care. What follows is a list of audiences that are typical consumers of nonprofit data and the primary reasons they are interested in that data.

Nonprofit Governance

In successful, high-performing nonprofits, the board is a primary consumer of data. Board members are interested in having data and information that will allow them to make intelligent decisions regarding budget allocations, more effective program management, and organizational needs. Busy board members appreciate having robust and reliable information that will help them make critical decisions with confidence.

Program Staff

To develop highly effective programs, program staffs need regular and accessible data and feedback on the success and impact of the program and services they oversee. They require information that will help them understand what is working and what is not. Data is most helpful to these consumers when it suggests how staff can improve the quality and delivery of programs and services. This information encourages and motivates program staff when things are going well. It also provides evidence that helps them accept and embrace program improvement and change. When acted upon by program staff, this data leads to the increased impact and effectiveness of programs.

Development Staff

Within a nonprofit organization, development staff members are responsible for fundraising and grant management. These administrative staff members need organizational outcomes and impact data to help them effectively tell the organization's story. They need valid and reliable data that documents the outcomes of the organization. They desire data that will motivate donors and funders to give resources. They also use information to determine the success of the organization's marketing and social media efforts.

Corporate Funders

Not all funders are created equal in terms what information will inspire them to donate to a specific charitable cause. Nonprofits need to understand the motivation behind their funders' giving patterns. Some corporate funders are interested in their company's being seen as a socially conscience business. These funders are motivated by measures related to the reach of their brand. They may be interested in how many people will see their logo or consume information related to their mission. For example, they may want to know how many people will be at an event or visit the organization's website where the company's logo will be highlighted in exchange for its donor or sponsor status.

Other corporate funders are interested in funding programs that are likely to further a specific cause. These funders desire to see outcomes measures related to social return on investment. For example, the PNC Financial Services Group, Inc., founded the PNC Grow Up Great program, which provides grants to innovative nonprofits focused on serving underserved children from birth through age five. Grant recipients include organizations that work to improve children's school readiness by providing support in one of the following key areas: math, science, the arts, and financial education (PNC Financial Services Group, 2014). Therefore organizations interested in receiving funding from this corporate donor may improve the chances of securing funding if they clearly demonstrate how their programs directly impact children's school readiness.

Foundation and Government Funders

Nonprofit organizations are often charged with furthering the mission of government organizations and foundations. Foundation executives and government managers who make such funding decisions are often concerned with and expect to receive data and information about how the nonprofit programs and services further advance their mission. A failure to demonstrate proven outcomes may result in a loss of funding.

In 2009, roughly $100 billion went to human service nonprofit organizations through some two hundred thousand contracts and grants (Boris, Leon, Roeger, and Nikolova, 2010). This represents 65 percent of the funding to this sector. These organizations are contracted to provide long-term care, mental health counselling, medical services, job training, homelessness prevention, and rehabilitation services, to name a few.

Another example of a large funder motivated by quality outcomes measures is the well-known and highly regarded Bill and Melinda Gates Foundation. According to the foundation's website (2014), it prefers to fund initiatives that "reduce inequities around the world. In the developing world, the foundation focuses on improving health and alleviating extreme poverty. In the United States, the foundation supports programs related to education. In its local region, the foundation promotes strategies and programs that help low income families." The website also states that the foundation is interested in working with partners to define and measure results rather than working on inputs and activities. It is unlikely that an organization with a low-measurement culture would attract funding from this foundation.

Private Donors

Typically, private donors are more likely to give to an organization to which they have a personal tie, in terms of either mission or relationship. Overall, these donors desire to give back to society and want to feel good about themselves as a result of their gift. The more information a nonprofit organization can give to a private donor about how their contribution is making a difference, the more likely it is that donor will continue to provide financial support.

In addition, private donors are becoming more likely to ask questions and seek out information on the efficiency of an organization when making funding decisions. They want their money to go to a cause they can trust. Having data related to the impact of programs and services will earn the trust of private donors.

Program Participants

Clients who benefit from programs and services offered by a particular nonprofit organization often have a choice whether or not to engage in those program offerings. Private schools, arts organizations, and counseling centers are examples of choice-driven programs. Participants need information that will motivate them to seek out the organization's services and continue their participation in program offerings.

Program participants want to know that participating in an organization's program or service will be a valuable use of their time. They want to be assured that they will receive the benefits or value promised by the organization. They are looking for information, such as program testimonials, that demonstrates how individuals similar to them have experienced positive results.

Partnering Organizations

Social change is complex and often requires the collaboration of partnering organizations to achieve the impact funders most desire. For example, many health-related nonprofit and public organizations have contracts with the Centers for Medicare & Medicaid Services (CMS), a division of the federal government, to administer or directly provide health care services. One desired outcome of CMS is to reduce the amount of unnecessary use of the emergency room and hospital readmissions. To reduce these admissions, a nonprofit hospital that is contracted to receive Medicaid or Medicare funding may need to partner with a local community health center to divert patients not requiring emergency-level care.

Other examples include a local housing agency partnering with substance abuse agencies to help clients be successful and sustain permanent housing and achieve desired outcomes for HUD funding. Similarly, an early childhood education program may partner with a local arts organization to help students achieve arts-related core standards required by Department of Education funding. Like foundation and government funders, partnering organizations are motivated to engage in a partnership by seeing data that indicates how a nonprofit organization has been successful at achieving the outcomes that will ultimately help the partnering organization improve its outcomes.

Barriers to Implementation

As Measurement Resources Company has partnered with nonprofits of varying sizes to help them increase their capacity for data-driven decision making, I have noticed common barriers that are red flags for the successful implementation of a high-performance measurement culture. These factors seem to be unique to nonprofit organizations and are often not prevalent in government settings. Understanding these barriers to implementation in advance will help nonprofit leaders clear potential blocks and eliminate frustrations that may impede progress.

The Bottom-Line Mindset

Boards of directors are responsible for setting the priorities and goals of the nonprofit organization. These members are typically high-achieving leaders from the for-profit world. They have a variety of assets and skills in disciplines such as accounting, law, marketing, and management. Typically, they choose to serve on the board because they have an interest in the mission of an organization and desire to give back to the community. Although they take their roles very seriously, many board members lack training in nonprofit governance best practices. Therefore they use the skills and procedures they know best and that have worked for them in the past. They lead and manage the nonprofit organization in the same manner they would lead a for-profit venture. In for-profit organizations, effective decision making concentrates on activities that will generate increased revenues. This approach works well in these settings, because the primary mission is to produce a profit for shareholders. Without an understanding that organizational outcomes are the true profit of a nonprofit, when these individuals are discussing organizational goals and strategic priorities the conversation often gravitates to the topic of increasing revenues. There is an assumption that greater revenue equals greater impact, even though this is not always the case in the nonprofit organization.

To assess whether board members are operating from a for-profit mindset when it comes to nonprofit decision making, I often ask, "If you had a crystal ball, what would you want to know?" In almost every case, the responses I receive from board members involved in a moderate- to low-measurement culture nonprofit concern money. Popular answers include "Will we have enough money to continue the program next year?" and "Will we be able to fully establish our endowment?" These are important questions; however, such an extreme focus on revenues can sometime get in the way of establishing a robust measurement culture.

One organization's chief operating officer and development director were excited about establishing performance measures and taking the steps to move toward a measurement culture. They wanted to allocate some resources to efforts that would increase their capacity and, as a result, allow the organization to increase its impact and value. The administrators were quite surprised and disappointed when the board turned their request down.

The reason behind the board's rejection was that this was not a priority, because the organization needed to focus on increasing revenues. What the board failed to realize was that, by investing in evaluation and capacity building activities, they would make it easier for the development staff to raise funds, build partnerships, and increase sustainability. Had the discussion been focused on how to ensure the delivery of the most impactful and highest-quality programming possible (that is, delivering on the organizational mission), making an investment in a measurement culture would naturally fit with their understanding of organizational priorities. By focusing on organizational outcomes, the nonprofit would naturally provide a foundation for fundraising activities and therefore increase revenues.

Leaders of high-performance measurement cultures understand the fallacy in this thinking. They seek data that will better help them achieve their missions first and increase revenues second. The tendency to rely too heavily on discussions related to revenues can be easily overcome. When board members are introduced to high-performance measurement culture training, attitudes can shift quickly. To sustain a high-performance measurement culture, it is important that this training is also incorporated in the onboarding process for nonprofit board members.

When new members join the organization's board, other members can familiarize them with the organization's desire to be a high-performing, outcomes-driven organization. Such an introduction stresses that decisions are based on data that will help the organization better achieve its mission as a priority. Effective training for this effort should discuss how measures are in place to help leaders run a more efficient, well-funded, and impactful nonprofit. Prior to the implementation of measurement culture strategies, nonprofit leaders interested in making such a change should assess the readiness of key leaders and board members within the organization.

The Overhead Debate

Traditionally, nonprofit effectiveness has been defined by the organization's ability to maintain low overhead costs. Good nonprofits are expected to demonstrate how they channel most of their financial resources to services that directly impact participants. The desire to keep overhead low can sometimes be in direct conflict with the organization's desire to focus on impact and excellence.

Investing in measurement activities often entails a slight increase in administrative costs. Depending on the size and capacity of the organization, measurement systems may require upgrades in technology or the addition of a part-time staff to assume responsibility for measurement activities. As this book was being written, the expectation that good nonprofit organizations maintain a very low overhead was beginning to be challenged, but this shift may take some time to permeate the long-ingrained expectations of donors.

To minimize this challenge, organizations should educate donors about how leaders are using data to increase the impact of programs and the ways participants benefit. The effort to increase positive use of data does not require layers of additional resources. Focusing on the return on investment of activities can actually help a nonprofit attract additional funds, and this must be conveyed to all constituents.

Staff Turnover

Turnover among top leaders and those responsible for data management at an organization can quickly disrupt efforts to establish a high-performance measurement culture. When an organization does not establish systems for training multiple staff members in the work related to data collection, tracking, and evaluation, the institutional knowledge and the benefits of such efforts are lost when that individual leaves the organization.

Other common issues related to staff turnover arise when a new top leader is hired who may not be accustomed to working with performance measures. This new executive director may not place a priority on using the data that is collected. When information is not used, staff members responsible for data collection quickly abandon the practice, which weakens the organization's measurement culture.

Developing a high-performance measurement culture takes commitment. For such a culture to thrive at an organization, leaders need to set aside time to educate all staff and board members about why certain data-driven activities are being performed. In addition, the processes, policies, and procedures should be written down in a formal document and made available to all employees. These efforts naturally lessen the possibility that positive measurement efforts will be abandoned when longtime staff members depart and new employees come on board.

Funders' Requirements

Because funders are interested in achieving desired outcomes, they often require nonprofits to measure and report certain activities and results. These requirements may or may not be related to the main mission of the funded nonprofit. And because these are requirements for receiving an investment from funders, organizations must devote both time and human capital to measuring these activities. Organizational leaders may assume they have a well-established measurement culture simply because they have a process for measurement. This can create problems when these requirements are not aligned with the nonprofit's mission.

Another common situation occurs when nonprofits receive funds from a variety of funders, each of which has its own unique data requirements. Nonprofit employees often invest much time focusing on divergent requirements in such a way that it becomes unwieldy to spend any additional time on measurement activities that are more directly related to advancing their unique mission. Leaders of established high-performance measurement cultures chose funders wisely (this is discussed further in Chapter Seven). They understand the missions of their respective organizations and seek only funders with aligned missions. When the funder is misaligned, measurement activities will be misaligned as well, moving the organization further away from the capacity to demonstrate how they are measuring the organization's unique impact and value.

Build on Strengths

Successful nonprofit organizations overcome known weaknesses and move toward increased effectiveness, efficiency, and impact by building on strengths. By design, nonprofit organizations have several components that make implementing the steps found in this book relatively easy. Once nonprofit leaders choose strategic and data-driven decision making that enhances the organization's mission, they benefit from increased flexibility, decreased bureaucracy, and direct contact with participants as well as quicker access to increased funding, compared to their government counterparts.

Flexibility

In many ways nonprofit organizations are similar to their for-profit counterparts. Nonprofits are typically started by an individual or a few people who set the direction and the culture of the organization. The board and the executive director are able to make decisions to start or discontinue various programs and activities based on their organization's goals and priorities. Beginning to measure outcomes and impacts typically does not require approval from anyone outside the organization.

Such flexibility is an inherent benefit to the nonprofit organization seeking to implement a high-performance measurement culture. Nonprofit leaders can get started quickly when they realize that they are operating with a low- to moderate-measurement culture and desire to take the next steps to measure and communicate their true impact and value. The most difficult step may be in educating the board or staff as to why they need to establish new policies and procedures for measurement and data collection. Having key players read and discuss this book and other resources on the benefits of a high-performance measurement culture is a great first step toward achieving a high-performance measurement culture.

Direct Access to Clients and Participants

Focusing on outcomes means understanding the lives and circumstances that have changed for the better because of a nonprofit's programs or services. To do this, organizations need access to data that systematically documents those changes. Effective methods for capturing data typically include collecting data directly from participants.

Nonprofit organizations have an advantage over their government counterparts, because their staff members often have direct access to the populations they serve. The organization can establish trust and rapport with participants, making it easier to ask for personal and sometimes sensitive information. Program managers and organizational staff often can communicate directly with participants at the beginning of the program and to establish an expectation that evaluation data will be sought at the end of the program. They also gather information from participants that can be used for a follow-up e-mail or phone call a few months after the program ends.

For many nonprofit organizations, collecting participant data is often expected as a way of doing business. For example, patients of health-related nonprofit organizations expect their physician or counselor to ask questions about their medical history and capture data related to their health status in their charts. The use of electronic health records makes it very easy for these organizations to start aggregating health data to form an overall picture of the collective change that many individual patients are experiencing. Because health outcome data is reported in aggregate and individual patient names are not released, analyzing the data this way, internal to the organization, does not violate any policies of the Health Insurance Portability and Accountability Act (HIPAA).

Control

Nonprofits have a great deal of latitude and control over activities and processes. Nonprofit governing bodies can decide what programs to deliver, which populations to serve, and how to deliver programs and services. Sometimes funders or government regulations dictate how money can be spent or how programs need to be delivered, but the organization has the power to accept or not accept these funds. If activities are not aligned with the organization's mission, it is often in the organization's best interest to decline funds offered by a particular funder.

This element of control is essential for success. Successful organizations own their data collection processes. Once they collect data, they have the power to use it to make changes that will increase their impact and value to the community. Usually all that prevents a nonprofit organization from collecting meaningful data and using it to make positive change are forces that are well in their control.

Ability to Seek New Funding

A major advantage nonprofit organizations have is their ability to quickly seek funding to support efforts to increase evaluation capacity. This capability allows them to quickly adopt the principles shared by those organizations that embrace high-performance measurement cultures. Many foundations have designated funds for organizational capacity building that nonprofits can use. Leadership development, information technology, and evaluation activities are all focuses of increased measurement culture and are expected expenditures for these capacity-building funds. In some cases, organizations can obtain funds from affluent board members or community members who understand the value of increasing the capacity of data-driven decision making in the organization.

One organization wanted to collect data on their participants' experiences and outcomes as well as conduct a survey of community needs to help support expansion efforts. This particular study was going to cost approximately $25,000—funds the organization did not already have. The organization's leaders approached a board member who passionately believed this was the precise data the board needed to move forward with decisions on expansion. The board member gladly wrote a check to fund the entire project. Had organizational leaders not gone to this board member, it could have taken years to raise the additional money required for the project. Either this would have slowed down progress toward their goal or, worse, decision makers might have forged ahead without the data required for effective decision making.

When foundations and donors make an investment in data and measurement, organizations can move forward quickly. If additional resources are required, leaders can approach foundations or individual donors, making a compelling case for how upgrading organizational culture and implementing data-collection and evaluation systems will allow the organization to become more strategic and, ultimately, more effective.

Next Steps

Nonprofits of every size and purpose can effectively use the strategies shared in this book to develop a high-performance measurement culture. Leaders of these organizations can quickly implement new measurement policies and procedures and seek additional funds to help support these new efforts. When nonprofit leaders remain aware of common roadblocks and create a plan to remove these obstacles, success is inevitable. The next chapter examines the unique factors connected to the successful adoption of measurement cultures in government organizations.

Impact & Excellence

Chapter Four Discussion Questions

1. What strengths discussed in this chapter are also found in your nonprofit? These strengths will support the strategic implementation of a high-performance measurement culture in your organization.
2. Who are the likely key audiences that might consume your organization's data? What type of data will best motivate each of these groups?
3. What common barriers to implementation do you believe currently exist at your nonprofit?
4. What action steps could you take to help overcome these barriers?

5

Government and Measurement Cultures

The purpose of government is to enable the people of a nation to live in safety and happiness. Government exists for the interests of the governed, not for the governors.
—THOMAS JEFFERSON

THE PUBLIC SECTOR CONSISTS OF national, state, and local governments; their agencies; and chartered bodies that play a significant part in the national economy, providing basic goods or services not provided by the private sector. Measurement cultures in government organizations are vital to a well-functioning society. It is essential that these organizations, which represent 35 percent of the entire economy (U.S. Office of Management and Budget, 2013b), adopt high-performance measurement cultures that ensure optimal efficiencies. The successful implementation of such cultures requires careful and sustained attention.

Unlike their nonprofit counterparts, government organizations are supported directly by tax dollars and fees for services rather than by individual citizens and funding by corporations. Although the public "owns" government organizations, citizens do not have a significant voice in how these organizations are run and operated. Elected officials, as well as individuals appointed or hired by elected officials, are charged with the administration and management of government organizations. These individuals become the stewards of resources needed to carry out the spectrum of programs and services managed by government agencies and related organizations.

Every member of society is impacted in some way by government on a daily basis. Public schools, libraries, and police and fire departments as well as courts, tax departments, commerce regulation agencies, and a host of agencies providing socials services are all examples of public sector organizations. Services provided by government organizations range from trash and sewer services at the city or county level to the construction and maintenance of highways, roads, and bridges locally, regionally, and nationally.

Measurement Cultures: A Moral Responsibility of Government

It seems logical to expect high-performance measurement cultures in a sector that controls over a third of the economy. Research shows that high-performance measurement cultures in government organizations lead to responsible spending and greater impact. The Measurement Culture Survey revealed, for example, that those government organizations that implemented data collection systems and used the data collected to make key management decisions experienced increased operational efficiencies.

Despite the clear link between the adoption of a high-performance measurement culture and smoother operations in public sector organizations, it is estimated that a scant 18 percent have adopted such a culture. This is almost 10 percent less than the incidence of high-performance measurement cultures among nonprofit organizations. This lack of focus on high-performance measurement cultures in government agencies is evidenced by less-than-impressive results. In the United States, studies have shown a steady decline in the positive impact of government agencies' organizational cultures. No nation can afford to accept mediocre results from its public sector. The consequences of systemic failure in a sector that represents more than one-third of the U.S. economy would be devastating.

The causes for the underwhelming evidence of measurement cultures in government organizations are varied; they include disengaged leadership, unwieldy organizational structures, a perceived lack of resources, and a shift in prevailing attitudes and beliefs about government. This shift in the quality and effectiveness of government is evidenced by the decline in public trust in the government. In 1958, 73 percent of Americans reported trust in the government. In 2013, just 19 percent of Americans indicated they trust the government (Pew Research Center, 2013).

A malaise has settled in like a persistent fog, resulting in the shared perception that nothing will ever change in government. The expression "good enough for government work" is believed to have originated during the World War II era and originally meant that something passed rigorous standards. In more recent years, this expression has taken on a much different meaning; it now suggests that the expected standard for government operation is merely passable.

Why should we care? The U.S. national debt currently stands at more than sixteen trillion dollars. This is largely a result of countless government administrations spending far more than the resources available from taxation. Despite all this spending, social indicators continue to remain flat or stagnant, and most citizens become further removed from and disillusioned by the functioning of government systems.

In addition, it appears that many government leaders have lost sight of whose money they are using to carry out their duties. It would be nearly impossible for the private or nonprofit sectors to survive with these results, yet we continue down this path with our government sector, expecting success.

Implementing high-performance measurement cultures in government organizations provides a path toward the reestablishment of trust with the people served by those organizations. Given the benefits of operating with data-driven strategies and the dire consequences of *not* using them, it can be argued that government leaders have a moral responsibility to gather the data that will provide clear evidence of program excellence and impact. The adoption of measurement principles will empower government organizations to use data to focus on efficiency without losing sight of impact.

Leaders who find the courage to look past their own needs and embrace the pressing needs of the country can transform the current culture of entitlement being propped up by unv bureaucrats into a network of efficient government opera It is not too late to change things, but lasting change will require leaders to stay focused on the mission and original purpose of the government organizations they lead. For the United States to remain strong economically and thereby retain its global influence, government leaders must reduce government spending and enhance the level of service provided.

The Outcomes of Government

Thomas Jefferson said the purpose of the United States government is to "enable the people of the nation to live in safety and in happiness." Through the years, public entities have been created to help individual citizens and groups in society to achieve this purpose. Leaders who focus on creating data-driven cultures designed for efficiency and impact must first understand the main mission of their respective organizations. (Chapter Eight provides greater detail on this imperative.)

The true purpose of government organizations can often be found in the documents that originally established them. For example, the opening preamble of the United States Constitution states the purpose of the U.S. government as envisioned by the founding fathers. This historical document captures the six fundamental functions of the federal government:

"We the People of the United States, in Order to form a more perfect Union, establish Justice, insure domestic Tranquility, provide for the common defence, promote the general Welfare, and secure the Blessings of Liberty to ourselves and our Posterity, do ordain and establish this Constitution for the United States of America."

State and local governments may have their own guiding documents, but the missions of these governments are always related to these six basic functions clearly outlined in the U.S. Constitution. Government leaders who make the shift toward managing to outcomes and ensuring effective and efficient government organizations must align performance measures to at least one of these functions. In the absence of such an alignment, citizens should ask why such government organizations exist at all.

The Six Basic Functions of Government

Democracies are created by and for the people and are owned by the people. Because it is not feasible to have millions of citizens govern at once, elected positions, public departments, agencies, and commissions were created to carry out the six functions of government. The six basic functions of government organizations are described in this section.

A More Perfect Union

The founders saw the opportunity realized through the formation of alliances between and among the original American colonies. In our modern era, government functions best when it provides programs and services that solidify and strengthen both individual states and the overall nation.

Establish Justice

Americans desire a society rooted in justice, and elected government officials are responsible for establishing, upholding, and administering the laws of our nation, which are founded on the principle of liberty and justice for all. Although there is often vigorous debate about whether this result is achieved by elected officials, the laws and the processes used to implement and enforce those laws are intended to be fair, unbiased, and logical.

Ensure Domestic Tranquility

Many government organizations and the laws and regulations those governments create and enforce are designed to meet the goal of establishing public order and peace throughout the nation.

Provide for the Common Defense

Government is responsible for providing a basic system of defense that protects national interests from "enemies of the State."

Promote the General Welfare

An important role of government is to provide for the common good. This is an area where government organizations must consistently adapt and evolve to meet the changing needs of the public. The adoption and administration of regulations to ensure the safety of food and water resources, clean air, public education, and consumer protection are examples of government activities intended to promote the general welfare.

Secure the Blessings of Liberty

America was founded on the ideals of life, liberty, and the pursuit of happiness. The role of the government is to develop systems and policies that ensure that the liberties of one individual do not breach the freedom of other citizens or groups of citizens. Therefore careful attention should be given to how laws and regulations enhance liberty without infringing on the rights or freedoms of other citizens.

Audiences for Government Data

The internal workings of government organizations look very similar to the operation of nonprofit organizations and corporations. Similar to nonprofits, governments and those agencies and organizations that carry out government programs and services strive to achieve a mission that is related to the greater good. In addition, governments are often focused on increasing the common interest of their funders, United State citizens. In these ways, the strategy required to manage responsive government organizations that employ data measurement practices and deliver impactful results is similar to those common in nonprofit organizations.

Despite these similarities, governments employ data in ways that differ from how similar data sets are used in nonprofit organizations. The most successful government organizations collect and use data that empowers leaders to more clearly understand how tax dollars are being spent and the impact of the government organization's efforts to meet the needs of citizens or effect social change. Elected officials also use this information to communicate to the public how dollars invested are achieving desired results.

Data can help elected leaders set key priorities, goals, and objectives in the organizations they fund. Performance measures guide administrators to understand how to manage programs more efficiently and provide needed insights into how to achieve stated goals more effectively. Like their counterparts in nonprofit organizations, government leaders must consider several different audiences as they decide what information to collect. Key consumers of government data include taxpayers, target demographic groups, the legislative and executive branches, and budget offices.

Taxpayers

Nearly all revenues supporting the public sector are generated by taxpayer contributions or from fees paid for services. As such, government organizations have millions of shareholders. Although taxpayers do not run these organizations, citizens do choose who they elect into office. In general, individual and corporate taxpayers desire government leaders to be good stewards of these mandatory financial contributions. Motivated by the need to tighten their own personal budgets and the need for businesses to become more lean and efficient, taxpayers want to know that their tax dollars are being used for programs and services that have superior impact. Historically, taxpayers have expressed a marked dislike of wasteful government spending. Voters will use data and information that shows how their hard-earned tax dollars are invested to evaluate the performance of elected officials. The availability—or lack—of such critical information may influence their choice of candidates to vote into office.

Target Demographic Groups

Many government programs are designed to serve or benefit a specific target demographic. For example, state governments often have departments devoted to serving individuals with disabilities, those with behavioral and mental health issues, the aging population, children, or business owners. In some cases, target population groups are directly served by government programs and services to address areas as diverse as health care, road maintenance, and job training. In other instances, government activities are designed to educate specific populations or change attitudes and behaviors as a means of achieving a certain mission;

government dollars have been used, for example, to fund education campaigns designed to reduce the number of drunk drivers, increase the number of new mothers choosing to breastfeed, and raise awareness about the importance of saying no to drugs.

Regardless of whether participants are directly served or are simply the recipients of information, these demographic groups must typically engage with the government organization in some manner. Data and information that discusses how participants' lives will be changed in desired ways will motivate further participation and will inevitably lead to more successful outcomes for the government organization.

As an example, the U.S. Small Business Administration (SBA) is an independent agency of the federal government designed to help Americans start, build, and grow businesses. Aspiring entrepreneurs and small business owners are not required to participate in SBA programs. Therefore, for the SBA to achieve its mission, it needs to deliver a message and provide data on how it is worth a business owner's time to engage in these programs. Providing data that (1) demonstrates the specific benefits and (2) outlines the ways in which the Small Business Administration has helped other business owners grow their businesses will likely motivate greater participation.

The Legislative Branch

Most government budgets are set by legislators. Depending on the level and type of government organization, audiences of budget data will include senators, representatives, commissioners, and boards. Functionally, these groups are similar to nonprofit boards, as they each have a role in establishing the priorities of the government organizations through laws or regulations. In addition, these stakeholders often approve the government organization's budget.

At the state and national level, the legislature has the power to create or dissolve government organizations. Legislative bodies may also fund or defund programs. Legislators are elected. In theory, they serve the best interests of their constituents. To make the best decisions, they require data points that help them decide how programs are impacting the citizens they represent.

Legislators are interested in how and how well government programs benefit the public they serve. The more effectively a government body can demonstrate with data that its programs and services are delivering high impact to citizens and helping the government preserve resources and eliminate wasteful spending, the more likely those organizations will receive full and continued funding.

The Executive Branch

From the president of the United States to state governors and mayors, government leaders in the executive branch have significant influence over priorities of government spending. In many cases, they provide a budget that goes to the legislature for consideration and further refinement. In addition, elected leaders can veto budget items. These officials are often elected on the basis of specific campaign promises. Government organizations that effectively communicate how their programs advance the campaign promises of elected officials are likely to receive favorable treatment in the budget process.

Budget Offices

Theoretically, the legislative and executive branches will use the data provided by government organizations to set priorities and fund programs. However, budget offices, which range from entities at the state and federal levels to accountants or treasurers at the local level, wield significant power over the funding of government. Regardless of the level, budget offices are responsible for helping the executive branch prepare a budget. They provide a level of accountability to the budget-making process. Because they have the ear of elected executives and often make recommendations, it is important that agencies collect data that is relevant to these agencies and their budget priorities.

In recent years, budget offices have become more interested in obtaining performance data along with fiscal information prior to sharing funding recommendations. Organizations that have moved toward a high-performance measurement culture will be in the best position to demonstrate their impact during the budget process. When performance measures provide evidence of sustained effectiveness, these organizations are likely to appear as favorable candidates for continued funding at the highest levels during the budget process.

The federal government took an even larger step in July 2013, when the Office of Management and Budget (OMB) announced plans to prioritize budget requests that strengthen the use of evidence and innovation. The OMB is implementing processes designed to strengthen the ability of all government agencies to continually improve and enhance program performance by applying existing evidence about what works, generating new knowledge, and using experimentation and innovation to test new approaches to program delivery. The rationale for this shift is rooted in the current fiscal challenges resulting from a deep national recession. Government agencies will continue to face challenging choices in how to meet an increased demand for services in a constrained, resource-poor environment.

The OMB is urging agencies to allocate resources to programs and practices backed by strong evidence of effectiveness while trimming all activities that are shown to be not effective by collected data (U.S. Office of Management and Budget, 2013a). The OMB defines evidence as evaluation results, performance measures, and other relevant data analytics and research studies and maintains a preference for high-quality, experimental, and quasi-experimental studies. Organizations that have not yet begun to move toward collecting and using data related to program impact in key outcome areas will encounter significant challenges in meeting this new request in 2015.

Other Government Funders

Many state and local government programs are funded by organizations that represent higher levels of government. For example, local courts may receive grants from their state's supreme court or from the state department of juvenile justice. These funders are looking for evidence of impact that aligns with that agency's specific mission.

Media

When it comes to government organizations, the press often scrutinizes and reports on government spending. Reporters and other media professionals are interested in data that shows how governments are delivering high-quality services at the lowest cost possible. The media is likely to be more favorable toward an agency that is transparent about how it is responsibly investing resources to solve problems in the community.

The media are also interested in learning how a particular government program delivers a high return on investment, wisely using taxpayer dollars to solve a problem that in the long run will reduce government spending. For example, government dollars spent on job training will likely reduce the level of future funding needed for food stamps and Medicaid programs because the individuals who have received training have acquired the skills needed to provide for themselves and meet their own basic needs.

Organizational Staff

Like nonprofit leaders and program managers, government staffs need solid data on the impact and outcomes of their programs. This data allows them to make program improvements and adjustments. In addition to the demonstration of positive results achieved through their programs, solid data also provides insight into why certain programs are working or not working. Such data empowers government leaders to institute changes that lead to even greater effectiveness. The better the data an organization collects about what is working and why it is working, the more easily government managers can improve programs and services, making them better stewards of public dollars.

Barriers to Implementation

Data-driven cultures benefit government organizations in a myriad of ways, allowing them to better utilize resources, improve and strengthen communities, and potentially reduce the tax burden on citizens. In spite of this, only a fraction of government organizations are performing at a high level. As state and federal budget makers require agencies to become more data-driven, these numbers will likely increase; however, the leaders of government organizations face several barriers to implementation.

While many government organizations collect data, this does not mean that leaders are using the information to deliver more impactful and effective programming. If government leaders truly want to move toward a high-performance measurement culture, they must remain aware of the forces aligned against their efforts to initiate change. Most of the unique barriers to success in government agencies stem from the historical structure of these agencies. Government was originally structured to focus more on compliance and monitoring and less on performance and impact. Leaders who anticipate and plan workarounds for these common barriers will be more likely to prevail when they face these common challenges to success.

Tangles of Red Tape

Our society assumes that government organizations are bureaucracies. The typical government agency has a vertical pyramid structure, with many more offices, bureaus, and employees located at the base than near the top management level. These organizations have a hierarchy of authority, division of responsibilities, and strict operational procedures. The officers and employees at lower levels of the organization must follow clear rules and regulations that dictate how they function. These procedural rules result in layers of documentation and multiple levels of checks and balances that are then made available to officers and administrators at higher levels in the organization.

Prior to the explosion of technological tools and easy access to data, these structures were necessary to manage a large, complex organization in an orderly manner. In addition, many regulations of government organizations were created to provide greater accountability and consistent levels of customer service. Yet many of the regulatory elements found in today's government organizations impede progress or are in direct opposition to the organizational structures needed for a successful measurement culture.

Greater impact and efficiency come when the organization quickly uses a program and processes data to make real-time program improvements. This is more difficult to do when there are multiple layers of red tape. Changes in office policies and procedures often require many levels of approval, resulting in slower implementation of data-driven strategies for program and policy improvements. Change agents working in government often become frustrated with the pace of change and either give up or move on to another organization that is more responsive and well-suited for quick implementation.

Although it requires a considerable investment of time and effort to transform a government agency into one with a high-performance measurement culture that adapts and adjusts quickly to current data and information, it is achievable. Agency leaders can help speed the process by examining every work rule and policy within their control that runs counter to the principles and structures of a measurement culture. Leaders should begin by identifying redundancies and built-in inefficiencies that are likely to delay or impede progress toward a reliance on data-driven strategies. It is also important to communicate regularly and consistently across all levels of the agency, and sometimes between agencies, as measurement strategies are being implemented. The better and more thorough the communication, the more quickly government organizations can successfully implement change.

Bargaining Units and Civil Service Regulations

Along with policy and program rules and regulation, many governments also operate under strict civil service rules and bargaining unit agreements with unions. Such rules and agreements are in place to protect employees and ensure that there is transparency in government hiring and employment. Yet many of these regulations have become so strict that they form a barrier and severely limit an organization's ability to adopt the measurement cultures that will enable them to become more efficient and effective.

In one state agency, professional employees were given the broad job classification of Management Supervisor II. Individuals across the organization had this title, including program staff, performance managers, human resources managers, and graphic designers. When the organization's budget was cut due to the recession, agency leaders were faced to lay off staff. Because of civil service statutes, layoffs in a job classification were based on tenure. Therefore, if the organization decided that the graphic designer position was not essential in this time of financial crisis and chose to eliminate the designer position, it would instead assign the designer to a new position. The designer would become the new data analyst.

This happened because the graphic designer had been with the agency longer than those in comparable positions. Based on civil service rules, this individual had the right to fill a job in a similar classification of a less-tenured employee. When situations like this occurred, employees who remained in the organization became dissatisfied in their assigned roles. Under-qualified individuals were often placed in key positions. This practice greatly lowers the performance quality of the organization and takes years to sort itself out. In addition, these regulations can make it very difficult to eliminate employees who are interfering with the move and efforts toward a high-performance measurement culture.

Although there are real barriers to implementation, government leaders should implement as many data-driven strategies as they possibly can as they move their organizations toward a high-performance measurement culture. Leaders will no doubt encounter a few more obstacles when they must move an organization from a decision-making system of compliance and rule following to one that operates from the measurement foundation of feedback and data. Lasting success is predicated on an increase in full communication with union representatives, human resources managers, and legal staff that details the reasons behind the shift toward a data-driven culture. As leaders are persistent and stay the course, the policies and staffing issues work themselves out. Patience and communication are the keys to success.

Elections

Agency leaders are the biggest driving force in achieving the full implementation of a high-performance measurement culture. Their diligence in asking for data and using data to make decisions will move an organization toward greater effectiveness and impact. Unlike the turnover experienced in private and nonprofit organizations, turnover at the executive leadership levels of government organizations is expected and built into the structure, as government agency leaders are often appointed by elected officials.

With each new election comes a new leader at the top of the organization's structure. Unfortunately, these newly elected leaders many not be familiar with the organization's data capabilities and use of performance measures. They may not recognize the need for the agency to become data-centric. In such cases, the organization may revert back to a level of mediocrity and find that its impact is diminished. In addition, newly elected officials may bring in new priorities, making the data that was being used and collected less relevant than it had been under a previous administration.

As budget makers continue to ask agencies to provide data and evidence of what works, organizational leaders can refocus on the need for data compliance and a system for data collection and utilization. Whether or not an agency director is familiar with measurement policies, a lack of trustworthy evidence will result in a lack of funding, and the situation will be at the forefront for constituents. When leaders take appropriate corrective action, data-driven cultures will replace the model of redundancy and inefficiency that governments often adopt by default.

No Direct Access to Clients and Participants

A key challenge that government organizations must tackle as they move toward a system of measuring performance and outcomes is determining how and where to obtain the data. As discussed in the previous chapter, many government organizations administer funding and rely on programs over which they have no direct control. For example, state departments of mental health typically do not serve clients directly; rather, they contract with independent social service providers who provide mental health services to clients, so access to data related to end users requires cooperation from local mental health boards and agencies.

Successful data-driven government funders will use agreements that require these agencies to provide performance data in exchange for awarded grants and contracts. This may require legal reviews and discussions to ensure that proper data-sharing agreements are established. Issues related to client, patient, and student rights and privacy are frequently raised as reasons why government organizations cannot measure outcomes and performance. Despite this barrier, solutions can be found when agency leaders commit to obtaining this data in order to operate more effectively and efficiently and provide the best possible service.

Large and Outdated Data Systems

Most government organizations have been collecting at least some data for decades. At a minimum, most have been tracking services delivered and expenses paid. As a result, most organizations have created systems to capture this information as a means of increasing public accountability and transparency. Such systems, typically decades old and antiquated by today's standards, can actually become barriers to focusing on outcomes.

Organizations that have already established data systems are sometimes most resistant to change. These organizations may invest time and energy entering data into a system that was designed at a time when reporting capabilities were not as flexible. It can prove difficult and cumbersome to extract and interpret that data.

When a court system wanted to better understand where delays were occurring in their court processing, they turned to a database that contained every case served by the court. This system was designed to warehouse paper files. The system helped judges and court staff easily access all the records related to each case. However, the data could not easily be downloaded into a spreadsheet format for easy manipulation of the aggregate data.

Efforts to address the original question of where delays were occurring required either an expensive upgrade to the existing system or a workaround. Once records of a random sample of cases became available, each individual case file had to be coded into a spreadsheet structured for analysis. This process required more than 120 hours of manpower. Had the original database been structured in a way that allowed for full reporting functionality, this tedious and time-consuming process could have been avoided. If the database had been designed so users could easily pull fields to collect specific data points, this task could have been accomplished in less than a day.

This tedious process did turn out to be worth the effort. The useful data it produced helped court officials understand that low-level misdemeanors were clogging up the docket. The court opted to dismiss many of these less important cases and used the information retrieved to seek a solution that would divert these cases in the future. As a result, fewer cases would be on the docket, freeing court time for more serious cases.

Although court leaders should be praised for embracing a data-driven approach to find a solution to the problems at hand, the outdated system made it difficult for the court to track results and know how effective the changes were. It could be years before the court can justify the expense to conduct another analysis. If the court chose to implement a case management system that allowed for better exporting of data, this study could be repeated regularly for consistent feedback and monitoring.

Government organizations with antiquated systems can expect to encounter ongoing challenges with accessing required data through these systems. When leaders enter organizations with an attitude that allows for flexibility, they are more likely to identify solutions that extend beyond current systems. If an organization finds itself with an outdated system that does not allow for the downloading and analysis of critical data, a recommended solution is to create a secondary system. This may require the implementation of workarounds, in which case government leaders must acknowledge the limitations until a new system can be purchased. Interim measures may require some duplication of data collection to ensure that data is gathered in a way that simplifies analysis. Once the secondary system has been successfully established, the organization may be in a position to approach budget makers about the need to update existing systems to support improved service delivery. When a new system is created, data users will know exactly what information they need, because they have been gathering and tracking data manually for some time.

An Inevitable Movement to Managing to Outcomes

Despite the many barriers that government leaders must overcome to achieve a successful measurement culture, there are also many forces that will help facilitate the implementation of effective measurement systems. In recent years, there has been a noticeable shift in conversation and practice that acknowledges that government organizations not only must be accountable for fiscal practices but also must track the results of following these practices. Government organizations no longer have the luxury of continuing to operate as they have in the past. The large federal debt and public dissatisfaction with the current economic crises require a move toward a more balanced budget. This is forcing government leaders to find new ways to make monetary cuts without failing in their obligation to fulfill the six functions of government.

The best way to achieve the change required is to take a data-driven approach, (1) investing money in programs and services that are proven to work well and (2) eliminating funding for things that are not working at all or are performing poorly. Noticeable shifts are occurring throughout the sector, and a clear movement has begun to affect change at the federal level as well as at many state and local levels. In recent years, the federal budget office has requested that agencies include new proposals for developing clear evidence that can be used to improve existing programs and inform decisions about new programs.

Given that the federal government enlists the help of state and other local programs to carry it out its mission, it is likely that these other levels of government are going to follow suit and begin to provide evidence of outcomes and impact. Early adopters of data-driven decision-making strategies will likely receive first-round funding. Organizations that choose to ignore this trend or struggle to make the changes to achieve a high-performance measurement culture may have difficulty obtaining funding.

Ample Resources

Compared to their nonprofit counterparts, government organizations are typically in a much better place in terms of the resources required to move toward a high-performance measurement culture. Many already have staff and resources in place to help carry out these functions. In such cases, it is a matter not of hiring new people but rather of realigning the workflow and staff assignments in the organization. For example, employees who in the past have focused on compliance and monitoring can shift their focus and start adding elements of outcomes and results to their activities.

Most government organizations already have some type of data collection system and do not need to create something out of nothing. The first step for the majority of agencies is to simply determine what data already exists and ask key questions about the most important data to collect and examine. What kind of information will help the organization or agency deliver more effective and efficient programs?

In many cases, the information needed to establish performance and outcomes measurement systems already exists somewhere within the organization. The focus can often shift to clarifying what needs to be measured, identifying where those measures already exist, and creating a plan for regular reporting and decision making about these measures. The remainder of this book will help agency leaders accomplish these critical tasks.

Public Demand for Change

The public is demanding something more than the status quo from government. Citizens want government leaders who are willing to stop fighting based on political lines and to work together. Using objective data is one of the best ways to move toward such bipartisanship and has the potential to replace the "I think" with "what is." As more government agencies become better at measuring and communicating how they are improving lives and changing circumstances, these organizations and the public sector as a whole will secure greater support from constituents and taxpayers.

In the last one hundred years, the government sector has continued to grow and establish more regulations, rules, and layers of bureaucracy with little improvement in societal outcomes. As a result, current systems are not naturally aligned with those critical elements needed for a high-performance measurement culture. Organizational change is possible, but it will take some government restructuring and a focus on using data to understand what is working and what can be improved.

Most government organizations have the resources needed to lead the movement to create better outcomes for the country as they perform necessary functions with less money. Inevitably, organizations must become more focused on outcomes as the access to data and information becomes more and more available. Early adopters will be in the best position to prosper during this time, because they will already have the evidence needed to demonstrate how programs will work. Organizations that implement a high-performance measurement culture position themselves to improve as other government organizations play catch up.

Next Steps

The processes outlined in this book can help those government leaders who see it as their responsibility to deliver more cost-effective services with the best possible results. Although they will experience challenges, with persistence and time, as these organizations move toward a high-performance measurement system their efforts will pay off. With decisive action, success is achievable across the social sector, including in public sector organizations.

The following chapters outline a clear path to move government and nonprofit organizations from mediocrity to excellence. Both nonprofit organizations and government agencies can follow this step-by-step plan, proven to create high-performance measurement cultures that contribute to the betterment of society.

Impact & Excellence

Chapter Five Discussion Questions

1. What strengths discussed in this chapter are found in your government organization? These strengths will support the strategic implementation of a high-performance measurement culture in your organization.
2. Who are the likely audiences that might consume your organization's data? What type of data will best motivate each of these groups?
3. What common barriers to implementation currently exist in your government agency?
4. What action steps could you take to help overcome these barriers?

6

Letting Go of Excuses

The "Five C's" of Easy and Effective Impact and Excellence

He that is good for making excuses is seldom good for anything else.
—BENJAMIN FRANKLIN

THE FULL POTENTIAL OF NONPROFIT and government organizations remains unrealized when the social sector fails to implement measurement cultures and instead clings to a series of excuses. Such excuses, often masquerading as barriers and obstacles, create and perpetuate a culture of mediocrity. They result in the organization's falling father and father behind. Potential funding and revenues do not flow to the organization. Staff morale declines. Communities remain stagnant or continue to struggle. Finally, the public becomes disengaged, and well-meaning organizations are often forced to close their doors or make severe cuts to critical services. Such negative outcomes are inexcusable and easily avoidable.

Those organizations that fail to collect and use data for decision making most commonly cite a shortage of time, resources, trained staff, and evaluation expertise as reasons (Carman and Fredericks, 2010). Too many government and nonprofit leaders give up in the face of these obstacles. But there are solutions and a clear path to easy and effective evaluation. Social-sector success is possible when organizational leaders find ways around obstacles rather than turning them into excuses that prevent success.

A Formula for Change

If social-sector leaders hope to create high-performance measurement cultures with a focus on measurement, thereby transforming their organizations, pursuing excellence, and increasing impact, three crucial elements must be considered: dissatisfaction, vision, and the first steps toward change. To achieve significant organizational, systemic, or individual change, all three must be present.

Richard Beckhard's well-known formula, outlined in *Organization Development: Strategies and Models* (1969), outlines the essential elements that result in change.

$$\text{Change} = D \times V \times F > R$$

This model, often called Gleicher's Formula, provides a way to assess the relative strengths affecting the likely success of organizational change efforts (Beckhard 1969). The formula suggests that in order for successful change to occur, dissatisfaction with the current state (D), a desired future vision (V), and the concrete first steps (F) must be stronger than the natural resistance to change (R). Dissatisfaction, vision, and first steps must be combined to overcome the natural resistance to change if organizational change is to occur. If any of these three ingredients is absent or present in a weakened state, resistance to change will dominate, and change will not occur.

The desire to lose weight provides a relatable illustration of this principle. Many want to lose weight, yet they frequently encounter significant obstacles and are unable to overcome resistance to change. This keeps them stuck in their current state.

As a personal example, after my third son was born, I decided it was time to lose the extra weight accumulated from my three pregnancies. I had a desired future vision. I visualized myself in a fabulous dress I had worn before delivering my first child. I imagined how great I would feel in the morning as I got dressed. I also knew the exact steps I needed to take to get there: I needed to eat fewer calories and exercise three to four times a week.

However, I was not really dissatisfied with my current state. After all, I was having fun with my family. I had not heard comments from my family and friends regarding my weight, and most of my prepregnancy clothes still fit. Because my level of dissatisfaction was not very strong, I never took the actions required to lose the weight. Quite simply, I was not motivated enough to accomplish the desired change.

Whether the goal is weight loss, the implementation of a new policy, or a complete overhaul of Medicaid, the root cause of a failure to change the current state can be traced back to the absence or lack of one of three factors: (1) dissatisfaction with the current state, (2) a clear desired future vision, and (3) the concrete first steps toward success.

Organizational change is especially difficult to effect, due to the number of people needed to engage in such change. The greater the number of people involved in an organization's change, the more detailed, strategic, and persistent the efforts needed to establish these three required elements and overcome the natural resistance to change.

The first three chapters of this book addressed two of the three required elements: dissatisfaction with the current state and the necessity of a clear vision for the future. The remainder of this book covers the third crucial ingredient to change: the concrete first steps that social-sector leaders need to take if they wish to pursue impact and excellence through the development of a high-performance measurement culture.

Rather than focusing on scarcity and lack, today's successful social-sector leaders are finding more effective ways to solve the world's most complex problems. As more organizations demonstrate clearly how they are changing lives, achieving greater impact, and providing social return on investment, increased numbers of government and nonprofits will fully realize their respective missions. This will create a ripple effect of stronger communities and will also result in decreased government reliance and contribute to a thriving economy.

An Urgent Call for Change

Thinking big and staying positive are important, but these actions alone are insufficient to achieve real change. To achieve the future vision of a social sector composed of strong leaders who are actively engaged in data-driven management, a clear dissatisfaction with the current state must motivate organizational leaders and stakeholders to take decisive action. Yet the social sector as a whole is not currently engaging in the practices required for increased impact, efficiency, and organizational change. Staff morale and positive press remain at historic lows, and less than a quarter of nonprofit and government agencies who participated in the Measurement Resources Measurement Culture Survey were found to have adopted a high-performance measurement culture.

At this point in history there is a swelling dissatisfaction with the current state of our national economy and with the strategies proposed by government leaders for dealing with pressing economic issues. The national debt stands at approximately $17 trillion. Without question, our nation's leaders will be required to make difficult decisions on what must be cut and then communicate their funding decisions to the public.

The stress of waiting to learn where those cuts may be made is currently creating a wave of dissatisfaction and concern throughout the social sector. Organizational leaders who are equipped to communicate with data and bipartisan facts will have a higher likelihood for success. In addition, donors are dealing with the uncertainty of tax increases, reduced deductions for charitable donations, and an overall decline in assets resulting from falling real estate prices and stock market losses experienced after the crash of 2008. Although giving is starting to recover along with the economy, it is still 8 percent from where it once was (Hrywna, 2013). Organizations that demonstrate how investing in their cause helps change lives and circumstances are more likely to capture a portion of these coveted dollars.

Despite this documented decline in funding, the demand for services is greater now than ever before and continues to rise. The Measurement Culture Survey revealed that nearly 70 percent of organizations reported an increased demand in services during the current year or an expected increase in services in the next two years. The rising need makes it clear: now is not the time to blindly reduce or cut programs and services. Rather, now is the time for innovative approaches and a change in the way social-sector business is conducted.

Learning from Baseball

A comparison can be made between the current state of the social sector and the state of baseball in the early 2000s as portrayed in the movie *Moneyball* (Miller, 2011). During this period, the Oakland A's were one of the lowest-funded teams in major league baseball. When the team achieved some success, they began to lose their best players to teams with higher payrolls. Instead of giving up and accepting the situation, General Manager Billy Beane used his dissatisfaction with the situation as motivation to do things differently. He created change.

Beane is credited with revolutionizing baseball by taking a data-driven approach to building his team. He used player statistics to achieve the goal of winning baseball games by securing runs and getting players on base. Based on the changes Beane made, the Oakland A's broke the record for the longest winning streak in American League baseball history. Although the A's did not become the American League champions and advance to the World Series, the team's innovation had a ripple effect on major league baseball. Two years later, the Boston Red Sox won the World Series using the data-driven principles implemented by Billy Beane.

My belief that the social sector can use the principles in *Moneyball* to get the sector back on track and move toward higher performance is shared by a growing number of those within the public sector. Moneyball for Government is a Results for America (2013) project launched to encourage governments at all levels to increase their use of evidence and data when investing limited taxpayer dollars.

This bipartisan group of government leaders is committed to helping improve outcomes for young people, their families, and communities. The group does so by building evidence about the practices, policies, and programs that will achieve the most effective and efficient results so that policymakers can make better decisions. They are investing taxpayer dollars in those programs that use evidence and data to demonstrate that they work. In addition, leaders are committed to directing funds away from practices, policies, and programs that consistently fail to achieve measurable outcomes.

The leaders of the Moneyball for Government program are building momentum toward high-performance measurement cultures in the organizations they serve. They are focusing on outcomes and changed lives rather than being content to focus on compliance and numbers served. They are using data to invest in and scale innovations that will make greater, faster progress in surmounting the challenges facing young people, their families, and their communities. Together, these organizations are focusing on funding communities that collaborate and use data and evidence to achieve significant community-wide impact.

Accepting mediocrity and failure due to crippling economic conditions is not an option for today's social-sector organizations. It is time to revolutionize how organizations are managed. The foundational step is to establish performance measures, managing to outcomes that lead to a change from business as usual. This, in turn, changes lives and circumstances. Innovation is imperative, and the time to take action is now, not later.

A Fork in the Road

There are two common approaches social-sector leaders take when faced with the current state. One path contributes to growth; the other leads to decline. When organizational leaders remain focused on the negative realities and allow these realities to overshadow the desired future state, fear drives them to deal with an anticipated decline in funding by uniformly cutting programs.

Worry begins to block innovative thinking and interferes with the organization's drive toward excellence. When new ideas or ways of doing business are presented, organizational leaders begin to raise roadblocks. "Now is not the time to take risks," they say. "We don't have the money to do that."

Rather than focusing on the organization's mission and vision, organizations that fall into this camp become consumed with budget-cutting measures and rapidly ramp up fundraising efforts. Program staff and organizational leaders start chasing dollars. All too often, they apply for grants that are not aligned with the organization's mission.

In some scenarios, the organization receives the misaligned grant funding and engages in work that is not congruent with its stated mission. Because of this discrepancy, the organization becomes less effective than promised in the grant application, resulting in disappointment for the funder. This downward-spiraling cycle ultimately hurts the very clients the organization desires to impact and weakens the organization's focus.

Alternatively, the prospective funder may realize the organization is not well suited for a particular grant and then make a decision not to fund the organization. This heightens the organization's fear and worry around funding and leads to further programmatic and administrative budget cuts. Either situation leads to an increase in turnover, a decrease in morale, and a continued decline in impact and excellence. This pattern was present in many of the nonprofits that have ceased operation in the past decade.

Substance Abuse Treatment Provider: A Case Study

A substance abuse treatment provider geared to serve *low-risk*, high-need juveniles was actively pursuing government grants that would enable the organization to provide the same services to *high-risk*, high-need juveniles. The organization based its decision to apply for funding strictly on the money available and not on an existing organizational strategy to expand services to the high-risk youth target population. The organization received the grant and then sought to fit services for high-risk juveniles into its low-risk programming.

The results were devastating. Not only did high-risk juveniles experience less-than-optimal success, but outcomes for low-risk youth were also reduced when the two populations were mixed. Staff members were not properly trained to deal with this new population, which quickly caused frustration and burnout. Ultimately, the organization lost both funding and its reputation in the community as a quality treatment center.

A Closer Look. Contrast this failed approach with the alternative. When faced with the same current realities, leaders at a second organization opted to confront the facts. Leaders in this organization were determined to meet challenges directly. They wanted to establish real and lasting change. They allowed the dissatisfaction of their current state to become a stepping-stone, using it to create a strong and vivid future vision.

Instead of arguing that the organization couldn't expand its services due to financial constraints, leaders of this organization asked, "How can we expand our services with the resources we do have?" They sought innovative solutions and further clarified their mission. These leaders were committed to doing whatever was required to move them closer to the future vision, no matter how distant it seemed.

Leaders in the second organization were strategic about the grant opportunities and partnerships they sought and quickly rewarded with opportunities that allowed them to grow. They bolstered their reputation as effective service providers. In spite of a weakened economy, they increased both the number and the strength of their strategic partnerships, achieved greater impact, and saw substantial growth in revenues.

Youth-Serving Residential Treatment Facility: A Case Study

Many residential treatment facilities across the country are closing their doors as child welfare and court agencies shift to home- and community-based treatment models. However, one youth service organization that was primarily known as a residential treatment facility was able to successfully expand its impact by 206 percent in a single year.

This organization had every reason to start cutting programs. The organization's primary funders, typically court systems and child service agencies, were reducing their reliance on residential treatment providers to solve their clients' needs.

Instead of making deep cuts to services, organizational leaders focused even more closely on their core mission, which was to create positive environments where children succeeded. They began to restructure some programs and to build on community-based services to create positive environments in the community. To do this, the organization formed strategic alliances with several community referral partners, such as the local children's hospital.

As a result, the organization expanded community-based services from 60 to 184 youth and grew from a team composed of just 4 members to a team of 13. These efforts not only provided increased revenues to the organization but also expanded both the organization's impact and its reputation in the community.

Letting Go of Excuses

Why did the group in the first case study fail, whereas the second group succeeded? The differentiating factor was the willingness of an organization's leadership to examine the reality and to take the first step. Leaders of the youth-serving organization took a no-excuses approach to arrive at their desired future vision; the substance abuse treatment provider viewed current obstacles as barriers to success, made excuses for playing it safe, and then rationalized those excuses.

To transform the 77 percent of social-sector organizations that have not embraced a high-performance measurement culture, it is imperative that leaders let go of excuses. Yet although many organizational leaders have seen the handwriting on the wall and would like to enact change, most of them fail to act swiftly.

"There's a difference between interest and commitment," says Art Turock (1988), a motivational speaker, author, and organizational researcher. "When you're interested in doing something, you do it only when circumstances permit. When you're committed to something, you accept no excuses, only results." The strategies that follow will achieve impact only when leaders do two things: (1) make the firm commitment to succeed and (2) follow that decision with the recognition and effective removal of common excuses for not pursuing implementation.

Common Excuses

As highlighted throughout this book, organizations with high-performance measurement cultures systematically collect and use a variety of data to manage operations and demonstrate effectiveness. Leaders who maintain high-performance measurement cultures are significantly more likely to report increases in positive press, funding, efficiency, staff morale, and organizational change. Though every nonprofit organization needs to engage in program and outcomes measurement, many remain resistant to change. Many nonprofit leaders incorrectly perceive program evaluation and data-driven decision making as a luxury they simply cannot afford.

The common misperception that organizations cannot afford to implement needed measurement activities prevents nonprofit organizations from implementing critical measurement tools. Although an overwhelming 81 percent of nonprofit leaders surveyed by the Center for Effective Philanthropy believe nonprofits should demonstrate the effectiveness of their work through performance measures (Brock, Buteau, and Herring, 2012), the Measurement Culture Survey reveals that only 27 percent of nonprofits are fully embracing a high-performance measurement culture.

The most dangerous excuses are those that masquerade as current realities. A 2010 study of nonprofit organizations revealed that only 45 percent of nonprofits were fully engaged in program evaluation activities, even though the majority of the organizations understood the value of these efforts (Carman and Fredericks, 2010). More than half of organizations cited not enough time, not enough funding, and not enough evaluation expertise as the top three barriers. Not enough staff and not enough trained staff were also identified. Barriers, challenges, obstacles; whichever word is used to describe existing blocks, these are, in reality, mere excuses. The good news is that such perceived barriers to success are merely persistent myths an organization's staff and stakeholders wrongly interpret as fixed reality.

Results from the Measurement Culture Survey also showed no correlation between high-performance measurement culture and organizational size and budget. As shown in Figure 6.1, 22 percent of organizations with budgets less than two million dollars were found to have high-performance measurement cultures, while 28 percent of organizations with budgets greater than five million dollars were consistently using data in management activities. Organizational size was not a determining factor in whether an organization embraced a data-driven, high-performance measurement culture.

Likewise, many small, single-employee or all-volunteer organizations achieve great success measuring their outcomes and using data to achieve organizational outcomes. At the other end of the spectrum, some organizations with a staff of more than a hundred and budgets in the millions struggle with the effective implementation of program evaluation and outcome measures. An organization's capacity for data-driven decision making has very little to do with its identified mission, geographical location, staff size, total budget, or growth trajectory.

Figure 6.1. Organizational Budget and Measurement Culture

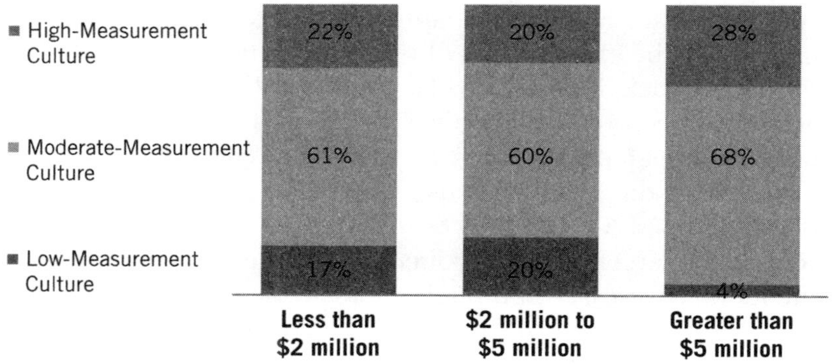

Pickaway HELPS: A Case Study

Pickaway HELPS is a small nonprofit dedicated to providing college readiness services in a rural county school district. Christy Mills, the executive director and the only paid staff member at the time of the interview, is a great example how a small organization is making a big commitment to creating a data-driven culture. Mills believes that "data are the answer to future success." Within a limited budget, Mills continually seeks the best ways to validate Pickaway HELPS's work and demonstrate organizational impact with data.

Mills selected three measures found in college preparation literature to link with increased readiness: increase in the percentage of students who took the ACT, increase in the number of students filing a FAFSA form, and increase in the number of college applications. The organization partners with and receives ongoing funding from area schools, thanks in part to Mills' continued efforts to demonstrate the success of the Pickaway HELPS program offering. Mills cultivates relationships with the school guidance counselors, and she obtained reports that contained key data. She instituted an annual review of this data, presenting it to the organization's board of directors and partnering schools.

Data has proven invaluable to the organization's efforts to increase student access to college. One example: Mills found that the data showed a decrease in the number of students taking the ACT, because students did not know what to expect from the test. Armed with this information, Mills made programming changes and was able to obtain funding to administer an ACT preparation workshop where students take portions of the ACT and to increase the number of students who had access to this important indicator of success.

A Closer Look. Measurement is an essential tool that helps government and nonprofit organizations achieve greatness. The path to organizational effectiveness begins with the commitment of leaders to move from simply gathering data to achieving excellence with the data they have collected. Once this commitment is made, organizations find the resources needed to successfully engage in the activities.

Great nonprofits let go of the excuse that performance and outcome measurement is "too expensive." Instead they ask, "How can we achieve the impact and excellence we desire to achieve?" Successful leaders find the required time and resources needed to establish performance measurement systems that fit within their budget and lead the organization to positive results.

Game Change

The trend toward outcomes-based funding and data-driven performance cultures in government and the nonprofit sector is comparable to the burgeoning popularity of the Internet in the mid-1990s. Think back to how business communication took place before the Internet became ubiquitous. Telephone calls, memos, and letters sent through the mail were commonplace means of communication. Organizations that opted not to invest in the new internet technology found it increasingly difficult to maintain the same level of productivity and effectiveness.

In a similar manner, outcomes measurement is radically changing the way the social sector does business. It has already had major ramifications in what funders and donors expect in terms of grant reporting. These swift changes will only be amplified in the years ahead. Leaders reluctant to embrace the emerging trend of managing to outcomes through the creation of high-performance measurement cultures not only will forfeit important organizational outcomes such as efficiency, staff morale and positive press; they also are likely to see declining revenues.

Across the public, social, and private sectors, there is an increasing call to engage in two dramatic shifts. The first call comes for those who fund government and nonprofit organizations, who increasingly support only mission-driven, high-performance causes that provide services aimed at solving our nation's social challenges. The second is a call for public and private funding decisions to be made based on merit instead of traditions.

Leaders who understand the importance of a data-driven culture engage in performance evaluation and outcomes measurement even when they are not required to do so by their funder. Others wait for funders to provide resources and guidance to engage in these efforts. Only 32 percent of nonprofit leaders agreed that their funders were helpful in assessing the organization's progress toward goals (Brock, Buteau, and Herring, 2012). This gap between shifting expectations on the part of the funding community and the typical nonprofit's measurement culture must be addressed.

On first review, it seems logical to expect funders who require outcome measurement to fund such efforts. Yet when viewed through a different lens, a funder's contribution toward measurement and assessment seems unnecessary. When funders give to an organization, they are paying for the expectation of changed lives and changed circumstances in exchange for the investment of funds.

This thinking is similar to parents who invest in a child's private school education. Parents are paying for outcomes—increased knowledge, skill, and future opportunities for their child. They want their investment to support their child's education and expect the school to do whatever it takes to successfully deliver that education as well as provide feedback about the progress and success of their child.

Parents do not expect to pay extra dollars for schools to administer tests and provide parent-teacher conferences. Rather, these activities are accepted as a standard way of doing business. The better the school is at achieving and communicating student outcomes, the more popular the school becomes. This results in increased enrollment and the ability to command higher tuition rates.

Corporate and foundation funders have widely varying views of whether it is their responsibility to pay for evaluation and outcome measurement efforts in the organizations they choose to fund. Some funders are investing in capacity-building grants that include dollars for efforts designed to increase organizations' use of evaluation and measures in their every day practices. Some allocate a small portion of grant resources, though generally no more than 10 percent, for evaluation efforts. Yet most believe that data-driven decision making is a cost of doing business and a required operational expense that allows the organization to achieve its desired impact and excellence. For most funders, evaluation and outcomes measurement are viewed as no different from an organization's investment in e-mail communication, internet access, and websites—activities not typically funded by grant makers.

Now is the time for leaders to make the commitment to gather required resources and respond proactively to this new expectation. Waiting for additional funding before taking action may put the organization in jeopardy. Mario Morino (2012) said it best: "This is not the time to be 'ostrich leaders,' burying our heads in the sand. Instead we need sector leaders, elected officials, powerful influencers, and people from all walks of life to stand up and say, 'Enough! It's time to change!'"

Five Easy and Effective Steps to Excellence and Impact

Even when organizations do not receive direct funding to implement measurement systems, they often can find a way to afford it. Leaders who choose to invest in a high-performance measurement culture, alongside the appropriate evaluation and outcome measures, soon realize that doing so does not require an abundance of additional resources. It is simply a matter of doing things differently.

Sometimes the decision to invest in a high-performance measurement culture means letting go of outdated models and releasing attitudes that no longer serve efforts to fulfill the organizational mission. Often, it means strategically examining the data already collected and devising a plan to use that data to make the best decisions. This may require a small investment to design new processes, select systems, and train staff on the new way of doing business. Committed leaders will find that there is no need to reinvent the wheel. Impact and excellence are easily within their reach.

The Five C's of easy and effective impact and excellence have the power to transform any organization. These five elements entail proven, practical strategies for all social-sector organizations, regardless of size, budget, and activities. These motivational strategies can be easily incorporated into any organization's culture and accommodated by any budget. They can often be implemented with current staff and volunteers and do not require an infusion of additional resources.

The bottom line for today's social sector: sustained success requires more than merely collecting data and running reports. Lasting change will depend on taking appropriate action as it relates to the Five C's:

1. Making changes to organizational culture and leadership
2. Clarifying organizational mission
3. Measuring the right things and capturing impact
4. Communicating the results effectively
5. Making data-informed changes and celebrating success

The Next Step

Countless organizations have implemented these methods and have experienced increased revenues, efficiency, and impact. The remaining chapters of this book outline these easy-to-implement strategic actions one by one. Together, they can lead any organization to greater impact and excellence.

Impact & Excellence

Chapter Six Discussion Questions

1. Consider your organization's recent attempts at organizational change and activities that proved unsuccessful. Were all three of the components necessary to achieving change (dissatisfaction with the current state, a clear desired future vision, and concrete first steps) present?
2. Which missing or inadequate factors do you believe blocked or hindered success by their absence? What could you have done to add and strengthen these three critical factors? How might this have contributed to a different outcome and led to successful change?
3. Common excuses include not enough time, not enough money, not enough staff, not enough trained staff, and not enough knowledge. What obstacles or excuses have prevented your organization from fully implementing outcomes measurement and data-driven strategies?
4. How can you turn a perceived barrier around and find a way to overcome the excuse? For example, rephrase the statement "We don't have enough money" as a question: "How can we implement outcome measurement strategies within our existing resources [staff, budget, and time]?"

7

Culture and Leadership

A great leader's courage to fulfill his vision comes from passion, not position.
—JOHN MAXWELL

MEASUREMENT FOR MEASUREMENT'S SAKE will not produce the widespread organizational changes needed to achieve high-performance measurement cultures equipped to realize greater impact and excellence. Organizations need the right measures, culture, and leadership in place to systematically use the appropriate data to manage programs, make improvements, and demonstrate unique impact and value.

To successfully adapt to the expectation of increased outcomes measurement, organizations must first ensure that leadership and foundational structures align closely with the principles of a thriving, high-performance measurement culture. Without a strong culture that supports the performance and outcomes measurement in place, data collection and measurement activities become a waste of time and in some cases may even damage the organization.

Early in my career, I was frequently retained to assist organizations as they developed evaluation plans and put in place foundational systems for measuring key outcomes. Yet I invested much of my time helping these organizations align their cultures to support measurement activities and quickly realized that culture was the foundation to success. It became clear that the widely accepted model of doing business in nonprofit and government organizations was not structured to support successful data-driven cultures.

For the past decade, an increasing number of organizations have been attempting to fit outcomes measures into a system that is not designed to support them. As such, many attempts to implement performance measures fail miserably. When they do, employees become jaded and understandably want to run the other way when they hear the term "outcomes." The implementation of data-driven measurement activities is critical, but organizations seeking to adopt a high-performance measurement culture based on outcomes measures must first consider their organizational culture. When leaders try to implement measurement activities prior to examining and investing in their culture, they may experience unnecessary struggles with system implementation and overall success.

At a recent workshop, a program manager shared his experience. It was one with which many others in attendance could relate. The manager shared that his organization had put measures in place before considering the organizational structure and culture. The organization had wanted to become more efficient and effective, and the leadership team decided that managing to spreadsheets was the way to achieve this goal. Frontline staff members were not included in the process of developing measures, and the new measures were mandated without much explanation. There was little or no discussion of how these new activities would help employees serve clients more effectively or support the achievement of mission-critical goals.

The measurement program failed in a dramatic fashion. Morale tanked; productivity decreased; clients sensed the stress and, as a result, disengaged from the organization's program and service offerings. As in many similar cases, the measures themselves were not necessarily the problem. Rather, the leadership's failure to fully communicate the rationale for new measurement activities, combined with the lack of a supportive culture, prevented the success of this strategic measurement initiative.

A Commitment to Data-Driven Excellence

An organization makes the leap into greatness when its leaders move from simply collecting data to achieving excellence by interpreting, analyzing, and applying collected data. I witnessed this firsthand when two organizations went through a major transition. Both organizations were fortunate to be led by executive directors who had invested in managing to outcomes. Both had allocated significant time and financial resources to developing and using performance and outcomes measures. A commitment to leadership and data-driven measurement led both organizations to experience increased funding, greater impact, and expanded services.

Then both organizations experienced turnover at the executive level. Well-meaning governing boards of both organizations selected new leaders. Each of these leaders had significant knowledge and experience in their respective fields, and both boards believed this knowledge and experience to be the most important criterion for an effective director. In the hiring, interview, and transition process, little attention was given to the new director's ability to cultivate vision and purpose, build partnerships and alliances, direct and manage work, enable constructive change, and encourage dialogue. These essential leadership competencies, each required to effectively manage a social-sector organization in the twenty-first century, did not appear to be part of the hiring criteria. Both new executive directors lacked these crucial skills.

Although the staff in both organizations remained engaged in measurement systems instituted under previous directors, within eighteen months these data systems were put aside. Partnerships and funding began to dry up. Turnover skyrocketed. The quality of service declined significantly. This all-too-common situation illustrates one striking conclusion that can be drawn from Measurement Resources' survey research: winning measurement systems alone are not enough to achieve desired impact. Likewise, neither excellent leadership nor a satisfactory work environment is sufficient to support those nonprofit and government organizations that must navigate times of great change.

Three Essential Ingredients

Achieving impact and excellence requires a combination of the ideal culture, the ideal leadership, and the ideal success measures, as shown

Figure 7.1. Impact and Excellence

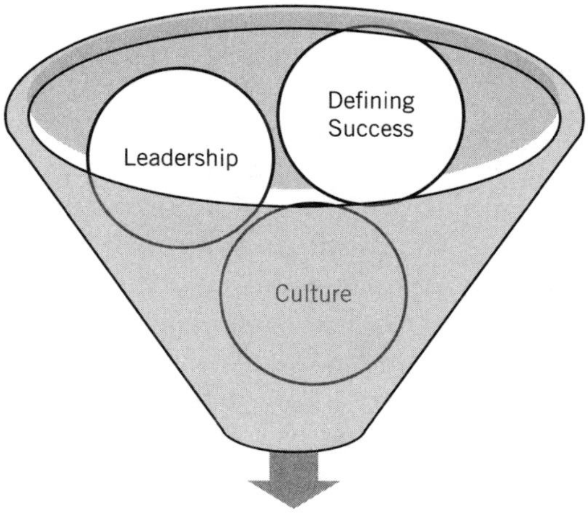

in Figure 7.1. These three essential ingredients are foundational to an organization's achievement of a high-performance measurement culture. Let's examine each of these factors in greater detail.

Ideal Culture

Successful social-sector organizations constantly strive to enhance the high-performance measurement culture they have embraced. They build from a solid foundation supported by performance and outcome measures that are strong and clear. Leaders of such organizations achieve such a culture by hiring and retaining the right leaders and staff for their particular organizations. They understand that talent can often compensate for a lack of resources, but money can never compensate for a lack of the right people (Morino, 2011).

To retain the best leadership and staff, successful nonprofit and government organizations create systems based on data and learning, feedback, and autonomy. These elements encourage, motivate, and reward high-achieving team members who are positive and self-motivated. Great organizations avoid the "doing more with less" syndrome by hiring the right people and creating the precise data-driven systems that naturally produce more with less.

Ideal Leadership

Great nonprofit leaders maintain a focus on the organization's core mission. They lead with humility and exhibit a clear passion for and alignment with the organizational mission. They do whatever it takes, in an ethical manner, to fully realize that mission by aligning organizational priorities and performance measures. When results are less than desirable, great leaders use performance measures to make necessary course corrections. In situations where desired targets are met, these leaders use data to demonstrate and celebrate success.

Ideal Success Measures

The most effective organizations measure success based on the distinct impact they are making and the effectiveness of services delivered relative to organizational resources. In addition to measuring the number of clients served, the amount of money raised, and the number of activities performed, these organizations measure outcomes—the extent to which their programs and services have positively changed lives and circumstances for clients, stakeholders, and the communities they serve.

The Link between Culture and Measurement

Nonprofit and government organizations that excel make it a priority to examine culture, ensuring that it aligns with high-performance measurement principles and incorporates appropriate outcomes measures. Contrary to a common perception among those employed in the social sector, many cultural changes require a minimal investment of money. Such changes do, however, require an abiding commitment to excellence. To break free from the status quo, leaders need to purposely and deliberately make the move toward a measurement culture.

Stakeholders must embrace a common definition of a high-performance measurement culture. Essentially, high-performing organizations adopt systems of knowledge with standards of perceiving, believing, evaluating, and acting that are influenced and informed by objective data and information. A high-performance measurement culture does not begin and end with the establishment of a set of performance metrics and running reports.

Leaders of high-performance measurement cultures leverage data and information to influence decisions and behavior that are consistent with organizational expectations. In a high-performance measurement culture, measures are both driven by and supported by leaders, and the values of selected measures are communicated and embraced at every level of the organization. These measurement systems unite staff and often result in employees' feeling valued and included.

Adaptive cultures are a hallmark of high-performing organizations. Organizations with robust measurement cultures have their finger on the pulse of both internal and external factors, continually refining and adapting to new data and information. Leaders in these strong cultures use measurement systems to help employees and stakeholders understand what has occurred and why it has occurred.

Culture Change

An organization's culture incorporates the values and assumptions shared by the people who work within the organization. It includes both what is important and what is not important to an organization. Consequently, it directs the work focus of everyone in the organization. Steven McShane and Mary Ann Von Glinow (2010) describe culture best as "the organization's DNA—invisible to the naked eye, yet a powerful template that shapes what happens in the workplace." All organizations have cultures, whether built intentionally or formed haphazardly.

Understanding the definition of organizational culture sheds light on why the implementation of the same outcomes measures works extremely well in one organization but fails in another. Thriving organizations develop a shared set of assumptions about the value of data. Within these organizations, individuals understand that measurement is helpful and necessary for growth and improvement. Executive leaders and employees also understand that measurement provides essential feedback information. They do not buy into the belief that measuring performance is difficult or time-consuming. Rather, they focus on the positive gains achieved by implementing them. Employees in these organizations naturally think in terms of evidence, proof, and outcomes in their decision-making processes.

Conversely, organizations that struggle with the incorporation of measurement systems typically exhibit a shared attitude that data tracking is "just another thing to do." Employees may view data measurement systems as cumbersome and complicated. Some within these organizations assume that the data collected will be used to punish. Others simply do not believe that data-driven evaluation is necessary for organizational growth and improvement.

When negative or even neutral attitudes toward data are ingrained in an organization's culture, the requirement of outcomes measurement activities does little to influence actual practice. Although the data may be tracked and reported, when the culture does not support measurement systems they are rarely used as an organizational growth strategy.

Most nonprofit and government organizations need specific strategies to shift practices and align the organization with the components of a high-performance measurement culture. As with any change, a change in culture must be precipitated by a level of dissatisfaction with the current state, a clear future vision, and concrete first steps to move toward the desired change.

We have established a clear basis for the necessity of a change in culture and demonstrated the positive results brought about by embracing a measurement culture. How does the organization take its first steps toward implementation of a high-performance measurement culture? There are clear and concrete steps required to move the organization toward the implementation of a successful high-performance measurement culture. We will take a closer look at four overarching strategies required for successful culture change:

- Taking decisive action
- Selecting and socializing employees
- Creating culturally consistent rewards
- Aligning organizational rituals, policies, and procedures

Strong cultures enhance the predictability of employee behavior; therefore stronger measurement cultures are more reliably predictive of actions that lead to impact and excellence. The greater the degree of movement within these four strategic action areas, the faster cultural change will occur. These efforts are also predictors of the strength and resiliency of an organizational culture that supports a data-driven approach.

Actions of Leadership

The basic definition of leadership relates to one's ability to influence others toward a particular outcome. Leadership is not a personality trait. Nor is it a fixed, unchangeable characteristic. If that were the case, U.S. companies would not have spent an estimated $13.6 billion dollars on leadership development in 2012 (Leonard and Loew, 2012).

Leadership encompasses a wide range of learned skills and behaviors, often called competencies. However, those qualities that make a good leader in one situation do not necessarily predict success in another setting. There are several instances of highly successful corporate leaders who retired from their private-sector jobs and moved on to run government and nonprofit organizations. Many were unsuccessful in their second careers. These individuals are not necessarily bad leaders. Rather, their inability to achieve success in this new setting is often due to undeveloped leadership competencies, particularly those essential for social-sector success.

For successful change to occur, a leader's actions, words, and deeds must be consistent with the desired new culture. Many leaders start try but fail to implement a high-performance measurement culture when met with staff fear and resistance. Unsuccessful leaders often discuss the implementation of metrics and measures without first considering their own leadership competencies and then determining whether these competencies are aligned with the high-performance measurement culture they seek to create.

Throughout the past decade, my work has involved the study, observation, and evaluation of the set of leadership competencies that lead social-sector organizations to greater success and those leadership traits that hold organizations back. A collaborative research project with David Sapper, a leadership development specialist and coach to government leaders, identified twenty-five essential managerial and core competencies for social-sector organizations that intended to make the shift to a high-performance measurement culture.

Leaders who wish to sustain and grow nonprofit and government organizations in this new focus of outcomes-based funding must have these qualities. Those who naturally excel in these areas and who actively seek to increase their competencies realize success in this new era of managing to outcomes.

Each of the twenty-five competencies listed alphabetically in Exhibit 7.1 are important. Depending on the circumstances and structure of a particular organization, some take on greater significance and importance. For example, navigating organizational politics is critical for government leaders who work in large, bureaucratic, and partisan systems, but the same competency may be less important for a flexible, two-person arts organization.

Exhibit 7.1. Executive and General Social-Sector Leadership Competencies

- Acting resourcefully
- Acquiring and applying technical, program, and industry knowledge
- Adapting to change
- Balancing strategy and tactics
- Behaving credibly
- Building partnerships and alliances
- Communicating in writing
- Cultivating organizational vision and purpose
- Developing self
- Developing talent
- Directing and measuring work
- Enabling constructive change
- Encouraging dialogue
- Fostering teamwork
- Innovating
- Learning with agility
- Making high-stakes presentations
- Making sound decisions
- Managing courageously
- Managing time
- Navigating political sensitivities
- Practicing sound fiscal management
- Prioritizing
- Relating to others
- Satisfying customer needs

Examining Leadership Competencies

A detailed and thorough review of all twenty-five competencies would require another book. As a first step, I recommend organizations assess how current leadership stands on the following five core competencies:

1. Cultivating organizational vision and purpose
2. Building partnerships and alliances
3. Directing and measuring work
4. Enabling constructive change
5. Encouraging dialogue

These five core competencies are nonnegotiable for the greatest degree of success in any organization. Let's look at each in greater detail.

Cultivating Organizational Vision and Purpose

Cultivating vision and purpose begins with a leader's demonstrated ability to align individual and team efforts with the organization's mission. The true profit of government and nonprofit organizations is not measured in dollars alone—the typical way profits are measured in these organizations' for-profit counterparts. In social-sector organizations, profit can be measured in terms of changed lives and circumstances.

Successful social-sector leaders ensure that all members of an organization are working toward the same goal. These leaders ensure that everyone in the organization, from the custodian to the board president, understands how the organization's work (1) impacts the bottom line and those the organization serves and (2) adds value to the community.

When I interviewed staff in a nonprofit mental health organization as part of an organizational development project, I learned that the organization's executive director was exceptional at cultivating organizational vision and purpose. A brief conversation with a part-time custodial staff member about working for the organization demonstrated the director's proficiency in this area.

During our conversation, the custodial staff member was able to clearly articulate the pride she had in her job and in the organization. With a vibrant smile, she shared how her role was critical to the mission of the organization, because the health and quality of life of the organization's clients were partially entrusted to her. If she did a poor job and skipped some steps in her duties, she said, individuals with already poor health could get sick. I imagine this staff member would have welcomed performance measures aligned with her ability to keep the facilities clean, thereby reducing client hospital admissions. Such a conversation would have further validated how valuable her role was to the overall mission of the organization.

Such a clear understanding of contribution to mission throughout an organization is not the norm. Staff satisfaction survey results from social-sector organizations consistently show that nonprogram staff typically have the lowest job satisfaction ratings among employees. These individuals also report less perceived connection between their work and the mission.

One of the most significant predictors of motivation and organizational engagement is a feeling that assigned duties make a difference in overall satisfaction. Given the challenging work, lack of corporate perks, and often lower pay found in social-sector organizations compared to for-profit organizations, cultivating organizational vision is even more critical for keeping them motivated and fully engaged. Leaders high in this competency are willing to employ a range of strategies and tactics to encourage employees to see the bigger picture and work toward a common goal. If an employee refuses to embrace a new direction designed to advance the mission of the organization, leaders with a strong capacity for cultivating organizational vision and purpose find the courage to either help that employee find an opportunity at the organization more suited for the employee's temperament or remove them from the organization.

In his book *Leap of Reason* (2011), Mario Morino underscores the importance of this concept, urging nonprofit leaders to step up and help people "catch the vision or catch the bus." Keeping employees around who continually distract others from the mission will prove detrimental. Removing these employees from the organization removes the distraction and allows the real work aligned with organizational mission to progress. Leaders who excel at this competency also look for opportunities to help team members succeed by removing tasks and activities that do not forward the mission. This frees up employees' time, allowing them to focus on the activities that help produce the intended organizational outcomes.

Building Partnerships and Alliances

In the twenty-first century and beyond, the social sector will need to work together to solve increasingly complex problems. Strategic partnerships and alliances are of critical importance if organizations are to achieve increased effectiveness and attract increased funding opportunities. The ability to find solutions for social challenges and effect change demands the experience, expertise, and knowledge of several different groups. For example, to overcome homelessness, individuals often need help from specialists in housing, education, mental health, substance abuse, and overall life skills management.

Success in social-sector organizations requires leaders who score high on measures that assess the ability to build partnerships and alliances. Collaborative leaders foster win-win opportunities and form interdependent relationships that help individuals, teams, and organizations advance organizational goals. Leaders who can successfully create strategic alliances and partnerships understand the underlying meaning of the common expression "There is no *I* in team." They take the time to develop trust and respect among employees and stakeholders. They listen to employees, clients, and partners and use the information they gather to start where they are, working diligently toward a solution to an identified organizational problem.

Data-Driven Leadership: A Case Study

An organization that provides subsidized permanent housing to individuals with disabilities who are also chronically homeless provides an excellent case study to examine the role of partnerships and alliances. The organization set out to compare move-out data between individuals who qualified for government-funded programs providing case management services and those who did not qualify for such assistance. Through analysis of collected data, leaders discovered that those who received case management services were significantly more successful in retaining their permanent housing.

Based on the data, to further increase the organization's success rate, leaders must form mutually beneficial partnerships to provide case management services to a greater number of clients. They also need to seek alternative funding streams if they wish to assist these clients who currently do not qualify for additional services.

When the executive director realized this need and acknowledged the need to bolster her skills in building such alliances and partnerships, she sought counsel on how to best meet this objective. The data held clues, and this leader responded by further improving her strong leadership skills. As she did, she was able to respond more fully to the challenge at hand and lead the organization to greater success.

A Closer Look. When an organization is populated with leaders who exhibit high competency in both cultivating vision and building partnerships, unprecedented success can occur. These leaders invest significant time in authentic conversation with key stakeholders, including them in making key decisions and learning from them in order to advance organizational goals. As part of this process, leaders build a rapport with stakeholders and solidify a sense of shared vision and purpose. This shared commitment to a common goal paves the way to win-win solutions, opening up new possibilities as the organization fulfills its purpose.

Directing and Measuring Work

High-performance measurement cultures are nearly impossible to achieve when leaders and managers are unable to direct and measure work. Performance cultures cannot exist without measurement activities aligned with the organization's mission, and leaders who excel at this competency use measures and milestones that support daily progress toward long-term goals. Leaders with this competency value feedback loops that monitor progress. They institute measures that identify waste and inefficiency, using the data to improve processes. Tactics may include satisfaction surveys, client surveys, and other ongoing performance measures systems.

In addition to welcoming and soliciting feedback, leaders strong in this competency also share feedback or offer rewards to those who excel and bring greater value to the organization. If the data shows an area of inefficiency, these leaders choose to communicate concerns and make recommendations. In situations where performance expectations are not being met, they often offer alternatives for improvement.

Leaders who score high in this competency area view measurement as a tool for growth and improvement rather than a means of punishment. Measures become guideposts that let employees know where they stand, how far they need to go, and how they can achieve intended outcomes. Once employees reach their goals, leaders celebrate their success. High scores on directing and measuring work demonstrate an ability to go beyond the activity of simply measuring success. Leaders choose to implement systems that look for strong returns on investment (ROI) and high levels of impact as a way to demonstrate success. We will examine such systems more closely in the chapters that follow.

Too often, nonprofit and government leaders underperform in this competency, becoming more concerned with activity than with the outcomes produced by the activity. Employees then begin to fear that collected data will be used for purely disciplinary reasons. At times, leaders who score low on this competency seem scattered and do not have clear expectations or measures in place to monitor progress. Within the organization, this type of leader may be perceived as a micromanager. These less-than-ideal behaviors contribute to a disengaged workforce. Over time, this creates and perpetuates a culture of mediocrity.

Directors and mangers who find innovative ways to work around barriers that stop other leaders in their tracks are among those who score highest in cultivating organizational vision and purpose, building partnerships and alliances, and directing and measuring work. These leaders possess the necessary skills to align performance measures with the organization's mission.

When the organization's partners and employees understand how their efforts contribute to the mission, the data gathered often motivates them to work harder and work smarter to achieve even greater impact. As this happens, leaders with the competency of measuring and directing work can further apply their skills to use collected data to build a common vision with strategic partners and further advance the mission of the organization.

Enabling Constructive Change

The challenges confronting the social sector are more complex than ever, and today's organizational leaders are being asked to solve problems with more efficient operations. Leading organizations across the sector must continue to clearly demonstrate how they have achieved their success. Without question, new challenges will continue to unfold within the social sector, requiring continued change in how nonprofit and government organizations conduct business.

Successful leaders create a space for constructive change to occur. Leaders with this competency can mobilize and, when necessary, redirect organizational energy in ways that enhance quality and improve effectiveness. They understand that change is difficult, and they choose to move forward in spite of challenges. Leaders with the capacity to embrace change often anticipate sources of fear and conflict and create a plan for dealing with these, clearing a path toward the organization's overall goal.

In contrast, leaders less developed in this competency typically prefer to play it safe and avoid conflict. They may engage in behaviors that support self-preservation or be reluctant to examine alternative information and data. This approach undermines and sometimes destroys a high measurement culture, which requires organizations to constantly examine and reexamine data, even when the data reflects negatively on the organization, and to make adjustments as need.

Enabling constructive change becomes less problematic when a leader has a team of employees and partners focused on the same vision. When leaders possess the critical competency, everything falls into place, and a high measurement culture is naturally established. Leaders who are proficient at managing constructive change use mission-aligned measures to direct and manage work.

Encouraging Dialogue

The most successful leaders encourage dialogue and create a culture where members openly express views and differences. High-performance measurement cultures are unlikely to form if management is unable or unwilling to allow open communication. When these skills are brought forward, leaders are often able to guide their teams to make critical decisions about change and hone the skills required to transform the organization.

Managers who encourage dialogue also ensure that the conversation remains focused on problems and solutions to those problems rather than on personalities. Data, information, and feedback sometimes provide unexpected and undesirable results. Leaders must deal effectively with unanticipated results by bringing everyone together, focusing on the most pressing issues, and removing personal attacks and blaming from the discussion.

Selecting and Socializing Employees

High-performance measurement cultures are sustained by the selection of employees who already posses the competencies that align with the new organizational culture. In the past, some organizations have experienced decline after adopting measurement cultures. This unwelcome occurrence sometimes results from the selection of leaders who lack the five core competencies. The smaller the organization and the more institutional power a new hire has, the more important it is to consider these key leadership competencies in the hiring process.

In addition to selecting highly qualified employees, organizations must develop a plan to train all staff on expected behaviors and performance standards. When change occurs at a faster pace, it is important to provide more frequent opportunities for dialogue around new or shifting expectations. It is helpful for executive leaders and managers to demonstrate new behaviors expected of employees, modeling them to support easy adoption throughout the organization. Organizations should also identify employees who already possess the desired traits and ask these employees to serve as mentors to other employees.

Organizational awards, such as employee of the month programs, can be established with a clear selection criteria matched to new expectations. In addition, desired competencies can be incorporated into performance reviews and goal-setting conversations. Over time, those unwilling to conform to new standards will naturally self-select out of the organization. At times, they may need to be encouraged to find positions that better fit their preferences either within the organization or elsewhere.

Leadership Development Strategies

For outcomes and performance measures to reach their fullest potential in the social-sector organization, the right leadership must be in place. Leaders committed to adopting a high-performance measurement culture in their organization first need to take an honest look within. Boards should assess their directors on the five core competencies. Likewise, executive directors and managers should assess staff. To assist organizations with this effort, Measurement Resources has partnered with Customized Perspectives to develop a tool that provides 360-degree feedback on the twenty-five most desired competencies (visit www.measurementresourcesco.com for more information).

This assessment gathers behavioral feedback on key competencies from a leader's superiors, peers, and direct reports and includes a self-assessment. The results of this assessment are invaluable for helping social-sector leaders gain insight and knowledge about their own leadership strengthens and weaknesses. It provides a data-driven approach for the leadership development required to sustain a high-performance measurement culture.

Improving Leadership Capacity

The first step to strengthening capacity comes when leaders actively and consciously choose behaviors related to the five critical competencies. For those competencies that need improvement, it is helpful to develop an improvement plan. Social-sector leaders can consider enlisting the help of an executive coach for guidance and accountability. Such an investment is warranted if it leads to increased impact and organizational effectiveness. An executive director or other leader can also engage in open dialogue and discussion with their team about changes they would like to make. In such a case, leaders can directly request the team's support and ask staff to hold themselves and executive leadership accountable for embracing needed changes.

Focusing on leadership first is a powerful step in the direction of achieving an enhanced measurement culture. Actions taken by an organization's founders and its present-day leadership are important for strengthening organizational culture and lay the foundation for the successful implementation of measurement systems that will serve the organization well into its future.

When a leader strengthens her competencies and demonstrates behavior aligned with a high-performance measurement culture, others within the organization naturally follow suit. A "new normal" is established. In many cases, these shared values and assumptions redefine the way employees collectively respond when faced with new situations, such as the establishment of strong outcomes and performance measures.

Putting Leadership Capacity into Practice: A Case Study

One large public agency's senior leadership underwent two years of intensive work intended to move the organization from one of making decisions based on personal preference and hunches to a more data-driven approach. Workgroups were formed to establish and use key performance indicators to solve agency issues. The organization began to see improved results externally: forging better partnerships with sister agencies, reducing wasteful spending, and generating interest from grant funders and the media. Unfortunately, in spite of all this positive work, the agency still experienced some costly workarounds, communication, and trust issues.

This case study provides an example of an agency that focused on working on the establishment of key measures prior to looking at the underlying organizational culture. In the years of working toward increasing data-driven strategies, they also saw declines and, when examining key culture issues in their organization's annual culture survey, consistently underwhelming results. A scant 20 percent of employees agreed that the organization had effective communication channels and felt the relationship between divisions was based on cooperation and trust. Although the key leaders had not changed in this time period, the percentage of staff who saw the organization's leaders as positive role models declined from 60 percent to 50 percent.

The director was committed to creating a culture of excellence and high impact. She believed that the current problematic levels of trust, tendency to work in silos, and perception of poor communication by staff was unacceptable. To address these problems, she asked her entire leadership team to go through the Leadership 360-Degree Assessment, based on a selection of seventeen of the twenty-five competencies required for social sector impact and excellence. In addition, each leader received up to five hours of executive coaching to work toward a specific leadership goal, based on the results of the assessment.

Leaders found this process very enlightening. They discovered some unique behavior trends that were contributing to the organization's success, as well as some issues that were holding the organization back from achieving the desired success. For example, one leader discovered that his peers and direct reports rated him low on fostering teamwork and encouraging dialogue, noting that he never had time to listen to them because he was always distracted by his smart phone. The simple shift of making his office a "no smart phone" zone helped immensely. The perception of his attention, communication, and support shifted almost immediately, leading to increased cooperation in that division.

Each of the eleven division leaders in the agency worked with an executive coach to come up with similar practical, first-step strategies based on the feedback from the assessment. These goals were shared with the leaders' supervisors and, in many cases, their direct reports. These efforts led to increased effectiveness in operations and significant improvements in the organizational culture.

The team also examined trends in the leadership team. A report highlighted the competencies that the group was typically strong in and those that still needed attention. Interestingly, findings indicated that the group was quite savvy at navigating organizational politics, valuing diversity, focusing on customer service, and striving for continuous improvement. These strengths most likely contributed to the organization's success with building external relationships and incorporating data into the work.

However, things were breaking down internally, because collectively the team was weaker in areas related to directing and measuring work, building productive internal relationships, and fostering team development.

It appeared that employees at every level of the agency were too busy setting the overall direction and mission of the department, focusing on external stakeholders and customers at the cost of internal management and staff development.

Seeing this pattern of strengths and weaknesses and how these were impacting overall operations was enormously insightful for this agency's leadership team. As each individual worked on an individual development plan, the group held a retreat to focus on developing a comprehensive agency plan based on the assessment feedback. Specific objectives included establishing regular meetings to discuss and review performance measures, focusing on setting clear expectations and deadlines, and increasing communication between the leadership team and staff.

A Closer Look. This agency's leadership team perceived this approach to be highly successful at increasing the leadership capacity of the organization because it raised the bar and expectations of the leaders' performance. Unlike many leadership capacity-building programs—which required one leader to attend an off-site training class or seminar to increase skills—these leaders gathered in one place, focusing together on both individual and collective strengths and weaknesses and considering how each strength or weakness impacted the organization's ability to fulfill its mission.

Attending a leadership seminar often proves less successful at increasing leadership capacity in an organization, because only the leader changes. When the leader returns, he or she still faces the same organizational culture and forces that are impeding positive changes throughout the organization. In contrast, with this more intensive and internal capacity-building method, the environment is changing at the same time the leaders are working on improving their personal development. In a survey conducted at the conclusion of the process, a full 100 percent of participants reported that they saw positive progress on at least one leadership development goals, and 86 percent of the participants agreed that the 360-degree feedback and executive coaching enhanced the organizational culture.

Organizational Structures

Strengthening leadership marks the first step toward creating high-performance measurement cultures and will help an organization increase morale and engagement. Social-sector organizations must also consider how well their organizational structures, processes, measures, and modes of communication support the new culture. Each is related to other critical factors of strengthening organizational culture, aligning organizational artifacts, and creating culturally consistent rewards.

When social-sector leaders possess the competencies described earlier during the initial phases of an organization's development, organizational structures aligned with a high-performance measurement culture naturally emerge. Similarly, when start-up nonprofits develop leadership and success measures before the first client is served or the first program introduced, they position themselves to realize the highest possible levels of impact and organizational success.

It is not always possible or realistic to break down every organization and start from scratch, yet most nonprofit organizations and almost all government agencies will need to undergo some organizational restructuring to achieve a high-performance measurement culture. Throughout an organization's history, the actions of various leaders shape structures and policies. Even when leaders shift their behavior, a state of inertia or a return to "the way things have always been done" can infiltrate organizational culture, blocking impact and excellence.

There are clear benefits to offering employees telecommuting opportunities, for example. Telecommuting has been shown to increase employee satisfaction, decrease overhead, and reduce an organization's carbon footprint. Despite this evidence, many government organizations struggle with a move toward this model. Often, existing policies and procedures have been put in place to prevent this type of innovative practice. There may have been a prevailing attitude that employees would not make the right choices without direct supervision or a belief that the public would not support such a practice. All too often, decision makers form opinions and make decisions before testing their assumption that practices such as telecommuting will be a failure.

Leaders of established organizations who wish to develop a strong performance culture need to overcome organizational inertia through a dedicated focus on leadership competencies and organizational structures. Successful organizations implement policies and practices that support their ability to gather and use data and information for optimal organizational success. In short, they put the structures in place to support success.

Putting Key Structures in Place

Based on my research and experience, I have identified thirteen organizational structures that correlate to strong performance cultures. These structures, listed in Exhibit 7.2, are consistent with research on job satisfaction and job performance (Hackman and Oldham, 1976).

Exhibit 7.2. Measurement Culture Organizational Structures

Training	Job satisfaction
Supervision	Policies and practices
Upper management communication	Innovation
Task significance	Intra-agency communication
Autonomy	Work/life balance
Feedback	Internal customer services
	Department culture

To begin to strengthen an organization's culture and its ability to use data and information, I recommend that organizations first explore existing policies and practices in three key areas: training, feedback, and autonomy.

Training

The need for growth is a successful motivator for change. Leaders who create strong performance cultures view ongoing training as the lifeblood of the organization. They support and encourage continual training in operations and employee development. Training occurs in a variety of settings, from workshops and conferences to job shadowing, trial and error, webinars, and books.

In addition to imparting new skills to improve organizational effectiveness, training is also beneficial for staff satisfaction and retention. Organizations with morale problems generally have little to no budget for training. These organizations can encourage engagement, innovation, and creative solutions by placing a high value on investing in and building on employee knowledge and skills.

Feedback

Feedback is a type of learning and training, and leaders of strong measurement cultures value feedback and accountability loops. High-performance measurement cultures establish practices to analyze feedback in the form of systematically collected data. After careful evaluation of the data, leaders make decisions for improvement. They implement predictable systems that encourage feedback from stakeholders concerning product development, operations, and satisfaction.

Such systems give staff natural opportunities for input—offering their observations about management style, ways to improve the work of the organization, and overall satisfaction with the organization and their place within it. The most successful social-sector organizations introduce policies and practices that specify how data and information is to be shared internally and externally. In thriving organizations, the data collected through performance and outcomes measures is used to improve operations and to inspire staff and stakeholders.

Autonomy

The best social-sector leaders create organizational structures that expand opportunities for innovation and initiatives from staff. When the staff is kept informed through continuous training and feedback, employees are more likely to share fresh ideas about how to improve the impact and efficiency of an organization. Successful organizations go a step further: they implement a process that allows staff members at every level of the organization to take initiative and implement new ideas. Leaders find creative ways to reward staff for their efforts in this regard.

Organizational norms that support pilot programs or the clear demonstration of new practices facilitate greater buy-in and enthusiastic participation. Successful leaders understand and accept that not all new ideas succeed. These leaders quickly adapt when data indicates a new program has failed to achieve desired results. They allow the data inform their decisions, rather than using the data as an excuse to give up on the problem at hand. Leaders who value autonomy take time to communicate to their staff that learning from failure is simply a part of the journey toward success.

Just as organizations must examine their leadership competencies on the way to a high-performance measurement culture, a second step requires a thorough examination of how well organizational policies, practices, and procedures support the move toward data-driven decision making. Practices that hinder training, autonomy, and feedback should be revised or eliminated in order to encourage innovation and change throughout the organization. Helpful questions include "Why does this practice or policy exist?" and "How might this policy or practice be altered to strengthen our culture?"

Government organizations are likely to face ongoing challenges as they seek to align policies and procedures. Many misaligned policies are established in the form of legislative rules or laws. Given the importance of the organizational culture shift, leaders should move forward with creating high-performance cultures in every area within their control. As they do, government leaders must consistently use their strengthened leadership competencies to communicate with executive and legislative bodies about the damaging effects of many existing rules and regulations, particularly those that block possible solutions to complex social problems.

As the social sector insists on a standard of excellence from organizational leaders, those leaders will begin to align policies and procedures and embrace high-performance measurement cultures. Over time, the incorporation of performance and outcomes measures in organizations will become easier and less costly. No longer will measurement seem like "one more thing to do." Rather, such measures and the systems that support them will become a bedrock foundation from which social-sector organizations demonstrate and communicate their effectiveness.

The Next Step

Now that we have established the importance of both the ideal culture and the ideal leadership in measurement cultures, we will focus on the ideal measures by turning our attention to the second element of the Five C's of easy and effective impact and excellence: clarifying mission.

Impact & Excellence

Chapter Seven Discussion Questions

1. Complete the Leadership and Culture Self-Assessment found in Appendix A.
2. Identify five actions steps your organization could take to enhance leadership competencies. What can you do to embrace each of these competencies in your own work?
3. How does your organization encourage training, autonomy, and feedback?
4. How do existing organizational policies hinder training, autonomy, and feedback? Which policies and practices can be revised, added, or eliminated to strengthen organizational culture?

8

Clarify Mission

People only see what they are prepared to see.
—RALPH WALDO EMERSON

PICK UP ANY GOOD LEADERSHIP, strategic planning, organizational development, business building, or wealth attraction book, and one of the first points sure to be discussed is the importance of a clear vision and mission statement. Creating a successful measurement culture always begins with this essential first step. Every organization must articulate a clear vision, and employees at every level of the organization must wholly embrace the stated mission.

A vision statement describes the ideal future state: something that does not yet exist. A mission statement describes what an organization will do or which initiatives it will take to achieve that vision. For example, the vision of Measurement Resources Company is to strengthen communities by transforming the organizations that serve them. How do we achieve transformation with the social sector and strengthen the communities that nonprofit and government organizations serve? We equip and inspire nonprofit and government leaders to establish high-performance organizations that continually seek impact and excellence. This is the mission of Measurement Resources Company.

Good mission statements clearly communicate to staff, funders, clients, and stakeholders what the organization is all about. They state the reason for the organization's existence. The best mission statements also guide an organization in terms of what goals, strategies, and tactics must be set in order to achieve the identified mission. The best leaders consistently rally the internal team and stakeholders to win support and spur action that contributes to the organization's cause. Movement toward the vision is impossible without a clear mission.

There is a second reason a clear mission is so important. This reason is rarely discussed and often hidden to many social-sector organizations. In successful, high-performance organizations, the mission is the very foundation that determines the organization's measurable outcomes. If the organizational mission has an unclear focus, then measures and outcomes will be equally unclear.

When funders and stakeholders ask organizational leaders to describe impact and outcomes, what they are really asking is "How well has the organization achieved its mission?" They want to know "What evidence of success do you have?" An organization cannot measure and communicate the extent to which it has achieved its mission if a clear mission does not exist.

Mission and Measurement

"What gets measured gets done." This popular expression underscores the importance of having measures that are aligned with mission. Decades of research have shown that the simple act of observing or measuring something frequently results in improved conditions. This phenomenon is referred to as the Hawthorne effect (Gillespie, 1991), a term based on research conducted by Elton Mayo from 1927 to 1932. Mayo's research demonstrated that employees are more productive when they know they are being studied. This pivotal research showed that an increase in worker productivity was produced by the psychological stimulus of being singled out, involved, and made to feel important within the organization.

The act of measurement itself impacts the results of measurement. Just as dipping a thermometer into a vial of liquid can affect the temperature of the liquid being measured, the act of collecting data where none was collected before creates a situation that did not exist before, thereby affecting the results. For measures to increase productivity and inspire lasting change, they must be relevant, and they must be communicated. Too often, organizations collect a variety of data for funders but fail to allot time to synthesize and discuss the data they collect.

In many cases, one person in the organization quickly pulls together data and compiles it into a follow-up report to a funder without another thought. The condition of relevant data that is not properly shared or communicated is prevalent. Our research findings show that 82 percent of the social sector has collected data, yet only 23 percent of organizations have successfully linked collected data to positive outcomes.

A recent example illustrates this all-too-common practice of putting measures in place but failing to use them. The question, "What do you do with the data internal to your organization?" stumped one collaborative community of data user: they responded with blank stares and silence.

The individuals gathered were responsible for collecting and inputting their respective agency's data for a large federally funded project. They were well versed in what data needed to be entered and how it was to be entered into their electronic case management database, and they knew how to read the reports on their organization's data compliance and errors. Yet many of these data users never thought to take the reports showing program outcomes back to their organization's leadership or to use them to validate meeting the mission or tweaking programs. Why was this oversight so common? What led to this incomplete use of valuable data?

The funder, in this case the federal government, placed a high importance on inputting the data in a specific timeline and wanted complete, accurate data. Data compliance and error rates were the measures most frequently communicated by the funder to those responsible for data collection and reporting in each organization. As such, these were deemed the most relevant measures and inspired the grantee's decisions to renew funding. As a result, the data users focused their attention almost exclusively on compliance.

The federal government was using each organization's data to improve programming and to measure and communicate the social return on investment for their funds. Yet, shockingly, the measures that truly told the organization's story—the number of clients served, changes in income, and successful completion rates—sometimes were not even communicated to organizational leaders. This data rarely led to evaluation of programming and organizational priorities.

Those responsible for reporting failed to recognize the value the measures had for their own organization's programming and daily operations. Therefore, they did not communicate the relevant data to leadership or share it within their own organizations. This costly mistake resulted in missed opportunities to improve efficiencies and strengthen the organization's practices to fulfill its mission.

Aligning Measurement and Mission

Without a clear and regularly communicated mission statement, an organization may fall into the trap of measuring things that seem good to measure but are not aligned with or relevant to the mission. When misaligned measures are communicated, there is often a flurry of activity that actually moves the organization further from its core mission.

One common but flawed social-sector practice is the use of administrative overhead to gauge and determine organizational effectiveness. Like many workplace giving programs, the State of Ohio's Combined Charitable Campaign (2012) asks state employees to donate a portion of their income to charities they select. To support informed giving, employees are given a resources guide that lists five pieces of information to be used in the decision-making process: the name of the charity, the address, a brief description of activities, a description of who the charity served, and, finally, the percentage of funds going to administrative costs. Any organization with administrative costs greater than 25 percent was marked with an asterisk, indicating that this organization was working on a plan to reduce administrative expenses.

Over the years, donors have been trained to use this metric to determine the effectiveness of a charity. Considering this measure alone, without carefully examining other measures, penalizes organizations that invest in the technology or high-quality staff needed to support impact and excellence. When viewed outside of the rich context of other outcomes achieved by the organization, the measure of administrative cost says nothing about how effective the organization is at achieving its stated mission. It is altogether possible that one organization could achieve a greater impact with only 30 percent of funding going straight to programs while another organization would require 95 percent of funds invested directly into programs to reach maximum impact.

Well-meaning government and nonprofit organizations often invest in highly communicated operational performance measures that, while important, are not directly related to the organization's ability to fulfill its mission. A juvenile justice organization partnered with Measurement Resources to conduct an analysis of its overtime policy. The client operated a 24/7 facility and was experiencing financial strain due to unresolved issues with overtime costs.

Our analysis revealed that the only communicated measure was related to keeping overtime low. As a result, managers were making their decisions based on overtime costs alone—and inadvertently ignoring decisions that could benefit the mission, unless those decisions simultaneously allowed them to control overtime costs.

Furthermore, the analysis revealed that overtime was spiking because staff members were burnt out. Staff called in sick, turnover skyrocketed, and staff morale plummeted. Only 10 percent of the staff indicated feeling safe in their jobs. At the same time, demand for services was increasing, and the organization was experiencing spiking enrollment with dwindling staff to serve program participants.

The facility was woefully understaffed. Yet, in an effort to save costs, managers were intentionally not hiring to full capacity. Instead, management was so focused on managing overtime, leaders were not devoting appropriate time to the delivery of adequate services, so youth were leaving their facility without the changes they needed to succeed. During this time the program participants' return rate into the program (recidivism) was increasing, which was obviously an unwanted outcome.

Staff originally came to work for this organization with the desire to make a difference for youth in the community. Yet this detrimental cycle was contributing to burnout and increased turnover, because individual staff members could no longer see how their efforts were making a difference. It was not the staff's fault that outcomes were not achieved. As the organization had lost sight of the mission, focusing on a specific measure rather than the larger vision, it had set them up to fail.

The core recommendation that emerged from the external study of this organization's practice was that leaders should hire new staff until the organization reached full capacity. In addition to its measurement of overtime, the organization implemented and communicated additional outcomes measures, such as number of incidents, percentage of staff who reported feeling safe, and youth recidivism. As a result of sustained efforts, the organization not only was able to save over $200,000 in overtime costs within a one-year period but also improved staff morale and safety and began working on a data-driven plan to improve client outcomes.

Concrete Steps to Clarity

Before an organization can develop relevant, well-communicated measures that drive effective and efficient services that lead to increased impact, organizational leaders, staff, and stakeholders must clarify the organizational mission. Once this is accomplished, many organizations rush to implement appropriate measures. But before establishing performance and outcomes measures, organizations need to establish a solid foundation from which to build a high-performance measurement culture. With the mission clarified, the organization must clarify its whys and develop a logic model.

All inspired leaders operate from a full realization of what drives them. Almost without exception, some greater purpose, cause, or core belief informs how leaders do things and the actions to which they commit. In his work, Simon Sinex (2009) has codified this principle and demonstrated how great leaders and innovators, such as Steve Jobs, Martin Luther King Jr., and the Wright brothers, achieved phenomenal success because they acted from the inside out. The whys or guiding principles that drive these individuals act as an internal compass, informing their choice to engage in every activity and communication.

Government and nonprofit organizations have proven to be equally as guilty as their for-profit counterparts in focusing exclusively on the "what" and "how," forgetting the whys at the center of their mission. When social-sector organizations fail to consider the "whys," they miss out on the opportunity to engage and inspire others to help the organization achieve its mission. As we have seen, stakeholders do not support an organization or donate to a cause because of what an organization does. Rather, funders are investing in the why that provides the basis for an organization's work. When leaders are clear on their "whys," they know the exact steps required to measure optimal success.

Government and nonprofit leaders who have created strong measurement cultures are measuring the whys and then communicating internally and externally, sharing specifically how they fulfill these whys through the organization's programs and services and daily practices that support the mission. As they share the stories of their organizations, they inspire others to partner and participate in their mission. Leaders take the first step toward effective measurement of the why by clarifying the organization's unique purpose—its reason for being in business. Doing so effectively can propel an organization forward like nothing else.

Five Whys

Adapted from lean manufacturing and the Toyota Production System (TPS), the "Five Whys" practice provides a series of pivotal questions that help an organization clarify the critical whys that drive the organization forward. Typically, this tool is used for understanding the root cause of a particular problem. Measurement Resources has modified this tool to help mission-driven organizations understand the underlying purpose that inspires them to fulfill their respective missions.

The "five" in the Five Whys is arbitrary. The questioning could continue as necessary. In most cases, five questions are sufficient to lead an organization's staff and stakeholders to clarify their underlying "whys." In the Five Whys process, answers to questions are followed by the facilitator asking another "why?" question. This process leads an organization to deeper and deeper meaning. The best way to understand this exercise is to observe it in action.

To illustrate the process, imagine a social-sector organization that provides job training and educational resources for individuals who are unemployed or underemployed. The facilitator would begin by asking each member of the leadership team the following question: "Why do you [your organization] do what you do?" Regardless of the answers given by individual leaders, the facilitator would follow up with a second question: "And why is that important?" The question is repeated after the next four answers.

Here is a hypothetical example of how the questioning might proceed.

Facilitator:	Why do you do what you do?
Individual:	To provide training classes and educational opportunities to underemployed or unemployed individuals.
Facilitator:	Why? Why is that important?
Individual:	So that participants can increase their skills and knowledge in a field of their choice.
Facilitator:	Why? Why is that important?
Individual:	So that participants can obtain jobs with decent wages.
Facilitator:	Why? Why is that important?
Individual:	So that participants can improve their quality of life and have the resources required to live a happy and productive life.
Facilitator:	Why? Why is that important?
Individual:	So that we decrease the unemployment rate of this community and make our nation a more vibrant and economically strong place to live.

As seen in this example, those responding to this line of questioning typically begin with a focus on what they do, such as "providing training and education opportunities." As the facilitator probes deeper, asking for further clarification, the true whys and the organization's measureable outcomes begin to emerge. In this case, continued questioning revealed that the whys were to increase the quality of life of the community's residents and to create a more vibrant and economically strong community. The "what" and the "how" included increasing the skills and knowledge of potential job applicants and helping participants move into gainful employment.

Focusing on the organization's whys allows the organization to evolve as it diversifies its program activities and adapts quickly to the changing needs of program participants. If the true purpose is to increase quality of life through economic sustainability, then the organization can offer training classes. However, it might also branch out and offer classes in life skills (such as managing a budget and stress management) that assist in removing barriers to maintaining employment. These classes will enhance the likelihood that unemployed individuals will secure gainful employment.

Understanding the why that lies at the core of the organization's mission might result in a new partnership with area housing organizations to help individuals find sustainable housing, supporting the goal of job placement. When an organization is pigeonholed as a training and development organization, opportunities are less flexible. A living example of the expansion that is possible when an organization intimately understands its whys comes from the corporate world. Apple's focus on its why has allowed the company to expand its product offering and meet consumer needs by providing music and phones as well as computers.

Knowing the organization's true why is critical, and it is also important that the organization align its purpose and core mission with the respective whys that drive an organization's funders and its clients. Often, organizational leaders make the assumption that their whys are identical to the whys of funders and stakeholders. In reality, these can vary significantly.

For this reason, social-sector leaders should conduct a minimal three-question why exercise for clients and stakeholders. Ideally, each organization should conduct a focus group and ask these two groups a series of questions. If formal questioning is not possible with individuals, these questions can be answered from that group's perspective. Continuing with the example of the training and education organization, here is what a conversation with the organization's stakeholders and donors might look like:

Facilitator: Why do you fund or partner with this organization? What do you hope to accomplish?

Funder: We want area residents to be provided with the skills required by our local employers.

Facilitator: Why? Why is that important?

Funder: So that we can have strong and stable workforce to meet the needs of our local employers.

Facilitator: Why? Why is that important?

Funder: So that we have prosperous companies.

Facilitator:	Why? Why is that important?
Funder:	So that we can continue to attract more companies to move to and invest and grow in our area.
Facilitator:	Why? Why is that important?
Funder:	So that our community is a strong, vibrant, and prosperous community.

By comparing the series of questions posed to the funder and those asked of organizational leaders, we learn that the ultimate goal for leaders is a strong and prosperous community. However, funders are more focused on increasing the effectiveness of local business by having a quality workforce than on improving the quality of life of area residents. This difference is subtle, but important to understand.

The implications and potential impact are significant. If the organization fails to measure and communicate how well they are meeting the needs of local business by producing a highly qualified and trained workforce, this funder may discontinue funding the organization and divert funds to an alternative organization that better communicates how this need is being met. Understanding a funder's whys may change the way an organization delivers services or the actual services it provides. The organization may decide to involve area employers more in training curriculum or launch a job shadow day for participants at these employers. Once the core beliefs and motivations of all stakeholders are understood, possibilities are expanded significantly.

The third important group whose whys must be understood is the group composed of clients and participants. It is unlikely that a program will prove successful if that program is not addressing the participants' needs. For example, a school is not successful if children are disengaged or drop out. Theaters and parks are not successful if people do not visit. Even a city recycling program is unsuccessful if residents place recyclables in trash bins. In these examples, public dollars and private donations are wasted on staff and overhead if lives and circumstances do not change.

For the organization to fulfill its funders' objectives and achieve its mission, leaders must earn the buy-in and participation of those they seek to impact. Even for programs that are free or mandated by law, the participants' whys are important. In the training and education organization, the participants' whys exercise may proceed as follows. For this example, we will assume that many participants are ordered by the court to participate in this program as part of their probation.

Facilitator: Why do you participate in this program? What do you hope to accomplish?
Participant: My probation officer said that I have to. If I don't, I'll go back to jail.
Facilitator: Why? Why is that important?
Participant: So that I can stay with my family and see my children.
Facilitator: Why? Why is that important?
Participant: So that I can teach my kids and be there for them, unlike how my dad was never around for me.
Facilitator: Why? Why is that important?
Participant: So my children can have a better life than I did and not make the same mistakes that I did.

For this participant, the ultimate why is to provide a better life for his children. He will be more motivated to continue to participate if he sees the direct relationship between completing the organization's training classes and providing a better life for his children. The participant is not there to increase the economic development of the community. Nor does he necessarily want to improve his skills so he can increase the profits of local companies. He is focused on creating a better future for his children. Therefore the more this organization communicates to this participant the specific ways that its programs and services have improved the lives of others like him and impacted the lives of participants' children, the more successful the organization will be at engaging him in programs and helping him through the difficult times.

Once organizational leaders and staff understand what matters most to employees, funders, and participants, they can begin to develop and implement measures and systems that lead them to a high-performance measurement culture. The next step is to turn these whys into key organizational outcomes. For example, the hypothetical training company can transform its list of whys into the following important outcomes:

- Increase the employment skills of participants.
- Increase the economic status of participants.
- Increase the number of qualified applicants who apply to positions with local businesses.
- Decrease local employers' job vacancies due to a lack of qualified applicants.
- Reduce unemployment in the area.
- Increase the profits of local businesses.
- Increase the number of new business moving into the area.

A large state agency serving seniors went through a process to clarify its mission and move toward thoroughly measuring and clearly communicating outcomes. Prior to clarifying its mission, the organization was segmented into distinct groups by program funding. Some of the organization's programs were funded through funds released as part of the Older Americans Act. Other programs offered by the organization were funded by state Medicaid funds and the state's general funds.

A disconnect and communication breakdown occurred within the agency between those running the federally funded programs and those using state dollars. To help unify the agency, the leadership went through an exercise that allowed them to clarify the organization's mission and purpose. They wrote the following mission statement: "To promote choice, independence, and quality of life for all aging residents of our state."

This particular statement helped unify the two groups within the organization, stating that, regardless of program funding, activities would be designed to increase (1) the individual's choice about how and where one would receive long-term care and aging supports, (2) opportunities for aging residents to remain independent, aging within their own communities, and (3) the overall quality of life through these efforts. This statement allowed the organization to establish a set of measures and indicators aligned with its purpose. All activities were then aligned to meet these objectives.

The Power of Logic Models

Once an organization has a clear understanding of its desired outcomes, it can move on to the process of linking the what and the how with the organization's core purpose and mission. This is most easily done using a logic model. Logic models come in all shapes and forms; they can be very complex or simplistic. Once leaders see the power and clarity a logic model can bring to the organization, they have a framework for selecting and communicating the organization's story through measures and outcomes.

Social-sector leaders often express doubt about logic models or fail to see the value in the tool. Sometimes it is the very word "logic" and the complex ways these tools have been presented that result in a leader's dismissal of a logic model. Nevertheless, the logic model is a tool that provides organizations with a strong foundation for embracing a high-performance measurement culture. Social-sector organizations and the programs within these organizations receive great benefit when they make use of a logic model.

Similar to most management practices, there are varieties of practice and terminology used in logic models (Knowlton and Phillips, 2009). Most of the various models have merit, and it is not the words used to describe the models or framework that drives success, but rather how an organization uses a particular model that determines the outcome. The key is for an organization to select a framework and terminology that fits within their particular culture.

For organizations just beginning to use logic models, I recommend the W.K. Kellogg Foundation's Framework (2006). The Kellogg approach provides the simplest and most flexible framework. The categories used in the Kellogg framework apply to nearly all social-sector organizations and situations. A sample logic model using the Kellogg framework is shown in Figure 8.1.

At its core, a logic model summarizes the program's whys, whats, and hows on a single sheet of paper. This powerful tool links organizational resources (inputs) to what it does (activities and outputs), to who it desires to impact (participants and audiences), and to what it hopes to achieve or change (outcomes). In the following section we review each component of the logic model.

Figure 8.1. Sample Logic Model: Jazz Arts Group

Program: Jazz Arts Group–Jazz Audiences Initiative (JAI) Theory-To-Practice Logic Model
Situation: To implement the Jazz Audiences Initiative data and findings and evaluate the success of best practices

Inputs	Outputs		Outcomes—Impact		
	Activities	*Participation*	*Short-Term*	*Medium-Term*	*Long-Term*
Jazz Arts Group Doris Duke Charitable Foundation Experiment Partners: • Jazz St. Louis • Hancher (University of Iowa) • MCG Jazz • Elastic Arts Foundation • Brooklyn Conservatory of Music Social media Jazz musicians Partnering organizations and musicians JAI Research Findings	Provide jazz concerts in intimate club settings Provide education to audiences about jazz Develop and implement marketing strategies Collect demographic data and audience feedback Provide BOGO and other incentives to participate in future concerts Provide genre-blending performances	18–34-year-olds unfamiliar with jazz Individuals with previous music experience Individuals who interact with technology/download music "Social butterflies"	Increased ticket sales Increased satisfaction—participants prefer the settings/experience Increased younger audiences Increased awareness of jazz Increased audience participation (i.e. dancing, involvement) Increased data and information regarding study hypotheses Increased creativity	Increased organizational capacity • Increased revenues • More effective marketing strategies Increased awareness of JAI research and JAG Development of a new and successful business model Increased engagement with the jazz art form Increased demand for jazz performances Increased knowledge about the jazz art form	Increased sustainability for the jazz art form Impact on the everyday practice of jazz (and other arts) organizations

Assumptions
Implementing the JAI study results will motivate younger audiences to attend jazz performances

External Factors

Inputs

Inputs include the organization's resources. This box should include anything the organization has at its disposal that supports employees and volunteers as they carry out the organization's work and achieve its mission. Common inputs include funding sources, partnering organizations, and physical space as well as technology, curriculum, and program materials. Typically, back-office activities such as marketing, human resources, finance, management, and development are also considered inputs, unless the organization is creating a separate logic model for its back-office operations. In this case, these functions would be listed as activities.

Activities as Outputs

Activities are what the organization does with resources to achieve its mission. These are the interventions used to bring out participant or community change and impact. Planned program activities as well as processes, tools, services, products, technology, events, and actions of service delivery are included in this category. Outputs include the measurement or result of program activities. Examples that fit this category include training classes held, units of services provided, and numbers of products sold.

Participation and Audiences as Outputs

Participation include those whom your organization desires to directly impact. Organizations can segment their audience to clarify the specific groups they serve. This practice proves helpful when measuring, managing, and communicating to outcomes.

For example, the logic model in Figure 8.1 represents a specific program designed to increase younger audiences for jazz performances. Instead of listing participants as individuals between the ages of eighteen to thirty-four who are unfamiliar with jazz, the organization listed specific groups, including individuals with previous music experience, individuals who interact with technology and download music, and individuals who might fall into the category of "social butterflies." The program's interventions are targeted to these specific groups, and segmentation supports targeted outcome measures. Common program outcomes often include a count of those served in each particular participation group (that is, the number of clients served). To evaluate the effectiveness of the program, outcomes measures must be tied specifically to this specific subgroup of the organization's larger audience.

Outcomes and Impact

This column lists an organization's whys along with the specific changes expected in a participant's attitudes, behavior, status, and functioning that occurs as a result of organizational activities. Short-term outcomes include results that occur immediately after an intervention. They describe the direct result of program activities, which may include an increase in knowledge or skills and a shift in attitudes.

Medium-term outcomes include results that occur if participants go out into the world and apply short-term outcomes. These are more indirect, because there are other factors that influence whether such outcomes will materialize. Examples might include the maintaining of new behavior, increased grade point average (GPA), or increased salary. Long-term outcomes or impacts are the results that occur if the organization serves a large number of people who consistently experience medium-term impacts, such as decreased usage of emergency rooms, increased graduation rates, or increased economic development activities.

The duration and intensity of the intervention will alter the time required for short-, medium-, and long-term outcomes. If an organization is engaged with a client for only a one-day event, the short-term outcomes could occur within one day to one week. If the program's intervention includes three years of early education, then short-term outcomes may be seen over the course of three years. The key is for an organization's internal stakeholders to define the timeline for which they expect to see the short-, medium-, and long-term outcomes. The next step is to communicate this timeline throughout the organization and to external stakeholders.

Another important element that should accompany a logic model is a statement of assumptions, especially if the organization does not engage in a theory of change process (see the next section of this chapter). This statement includes a brief description of why the organization believes its approach or key activities will be effective in achieving desired outcomes. The best assumptions are based on research specific to the organization's field or evidence-based practices and models.

The assumption for the logic model in Figure 8.1 is based on the Jazz Audience Initiative Market Segmentation Research (Brown et al., 2011), which found that younger audiences were more likely to explore new areas of music if they were invited to attend a show with a friend, had an opportunity to hear a sample of the music before attending the show, and were exposed to an experiential education component beyond the actual show. The logical conclusion is that incorporating these components into jazz performances will increase attendance by individuals between the ages of eighteen and thirty-four.

Creating a Logic Model: Best Practices

It is preferable that a cross-functional team creates the logic model rather than entrusting this task to a single individual in the organization. Leaders and staff should avoid using jargon when gathering information for the logic model, since the logic model process is easier to conduct when the language mirrors everyday speech. Organizations can use a basic questionnaire with select staff and stakeholders who represent all program functions.

The following is a list of basic questions to ask these audiences, along with an explanation of how each question is related to the logic model.

Questions used to fill out inputs:

- Who pays for your services?
- What materials and resources are required for you to deliver your services?
- Who helps you provide your services (partners, key stakeholders, and so on)?

Questions used to fill out activities:

- What activities do you perform throughout the day?
- What services or products do you provide to your clients?

Questions used to fill out participants:

- How old are your clients or participants? (List a range or group of ranges.)
- What sets your clients apart or differentiates them from the general population?
- Are your clients a specific gender, race, educational level, or social or economic status? (List all distinct groups.)

The "Five Whys" exercise results can be used to identify the short-, medium-, and long-term outcome sections of the logic model.

Once these questions are answered, the organization should assign a single individual to create the first draft of the logic model, using the collected data. The draft should then be reviewed by a variety of key stakeholders and staff until consensus is reached. The key is that the logic model is descriptive of what the organization does, how it does it, and what it is trying to accomplish for those it serves.

Key Benefits of a Logic Model

Once a logic model is created, organizations have in place a simple yet extremely effective tool to support a sustainable high-performance measurement culture. With careful attention and buy-in, the logic model becomes an essential tool for program planning, resources management, and communication with stakeholders. The logic model becomes the foundational support for outcomes and performance measurement.

Program Planning and Management

A logic model provides a guide for current and future program planning. If a new program or grant opportunity is presented, decision makers can refer to the logic model and decide if this particular opportunity is aligned with the organization's goals and objectives. If the answer is no, leaders quickly move on. If the answer is yes, designated leaders move forward with developing the new program or writing the grant.

Communication with Stakeholders

A thorough, simple logic model will prove invaluable to development officers and grant writers. It clearly communicates the goal of the organization and what the organization does. A logic model provides evidence that the organization is strategic in its resource use. The logic model describes the precise return on investment it strives to deliver to its funders, and the logic model itself can be used as a communications tool to educate new board members on all facets of the organization.

Outcomes and Performance Measurement

The logic model provides the framework for selecting the ideal success measures for an organization. It is neither possible nor necessary to measure all of an organization's outputs and outcomes. Logic models help leaders to avoid guessing games about which measures are most important and to support those leaders as they guide their organizations into the future. They provide a measure of confidence for leaders who want to quantify their organization's story, guiding the process for selecting success measures and capturing data that illustrates the organization's impact. (Chapter Nine explores this topic in greater detail.)

Going Deeper: Theory of Change

Leaders of organizations that adopt a high-performance measurement culture meet with greater success as they create and implement effective programs that lead to desirable social change. The quickest path to high-performance programs comes when an organization takes a theory-based approach to program development. Once the organization has developed a logic model and leadership is clear on the outcomes and impacts directly linked to the organization's core mission, it is time to create the theory of change.

A theory-based approach is significantly different from the manner in which most social-sector organizations develop programs. The typical, less-effective approach is trial and error. In this scenario, a group of well-meaning people have an idea for a needed program or service. This group secures the resources needed for the program and begins to implement the program. The program springs from a good idea that is not necessarily rooted in data or research.

Those who employ data-driven strategies will eventually stumble upon an effective program by delivering the services, measuring the outcomes, and then revising the program based on the outcomes until they achieve the desirable results. This process may take years and years of ineffective programs until the revisions are completed. Other organizations that have not moved toward managing to outcomes may continue to deliver these programs year after year without even knowing the true impact of their programs.

In contrast, a theory-based approach to program development requires leaders to take a step back and articulate why they believe that the program activities will lead to the desired program outcomes. It is a process of generating and reaching consensus on the explicit or implicit theories about how and why the program will work (Weiss, 1995). These assumptions and the hypothesis for success are often referred to as the program's theory of change.

Theory of change asks program stakeholders to predict exactly who or what is going to change, over what period of time, and by how much, at every single step in an often complex process (Anderson, 2005). Program leaders specify how and why they expect change to happen in a particular way. Theories of change often address how programs and initiatives are going to bring their resources to bear on creating early and intermediate changes that add up to their ultimate goal.

These often seem like simple questions, but in practice they can be hard to answer. Doing this difficult work and thinking about program outcomes *prior* to implementation or even measurement will lead to the creation of more impactful programs as well as more successful evaluation plans. Theory of change planning builds on the foundational work of the five whys and the logic model one step further and plans specifically how the organization is going to achieve the desired outcomes.

Let me use a fatherhood initiative program as an example. This specific program provides support groups, training, and one-on-one coaching to first-time dads aimed at eliciting greater parental engagement from the father. The ultimate goal is a healthier outcome for children. This shows up in the data as increased child support and decreased referrals to child welfare. The community outcome will be strengthened family ties and a reduction in crime.

- The fatherhood initiative program provides new fathers with training and mentoring in caring for an infant and basic parenting skills. The program's theory obviously assumes that fathers do not participate in fatherhood because they lack the proper attitudes, role models, and skills for their new roles as fathers. At the program level, the program theory is based on a series of micro-steps that make important assumptions: Training for new dads is (or can be) provided in accessible locations.
- Information about its availability will reach the target audience.
- When new fathers hear of the program's availability, they will sign up for it.
- New fathers will attend regularly.
- Where necessary, childcare will be available to fathers while they are in training.
- Trainers will offer quality training.
- The training will help fathers learn important parenting skills.
- Trainers will attend regularly and provide helpful and supportive counsel.
- Fathers will learn the lessons being taught about good parenting and fatherhood.
- Fathers will internalize the values and absorb the knowledge.
- Having attained the knowledge and skills, fathers will increase their engagement with their children in ways that will improve family and child outcomes.
- The children's mothers (or legal guardian or social services agencies) will be supportive and will not impede the fathers' efforts to father their children.
- New fathers will persist with these positive activities and stay involved with their children.
- Fathers will actively pay child support.

When the theory is examined, an organization can see how many of the linkages could be problematic and disrupt the overall success and impact of the program. At the program level, program leaders may know that the quality of instruction may be below par. It can be difficult to recruit new fathers to the training program. Many fathers may drop out of the programs, and those already participating may attend erratically.

In some situations, a mother may circumvent the father's willingness to use his new skills with his children. Many fathers may start to engage but stop after a few months, impeded by circumstances. An awareness of these potential problem areas as the program is being developed enables program leaders to try to prevent or address these factors and to develop more systematic data collection systems to highlight which factors are indeed impacting the effectiveness of the program.

In addition to being effective for outlining how and why a program works, good theory of change models are plausible, doable, testable, and meaningful (Connell and Klem, 2000). *Plausible* means that stakeholders believe the logic of the model. In other words, if the organization does these things, the organization will get the results they want and expect. *Doable* means the required human, political, and economic resources exist in sufficient supply to implement the action strategies in the theory. *Testable* means that stakeholders believe there are credible ways to discover whether the results are as predicted. *Meaningful* means that stakeholders see the outcomes as important and see the magnitude of change in the outcomes being pursued as worth the effort.

Although designing a theory of change model appears relatively simple and straightforward, it is likely to be difficult at first because most program leaders have not really thought this through. They have been using their professional training, experience, common sense, observation, and informal feedback to make important programming decisions. Using the theory of change process that follows can help facilitate the development of better programming and lead to positive change by way of an easy-to-follow pathway to greater impact.

The following steps are a map that illustrates the relationship between program activities and outcomes and how outcomes relate to each other over the lifespan of the initiative. The pathway map alone cannot tell the whole story of a program theory, but it is a framework to which successive waves of detail can be added to create a compelling theory of change. There is much more detail to add in order to tell the full story; however, this document is essential for better future program development and evaluation.

Step 1: Start with the Logic Model

When developing a program's theory of change, it is important to make sure all program leaders are in agreement regarding the ultimate purpose of their work. Using the outcomes of the logic model is a great place to start the conversation about creating a clear definition of the long-term outcomes the organization hopes to achieve through the program activities.

An organization's logic model may list several medium- to long-term outcomes. When creating the project change map, it is important for decision makers to be as specific as possible in the definition of their long-term outcome or overall impact. Overall impact includes big, complex, long-term goals, such as "improved family functioning" or "increased quality of life for seniors." However, although outcomes such as this sound good in mission statements and grant applications, they are too vague for the foundation of the theory of change.

As will be evident in the logic model, most social interventions have goals with many components. The creation of a map capturing the pathways to change becomes simplified when program leaders take the time to unpack larger goals, breaking them down into smaller components at this initial step. The following are some helpful questions to specify outcomes during this process.

- What are the ultimate goals of this program or initiative?
- How will we define success in this program?
- What are funders or program participants expecting to receive from their investment in the program?
- Given what we know today, what will be different in our community in the long term as a result of successfully reaching our goal?

Step 2: Identify Preconditions

This is the most time-intensive step of developing a theory of change, especially when a group has already done the work to establish whys and create a logic model. It is also the centerpiece of the theory development work. The goal of this step is to identify and sort through all of the preconditions related to the ultimate outcomes of interest. Leaders must funnel these preconditions into a pathway to change that moves in a linear fashion, proceeding chronologically toward the long-term goal.

The process used to create the map is "backwards mapping." This means that program leaders should imagine they are starting at the end of the successful initiative and mentally walking backward in time to determine what were the primary preconditions for success with regard to a particular expected outcome. In other words, leaders and program staff must ascertain which interim outcomes had to occur before an organization could achieve the ultimate outcome.

The pathway to change map depicts the relationship among nouns. Only outcomes (results, accomplishments, states, and changes, for example) are shown in the boxes at this point. All of the "stuff" that must exist in order for the long-term outcome to be realized is linked together on this map. The goal here is to depict the complete set of necessary and sufficient preconditions, including requirements, ingredients, and building blocks that must be in place.

Leaders must identify what conditions must exist prior to the realization of the long-term goal. Often participants are inclined to focus on what they must do or what must be done to others in the process of creating the change. This trap is avoided by remembering that *verbs are not allowed* on the pathway to change at this point. Figure 8.2 dictates this process of determining preconditions to the long-term outcome.

Figure 8.2. Theory of Change Pathway

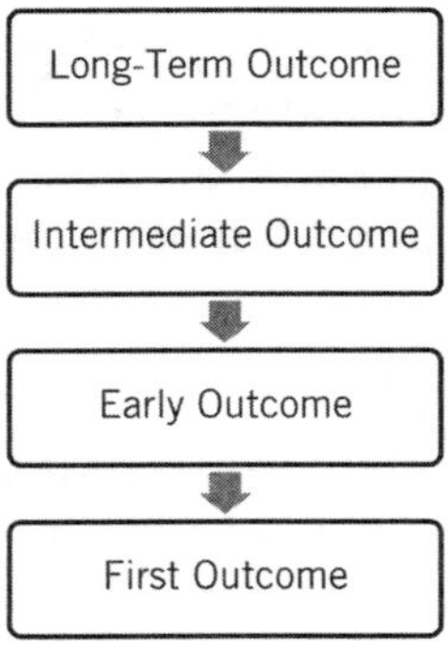

Step 3: Determine Indicators

Determining indicators means that for each precondition in the pathway to change, program leaders answer the basic question "What evidence will we use to show that this has been achieved?" The answer becomes the indicator that will be used to track progress and document success. At this stage it is important for leaders to clearly think about the best indicator first, regardless of how it will be measured. (In Chapter Nine we discuss determining how best to measure it.)

Step 4: Identify Activities

Once the pathway to change has been created and each of the preconditions in the pathway has been made operational, leaders can discuss the program activities, policies, and other actions that may be required to bring about the outcomes on the map. For each precondition on the map, the activities or policies that will be required to bring about that success should be identified.

Step 5: Identify Assumptions

Up to this point, assumptions have been unstated but have been used as the basis of creating change. The value of this approach lies in the ability to identify these underlying assumptions and capture the thinking that in the past the program leaders have taken for granted. This step allows leaders to clarify the underlying assumptions that make up the theory of change. The first group of assumptions addresses why each precondition is necessary to achieve the desired result in the pathway to change.

Completing this process, leaders begin to see why this set of preconditions will be sufficient to bring out the long-term outcome. To strengthen a program's theory of change, leaders can seek out theories and existing research that connect program activities to specific outcomes. This step may include gathering findings from best-practice research as well as collecting evidence from academic or basic research.

Communities in Schools: A Case Study

Similar to logic models, good theory of change maps can look very different from each other, depending on the organization, the particular program, and the audience served. They may contain multiple boxes with divergent arrows indicating how one action or activity leads to other actions, which ultimately lead to the program's long-term outcome.

Sometimes theory of change maps can become very difficult to understand and digest. Good models are clean and easy to understand by individuals both internal and external to the organization.

Communities in Schools developed a theory of change model that provides an excellent example of a simple and clean model that other nonprofit and government organizations can learn from.

Communities in Schools (CIS) serves students in grades K–12 and provides support to students who enrolled in college by surrounding them with a community of support, empowering them to stay in school and achieve in life. CIS works within the public school system, determining student needs and establishing relationships with local business, social service agencies, healthcare providers, and parent volunteer organizations to provide needed resources to students and schools.

Communities in Schools has spent some time thinking through their theory of change. The organization developed the following document to represent the change they bring about through permanent institutional change and positive outcomes for schools and students. The Communities in Schools theory of change statement reads as follows: "When CIS develops partnerships with high-quality local service providers and coordinates the delivery of services to school sites, the ultimate result is permanent institutional change, ensuring positive outcomes for children now and in the future" (Communities in Schools, 2013).

Usefulness of Theory of Change Models

Leaders of high-performance measurement cultures understand that having a well-thought-out and well-documented theory of change makes implementing data-driven strategies much easier. First, it helps ensure that program activities are thoughtful and truly linked to the organization's mission and vision. In addition, it forces decision makers to think through assumptions that underscore why certain activities are undertaken and also ensures that staff and agency leaders are working toward the same goals.

In addition, these maps become the framework for the successful evaluation of future programming. Most organizations have resources constraints when it comes to data collection and analysis. Leaders need to make choices between program evaluation activities and other important tasks, making program planning tools such as the theory of change map even more important. Most organizations, when conducting evaluation and performance measurement strategies, are unable to look at a wide range of program processes and outcomes. When there is a detailed project map, however, program leaders can make careful choices of where to invest an organization's limited resources and evaluation energies.

Central hypotheses about the program appear to represent potential issues that evaluation should address. Often, sufficient knowledge already exists and is available within the organization on a particular point, letting program leaders change a label from "assumption" or "hypothesis" to "fact." This allows leaders and program staff to divert their attention to other measurement priorities. If the central tenants of the program are still in doubt or unproven, this might present a question for which evaluation is well suited. In the next chapter, we will turn our attention to how to identify the best measures.

Next Steps

If an organization attempts to establish a measurement culture without a clear mission in place, it runs the risk of measuring the wrong outcomes. Such a mistake can prove costly, taking the organization further away from its desired state. A clear mission can guide the appropriate activities and measures needed if the organization is to advance to greater impact and excellence. The next step on the journey to excellence and impact is to capture data by using measures related to the organization's whys and its desired outcomes.

Impact & Excellence

Chapter Eight Discussion Questions

1. What is your organization's mission? How well does the stated mission relate to why your organization exists? How might your organization's mission statement be clarified or improved?
2. Conduct the "Five Whys" exercise by answering the following questions five times.
   a. Why does your organization do what it does?
   b. Why do your partners or funders support your organization?
   c. Why do your clients participate? What do clients hope to accomplish through their participation?
3. Use the logic model planning questions to develop your organization's logic model. Use your organization's whys to build the outcomes section.
4. What are your organization's assumptions? Why do you believe identified activities will achieve your outcomes? Use your answers to these questions to develop a theory of change map.

9

Capture Impact: Getting Started

Garbage in, garbage out.
—UNKNOWN

GREAT SOCIAL-SECTOR ORGANIZATIONS DEFINE THEIR SUCCESS BY the distinct impact they are making and the effectiveness of the services they deliver relative to the resources at their disposal. Leaders of these organizations ensure success and improve on the success they achieve by gathering data through measures aligned with stated goals and outcomes. They carefully select only the best measures to improve operations and tell the organization's story. When aligned with the ideal organizational culture, the measures contribute to the organization's sustainability and enable it to attract additional funds and opportunities.

Capturing impact lies at the heart of a high-performance measurement culture, yet it remains an area where organizations continue to struggle. Leaders know the value of measures and metrics but often are unsure about what to measure to drive results. Selecting the correct measures can be a relativity simple and empowering process. Two decisions are key: leaders must determine what they want to *know* and what they want to *do* with data collected through the measures they choose.

Qualities of Good Measures

The best measurement systems quantitatively reveal important information about the organization's products and services as well as the processes that support them. They are tools to help decision makers and constituents understand, manage, and improve what the organization does. Good measures also tell the story of how well an organization is fulfilling its mission. They provide insights into whether processes are supporting improved performance as intended.

The best performance measures indicate whether organizational goals are being met. Measurement data will show if improvements are necessary, where they are needed, and whether customers and stakeholders are satisfied with the changes an organization implements. The most effective measures excite and inform staff and stakeholders.

There are a number of common mistakes made by nonprofit and government organizations that choose to implement performance measures. Leaders may focus too narrowly, for one. An organization will often meet with a greater degree of success if, rather than selecting a single performance measure, leaders choose between five and seven diverse, powerful measures to tell the organization's story.

Many leaders also fail to consider how the selected measures will be perceived. The foundational reason to invest in a performance and outcomes measurement system is to establish measures that reveal the facts needed to take an organization to the next level. Outcomes measures support the organization's aim to achieve greater impact and excellent. However, when leaders fail to communicate this fully and to secure essential buy-in from line and management staff, the organization runs the risk of inadequate data entry, a declining attitude toward performance measures, and the creation of a work-around by those tasked with data collection and evaluation.

Lackluster or incomplete buy-in leads to lackluster or incomplete results from measurement activities. To avoid this pitfall and secure the necessary buy-in from staff, it is essential for social-sector leaders to include staff and other stakeholders from the beginning. It is important to communicate clearly and consistently how the selected measures will help these contributors make informed decisions, inspire them in their particular contribution to the organization's overall mission, and motivate them to make enhanced efforts to fulfill that mission. To increase acceptance of newly instituted performance measures, organizations can consider the following four traits of successful performance measures.

Effective Measures Have Face Validity

Face validity means a measure is perceived to measure what it is intended to measure. For example, if a set of measures is designed to assess program performance and management, line staff and stakeholders must agree that these are, in fact, good measures of their program's performance. Not all face-valid measures are good measures. Yet if face validity is not established, buy-in remains nearly impossible. It is essential to ask whether the value of the proposed performance measure has been clearly demonstrated.

Effective Measures Reflect the Needs of All Stakeholders

Good measures not only are important to the leadership of the organization but also are valued by staff, clients, and other key stakeholders. Before implementing measures, it is critical to understand what these different groups value most. Organizational leaders must consider how selected measures help these groups achieve identified goals. Good measures are those aligned with the "whys" important to the organization, stakeholders, and participants.

Effective Measures Are Simple to Understand

The best social-sector measures are easy to explain and understand. If staff or stakeholders must invest significant time learning how to interpret a measure, they may stop trying to collect and consider data. If the measure itself is difficult to understand, the measure will then lack face validity—the first of four traits that successful performance measures share. Leaders must ensure that each selected measure is clear and that all parties understand the value of this measure to their specific roles in the organization and to the organization as a whole.

Effective Measures Are Timely

The sooner data and results can be communicated, the more powerful and useful they will be to the organization. A twelve- to eighteen-month lag between the time data is collected and performance measure results are shared is typical, but in our fast-paced society, basing decisions on year-old data is not ideal. By the time data becomes available, it is nearly impossible to decide whether current organizational efforts are having the desired impact.

As an illustration of the importance of timely communication, consider the United States Census. The data collected from each census is a great source to use when planning, communicating, and supporting the social-sector organization's mission, programs, and services. However, the information gathered is not timely enough to use it as an organization's sole performance measure for guiding day-to-day decisions or for determining the immediate effectiveness of actions.

A Variety of Measures

Social-sector organizations are complex; therefore it would be highly irresponsible to evaluate the effectiveness of a government or nonprofit organization with a single measure. In an earlier chapter, we examined the danger of using administrative overhead as the sole measure to determine whether an organization is worthy of an investment. Overall revenues and the allocation of resources within the organization are other important indicators of what results organizations are achieving. It is important that leaders use a variety of measures to evaluate performance.

Sometimes organizations or funders rely on one specific outcome measure to evaluate success. Popular measures frequently used as standalone measures of success include graduation rates, recidivism rates, increased test scores, and cost. Each of these is an important and useful measure, and organizations with missions aligned with these outcomes should certainly be tracking them. The problem lies not with the effectiveness of the measures themselves but with an imbalanced reliance on them. When one of these measures becomes the only data point shared, the picture of overall effectiveness is incomplete.

Using a single indicator of success makes it more difficult to take appropriate, data-driven actions. If the outcome is less than desirable, that one measure is unlikely to provide decision makers with insights about why things are not going as planned. Is it because participants are not satisfied with services and are therefore less engaged? Or is it because there is inadequate funding to provide the proper services to achieve these outcomes?

Alternatively, if the outcome is desirable, a single measure is unlikely to indicate whether different groups are successful at different rates. A single measure is also unlikely to indicate whether the program could be delivered in a more cost-effective manner. Using just one measure limits the organization's chance of gaining the fullest understanding of what, specifically, is contributing to a success or failure.

To answer these important questions, organizations must use a variety of measures to tell their story. At a minimum, organizations should track data on participant demographics, services delivered, cost and revenues, participant and stakeholder feedback, and key outcomes. In addition, social-sector organizations should be tracking performance in terms of increased services to their target population. The mission and logic model of most organizations will clearly state what population is being impacted. Therefore it is important to collect data that demonstrates the organization is indeed impacting the targeted group.

Instead of solely focusing on number of clients served, a good measure is often stated in terms of percentage of total market served. Consider the following example. One thousand children receive free and reduced-price lunch through an after-school program. This particular program has a goal of reaching low-income elementary students with an after-school enrichment program. If the program is serving fifty of those one thousand students, then it is currently serving 5 percent of the target population.

A measure of increased success would be demonstrated by data indicating the program's ability to provide services to more students in the target population. One goal might be to increase market share by 2 percent each year. This performance measure captures impact, telling the story of the organization's reach much more effectively than a measure that simply captured how many students were served.

Outcome and Output

Outcome measures do not replace the need for output measures. Output measures provide valuable information and need to be tracked. Organizations should measure and regularly report the units of services. It is also important to understand the number of services received per client. Coupled with outcomes measures, output data allows the organization to examine the number of services offered as a predictor of its overall success. An organization may find that it can reduce the number of sessions or classes required to achieve such impact. Or output measures may show the need to increase the number of sessions or classes offered in order to achieve the same results.

A girls' empowerment program provides another example of how service unit data coupled with outcome measures allowed decision makers to increase program effectiveness. From her previous experience as an academic researcher, the executive director and founder of this organization understood the value of data-driven program development. Following the launch of a pilot program, the leadership team discovered the outcomes achieved were less than those desired.

If program managers had only had access to outcome data, leaders might have concluded that the program was not effective and ceased operation. But the organization had also collected data that enabled leaders to theorize that the program did not incorporate enough sessions to build the necessary rapport and trust among students. The resulting lack of group cohesion prevented participants from engaging with other students and program activities in ways that would most effectively produce lasting change. Instead of deeming the program a failure, decision makers added four sessions to build trust among these participants. This brought about the positive outcomes the organization had desired when it implemented the program.

Of course, all organizations should implement measures of costs incurred and revenues earned. An effective performance measure associated with cost is cost per outcome or cost incurred per successful participant. The cost per participant is calculated by dividing total program costs by the number of successful participants. This particular measure gives organizations a way to assess program effectiveness and efficiency as well as demonstrate success to prospective funders. As the organization provides better outcomes and finds a way to deliver services more efficiently, the cost per participant will decrease.

Another important outcome measure is the consistent assessment of participant and stakeholder satisfaction. This might include a participant's perception about whether the program achieved desired learning objectives as well as the participant's overall satisfaction. Depending on the program, reliable measures might include questions such as "Would you participate in this program again?" or "Would you recommend this program to a friend?"

These specific measures are not useful in all programs. If participation in a program is involuntary, such as a court-ordered program, asking participants if they would participate in a program such as this again may skew results. For mandatory programs, it is more beneficial to ask questions such as:

- Was this program a valuable use of your time?
- Did you learn new things that will help you in your daily life?
- Did this program exceed your expectations?

Outcome Categories

It is neither necessary nor practical to measure all organizational outcomes listed in the logic model. Just as too little information will not be useful, too much information can lead to overwhelm and a lack of clear direction. The goal should be to select three to four outcome measures that meet the requirements of good measures.

Social-sector organizations are best served when they start with outcomes that overlap with the outcomes funders and participants most desire. Typically, the outcomes of social-sector organizations fall within one of the following ten categories:

- *Increased Knowledge and Learning.* These measures relate to the percentage of participants who increased their skills and knowledge as a result of a program or service. This can be measured by a simple pre- and post-test design, in which participants are given a knowledge assessment prior to the training or intervention and a second assessment at closure. Increased scores on the post-test indicate increased learning. Depending on the nature of the content delivered, increased knowledge can be measured by asking participants in a post-evaluation survey to assess whether they believe they met identified learning objectives.

- *Changed Attitudes.* This category of outcome measures relates to the percentage of participants who report improved attitudes as a result of the program or service. Such measures can be reported through ratings from the participant.
- *Increased Readiness.* A participant's level of readiness is often measured by the percentage of total participants who meet the minimum qualifications for the next level. Examples include kindergarten readiness, college readiness, job readiness, or even readiness to begin treatment. Readiness is often measured by a skills and knowledge test that includes next-level concepts. Depending on the type of program, readiness can also be assessed using an attitude survey that asks participants to rate how comfortable they feel about moving on to the next level.
- *Reduction of Undesirable Behavior.* Reduction in smoking, drinking, drug use, or texting while driving are examples of this type of measure. The level of reduction can be measured by the incident rate of undesirable behavior on the part of program participants following program participation. Reduction level is often measured by relapse, recidivism, or self-reported behavior frequency. The smaller the incidence measured, the greater evidence of effectiveness can be inferred.
- *Increase of Desirable Behavior.* These measures relate to the percentage of participants who achieved a desired goal. This can be measured by predetermining the goal and recording success after a specified time frame. This is a particularly good measure to track for organizations that design individual service plans for participants. One ideal measure would be the percentage of participants who successfully achieve their goals outlined in the service plan.
- *Maintenance of New Behavior.* Outcomes such as increased exercise, medication compliance, or attendance are example of new behavior maintenance. Maintenance is often measured by the percentage of participants who proceed to the next level when they achieve behavior compliance or the number of participants who do not reenter a particular program or system.
- *Increased Social Status.* Examples of increased social status include employment, increased income, or increased education level. Increased social status can be measured by the percentage

of participants who improve or develop positive relationships. Increased social status is often measured through observation or through self-reporting.

- *Increased Economic Conditions.* Measures of economic conditions include factors such as the percentage of participants who retain employment, move from temporary to permanent housing, or increase their income. Increased economic conditions are typically measured through self-reporting or observation.
- *Improved Health Conditions.* This measure relates to the number of participants with reduced incidence of health problems. Improved health conditions are often measured by self-reporting, a review of medical records, or a survey of health care providers.
- *Increased Economic Development.* Examples of economic development measures include the number of jobs created, total money invested in a community, or the number of new businesses started. Data for each of these measures is gathered by establishing the desired outcome prior to program inception. Organizations can then track key success indicators.

Real-World Measures

The fact that mission, programs, target population, and outcomes are unique and specific to each social-sector organization presents both a challenge and a reward. Although the concept of selecting the right measures is shared by every nonprofit and government organization, each organization requires a unique set of measures to accurately tell its story. Those organizations that take the time to determine the best measures, rather than simply adopting measures forced on them by prospective funders, are more successful in achieving desired organizational outcomes.

We now consider two real-world examples of social-sector success measures. First we examine a government-funded nonprofit organization supporting permanent housing. Then we turn our attention to an early childhood education program primarily funded by government grants. These two case studies highlight distinct examples of diverse and real-world measures.

Permanent Housing Success Measures: A Case Study

The first set of success measures includes the performance and outcome measures established by a permanent supportive housing organization in a large and urban Southern city. The organization's mission is to provide affordable housing and economic opportunities to low-income residents, especially those who are homeless or disabled. Using the Quick-Start Performance Measurement Program offered by Measurement Resources, this organization identified the following seven evaluation and performance measures.

Unsuccessful Participants

This measure looks at the percentage of residents leaving for negative outcomes—that is, the percentage of residents who left the organization unsuccessfully. This is an undesirable outcome, and the organization's goal is to reduce this number. Reasons participants exited the program included eviction, suicide, overdose, jail, and noncompliance.

The number of unsuccessful participants is measured by analyzing data in the organization's property management system, which tracks the reason an individual leaves the organization. The specific measure is calculated using this formula: number of unsuccessful move outs divided by the total number of move outs multiplied by 100. Results are reported and examined every six months.

The collected data is used alongside other measures to determine if strategies can be employed to decrease the unsuccessful move-out rate. In addition, the comparison between program residents and nonprogram residents supports the organization as it seeks to communicate its need for increased funding. Doing so successfully enables the organization to provide additional services to nonprogram participants.

Cost Per Successful Client

This measure examines the costs for each successful client. This measure allows the organization to communicate the monetary investment required to pay for the average client's success. In addition, it is a measure of effectiveness and efficiency. The formula for this measure is: [total program operational costs divided by (number of positive move outs + number of current residents)].

Financial data and other data collected through the property management system are used to calculate this measure. This measure is calculated and examined every six months, in January and July. This measure is compared to previous costs to determine if the organization is becoming more efficient.

Stability of Health

This measure examines the percentage of clients who are maintaining their health while enrolled in the program. Health maintenance measures look at the number of clients who attend medical appointments, comply with medication guidelines, and attend groups or treatment programs. The organization uses both health-related goals established by its federal funder, Substance Abuse Mental Health Services Administration (SAMHSA), and a self-sufficiency matrix developed internally to assess these goals.

The stability-of-health measure includes the percentage of clients whose responses indicate maintenance of these behaviors. Data is analyzed every six months to ensure that these behaviors are being maintained at desired levels. This measure is used to communicate success in reaching stated goals as well as program improvement.

Increased Quality of Life

This measure examines the percentage of clients who increase their quality of life while enrolled in the program. This measure includes reaching identified goals, volunteerism, employment, and increasing social relationships, among other factors.

Items related to quality of life, as previously established by their federal funder's goals and the self-sufficiency matrix, are used as tools to assess these goals. Data is analyzed every six months to ensure that positive changes are occurring. This measure is used to communicate successful outcomes outlined in the logic model as well as for program improvement.

Increase in Income

This performance measure captures the extent to which a participant's income increases during his or her enrollment in the program. Increases in income include new employment along with new benefits, cash benefits, or a combination of both. The data for this measure are found in the organization's HUD-funded Homeless Management Information System (HMIS).

Data is analyzed annually to ensure that residents are receiving services and supports that allow them to increase their income. This is important, because it is related to participants' quality of life and helps them maintain their housing. This measure is used to communicate with funders and make program improvements.

Length of Stay

This measure of the percentage of program participants who maintain permanent housing is directly related to the mission of the organization. Data from the organization's property management system are analyzed and used to determine the number of residents who have lived in the organization's housing units for the following timelines: less than three months, three to five months, six to eleven months, one to three years, or more than three years.

The average length of stay is calculated by adding the total days that housing is provided for each resident and dividing that number by the total number of residents served for a particular period. As this number increases, the organization can be confident that it is achieving its goal of sustainable permanent housing. These measures are examined every six months, and the resulting data is used to communicate to funders and cited in discussions of program planning and sustainability.

Resident Satisfaction

A resident satisfaction survey evaluates resident perceptions of safety, increased quality of life, satisfaction with case management and with the facilities, and areas of organizational strength and weakness. The survey also assesses unaddressed resident needs. Data is used for program planning and improvement.

Early Childhood Education Success Measures: A Case Study

The mission of an early childhood education program in a rural Midwestern county is to promote healthy outcomes for pregnant women, enhance the development of very young children, promote healthy family functioning, and give low-income preschool children a developmental edge when entering kindergarten. The organization accomplishes this by providing early childhood care and preschool programs for children from birth to six years old.

The organization also connects families to required resources and provides education to parents. This nonprofit also participated in the Quick Start

Performance Measurement program and identified the following five measures that allow them to measure and communicate impact and value.

School Readiness

This measure represents the extent to which students are prepared for the next level of education. The measure evaluates early education to preschool or preschool to kindergarten. The first school readiness measure is the teacher's perception of a child's readiness. A survey asks the community's kindergarten teacher to assess the extent to which they believe this program prepared students for kindergarten. It also asks teachers to assess a child's specific strengths and weaknesses. A second objective measure of program results is based on a kindergarten screening assessment.

For children moving from the early childhood program to the preschool program, school readiness is assessed by an internal teacher survey. This assessment includes a natural control group, as not all participants enrolled in the preschool program are involved in the early education program. Results are reported annually to the board, staff, management, and key partners. These measures are used for program improvement and communicating to schools about how the program helps the kindergarten teachers to be successful. This sharing of data leads the organization toward significant improvement and partnership with other organizations focused on a similar mission.

Child Progress

This measure examines the percentage of children participating in the program who experience improvement on pre- and post-tests for each education domain. The percentage of students meeting expectations is also measured. This data is collected and maintained in the organization's case management system.

Children are assessed three times annually, and data is analyzed annually and sometimes more frequently. The information is reported in two ways: as an individual's readiness and as an overall average of scores. Results are communicated to teachers, management, the board, and the community. This measure informs program improvement.

Percentage of Families Reporting an Increase in Self-Sufficiency

This measures the extent to which parents are satisfied with the family's goal in moving toward the desired goal of self-sufficiency. This outcomes measure captures a parent's goals prior to a child's enrollment and then assesses parental perceptions of goal achievement at the end of the school year.

In addition, teachers' perceptions are gathered, and a checklist kept in the case notes is used as a part of the overall assessment of the family's perceptions of program effectiveness. These measures are evaluated each spring. Data is analyzed annually and used to report to staff, management, boards, clients, and communities. This information is used to inform outcomes and improve program components relating to family goals.

Increase in Comprehensive Health Services

This measure examines the extent to which individuals who are identified as needing health services (prenatal, dental, physical, and mental) receive such services over the course of the program. Data is collected in a case management system. Information is reported by overall health care, and then broken down by specific treatment area. The data is analyzed and reported annually to staff, management, community stakeholders, and families. These measures are used to educate the community about needs and to introduce value-added services that the program provides as well as to guide program improvements.

Parent Engagement

Parent engagement is measured by two specific measures: the teacher's perception of parent engagement and the percentage of parents participating in engagement activities, including parent meetings, homework, and volunteer opportunities. These measures are deployed twice annually, once at the midpoint of the year, and once at the end of the year. Data is analyzed and communicated to staff, management, board members, and families. This measure is important for building an understanding of the benefits of the program in the community and for program improvement.

Gathering Data

As is clear from these two real-world examples, there are a variety of ways to gather data. Most performance measurement programs include a mix of collecting hard data and survey data. Hard data includes financials, program activities, and quantitative counts as well as percentages of test scores and completion rates. Survey data covers both participants' and key stakeholders' perceptions of program services and the achievement of identified outcomes and goals.

The common, limiting belief that an organization lacks the appropriate technology or funding to develop a sophisticated data collection solution prevents many social-sector organizations from implementing a powerful performance measurement system. Technology does help automate and sometimes simplify the data collection process. However, expensive case management systems do not always generate good data collection measures. The defining factor of success is the system's ability to track the right measures and organize the data in the most useful format. When technology solutions are not available, an organization will need to invest time in manually designing a process to synthesize the data in a manner that provides maximum insight and benefit.

Each organization can establish its own success measures and pilot them on a low-technology, manual basis before investing in an expensive case management system. This allows the organization to define what the new system must achieve and prevents wasteful spending on technology systems that do not deliver what's needed.

Low-cost and no-cost ways to get started include:

- Establishing spreadsheets and databases using software tools, such as Microsoft Excel or Access
- Using collaboration tools such as that provided by Microsoft SharePoint software
- Using inexpensive survey software such as Adobe Central or SurveyMonkey

Using already established statewide or community databases is another option. These databases are often supported by state and federal governments or large nonprofit organizations. They frequently house relevant information related to an organization's desired outcomes. Examples include the Bureau of Labor Statistics and the National Student Clearinghouse. Such databases often have data repositories, which allow users to download data tables specific to a region or population.

Survey Best Practices

Conducting good surveys for research is no longer cost-prohibitive for nonprofits and government organizations. Online survey tools, such as those just mentioned, provide an optimal way to establish internal databases to help organizations track critical information. These tools offer some synthesis capabilities and, compared to manual tools such as Microsoft Excel, save users time in data analysis. Thanks to inexpensive and user-friendly web-based survey sites, any employee can quickly gather quality data.

Surveys can be used to gather useful information that makes it possible for organizations to improve services, understand outcomes, and engage the community. As with all tools, there is an optimal way to use surveys for maximum results. Organizations must heed the warning offered in the common saying, "garbage in, garbage out." Too often, managers hastily design a survey to collect data from clients, staff, or stakeholders but collect information that does not support the best possible measurement. Careful survey design will ensure that an organization is asking the precise questions that allow them to draw accurate conclusions and make the best recommendations based on survey findings.

The first step to developing a good survey is to focus on actions desired as a result of the survey. Before writing questions, leaders need to be precise about their plan for using collected data and identify what specific information is needed to take action. Before a survey question is posed, leaders should ask, "What would I do with this information?" The results gathered from transformational survey questions will help tell the organization's story, generate solutions to problems, lead to suggestions for improvements, and demonstrate outcomes.

Once a survey plan is established, staff should invest sufficient time in crafting questions to ensure each one is objective. A common problem with surveys is the use of biased or leading questions. Poorly worded questions lead to questionable results and ineffective conclusions. For example, respondents should not know where the organization stands on a particular topic. Instead of a question such as "How did our program help you?"

an improved survey question might read, "What, if anything, did our program help you accomplish?"

Surveys are often unsuccessful because they contain too many open-ended questions—that is, questions that allow respondents to enter anything they wish. Such questions reduce the organization's ability to analyze the data effectively. They also impact the response rate, as people feel overwhelmed having to think about and then compose a response in the space provided.

Successful surveys are brief. The shorter the survey, the higher the response rate, and, typically, the more meaningful responses an organization will gather. Respondents generally begin to abandon a survey after twenty-five questions. Therefore, the organization should identify the most important categories of information needed to assess impact and limit survey questions to those that provide only the most significant insights and data.

One way to ensure efficient use of participants' time is to use the skip function, allowing participants to omit sections that do not specifically apply to them. It is also critical to provide survey results to participants and complete the feedback loop. Great survey efforts use the survey as an opportunity to strengthen relationships by sharing the data with relevant communities and discussing what actions the organization is taking based on the feedback provided. Taking such an action communicates that the organization values its stakeholders, increases accountability, and enhances the likelihood of success.

Survey Scales

One key element of a well-crafted survey is the use of a four- or five-point scale designed to measure attitudes or perceptions. Such a tool is often referred to as Likert-type scale (Likert, 1932). Good scales have symmetrical labels, capturing the intensity of the respondent's feeling about an item. The most common Likert-type items ask respondents to rate how much they agree or disagree with statements. A five-point scale typically contains a neutral point to allow decision makers to understand the strength of attitudes.

Five-Point Scale

Strongly Disagree	Disagree	Neither Disagree nor Agree	Agree	Strongly Agree

A four-point scale will force participants to choose a side, thereby providing decision makers with insights on whether the majority of participants are mostly in agreement or disagreement.

Four-Point Scale

Strongly Disagree	Disagree	Agree	Strongly Agree

Sometimes the agree or disagree scale is not the most appropriate format for measurement purposes. The following are some other common types of scales that can be used in outcomes surveys:

Likelihood Scale

Definitely would not participate	Probably would not participate	Might or might not participate	Probably would participate	Definitely would participate

Importance Scale

Not Important	Somewhat Important	Very Important	Critical

Satisfaction Scale

Very Unsatisfied	Unsatisfied	Neither Unsatisfied nor Satisfied	Satisfied	Very Satisfied

Frequency Scale

Never	Rarely	Sometimes	Very Often	Always

Quality Scale

Extremely Poor	Below Average	Average	Above Average	Excellent

Effectiveness Scale

Very Ineffective	Slightly Ineffective	Neither Ineffective nor Effective	Slightly Effective	Very Effective

Testing Survey Questions

Because many nonprofit and government organizations are going to turn to surveys to achieve their outcome and impact data, sufficient steps should be taken to ensure that high-quality survey data is obtained. It is important that respondents interpret the questions in the way the organization intends. The familiarity and meaning of words may not be the same among all members of the sample. To increase the likelihood of obtaining high-quality data, organizations should considering including a process called cognitive interviewing as a way to pilot test the survey design (Willis, 2013).

Cognitive interviews are used to detect survey items that are not understood by respondents as intended by the survey developers. Generally, cognitive interview methods involve four stages: comprehension or interpretation, information retrieval, judgment formation, and response editing (Beatty, 2004). In other words, the respondent must first understand the question, then recall information, decide on its relevance, and finally formulate an answer in the format provided by the interviewer.

Cognitive interviews help survey designers understand how participants interpret and answer questions. They help organizational leaders understand the conceptual adequacy of a self-report measure for a desired population (for example, youth, various socioeconomic groups or race, and ethnicities). Cognitive interview results can be used to revise or develop new items so that they are appropriate to respondents' cultural context and lifestyle.

Cognitive interviewing can reduce respondent burden by removing ambiguity and adding clarity so that when the survey is launched, respondents will have an easier time completing it. This ensures the more accurate information needed for evaluation and assessing outcomes. For surveys, cognitive interviewing involves fielding the survey with a small group of individuals from the target sample population and asking the following types of questions for each item:

- Are you able to answer this question? If not, why not?
- Is this question clear? If not, what suggestions do you have for making it clearer?
- How do you interpret this question? *or* How do you interpret specific words or phrases within a question?
- Do the response options make sense? If not, what suggestions do you have?
- How comfortable are you answering this question?

This approach does require the investment of time in the process of survey design, but it can save the organization the hassle and expense of conducting a survey and receiving data that is not useful because participants interpreted the questions differently from how the organization intended them. Organizations must weigh the time and resources it takes to do this against the benefits that will be gained.

One cost-effective way to obtain participant feedback is to use a group approach rather than individual interviews. In this case, the organization can invite a diverse group of target clients or the survey population to the organization and provide participants with a meal, such as a continental breakfast, a box lunch, or pizza. Only more complex survey questions should be shared in the group setting. More straightforward demographic and open-ended questions do not need to go through this process.

Once the group is gathered, organizers invite participants to read and answer a specific survey question independently. The interviewer then follows up with probing questions for their consideration. Once respondents have completed the task individually, the discussion leader can then ask the group to discuss their responses to the probing questions.

The group leader then has the group examine the next survey question and repeat the process. This continues until all the survey questions have been discussed. This technique works well for new for respondents, as they will be inclined to talk about their answers to the survey questions rather than talk about how they think about the question. Asking the specific, probing follow-up questions is a vital and important step in the process.

Cognitive interviewing does not replace the need to also pilot test the survey prior to implementation. A pilot test should include asking a few people to take the survey to understand how long it will take and the ease of administration. This may detect more concrete problems such as technology problems with an electronic survey or difficulty accessing completed surveys. Identifying these issues up front will help ensure a better response rate and a more successful process.

For example, an organization may want to pilot test which method will deliver better results: the paper and pencil method or an electronic survey. In a pilot test conducted for a client's outcomes and impact survey, we were surprised to learn that a much higher response rate was achieved by mailing the surveys with a return stamp than by providing a link for individuals to click in order to complete an electronic survey. This was the exact opposite of our hypothesis. Knowing this up front allowed the organization to build in the cost of postage and, as a result, yielded a much better response rate.

Other Measurement Questions to Consider: The Measures Test

Every organization has the capacity to measure and communicate impact. Implementing strong outcome measures requires systematic planning and an understanding of the goals of both the organization and its stakeholders. It also requires access to an existing measurement system or the development of simple, low-technology data-gathering tools. Once the measures are established, the organization should examine plans to ensure selected measures meet the qualifications of good measures and are likely to result in the collection of data needed for important decision making.

Here are five suggested questions to ask before implementing a measurement survey:

1. Are these measures related to important policy and practice issues?
2. Are these measures relevant, and do they apply to practitioners?
3. Can these measures be communicated in a way that will influence outcomes?
4. Are incentives built into the system for collecting and acting on these data?
5. Are the measures linked to the stakeholders' interests?

Next Steps

The methods described in this chapter are designed to help nonprofit and government leaders understand the best success measures needed to tell their organization's story around impact and performance. These measures alone do not necessarily isolate the causes of a program's impact or reveal why the program achieved success. To understand the extent to which the program's impacts would have occurred if a participant did not participate in the program or to know how these impacts differ from the impact achieved by other groups, evaluation and measurement design must be considered. The next chapter presents the various strategies that will help organizations improve their measurement design to answer more complex questions related to causation and generalization.

Impact & Excellence

Chapter Nine Discussion Questions

1. What are four to seven measures that best reflect the whys that matter to the organization as a whole, to funders, and to participants?

2. For each measure, list why it is reflective of the organization's mission.
3. For each measure, list how knowing this result will improve operational or organizational outcomes. Why will the measure be helpful?
4. Review the Measures Test in this chapter. Do your measures meet these criteria?
5. For the measures that do meet the criteria, develop an implementation plan.

10

Capture Impact: The Next Steps

All life is an experiment. The more experiments you make, the better.
—RALPH WALDO EMERSON

LEADERS OF HIGH-PERFORMANCE MEASUREMENT cultures are interested in a consistent cycle of learning and feedback. They use this information to consistently improve an organization's programs and services. The strategies for measuring impact shared in the previous chapters provide a framework for developing organizational measures that tell an organization's story and communicating the difference this is making for participants and the larger community. This framework is also useful for organizations that want to measure improvement on an ongoing basis to make adjustments to programming that will drive even greater success.

The power of the organization's story that can be told from the data collected through measurement activities often depends on the organization's evaluation or measurement design. If an organization focuses only on measures related to their own participants and the organization's programs and services, the impact they can communicate will be limited. In addition, measures must be repeated over time for greater impact.

For example, if managers of a job training program know that 89 percent of participants receive a job after successful completion of its program, that organization can claim this result for the people who participated in that particular training year. Their story becomes even more robust, however, if program staff can show that year after year, on a consistent basis, 89 percent or more of program participants received a job. This demonstrates the reliable results achieved through the program.

An organization with such documented success has much to celebrate and is well ahead of the average nonprofit organization. However, there are limitations to only having outcomes data from the program itself. First, an organization cannot rule out the possibility that the participants who found jobs could have found them even if they had not participated in the job training program.

A funder looking to reduce program funding may feel less inclined to fund a program that cannot prove that it was the precise program that led to changes in participants. If an organization cannot demonstrate that its programs are making a difference in participants' lives *above and beyond what these participants could do on their own,* funders are less likely to donate. A skeptic could argue that these participants were highly motivated to get a job. In such a case, it is plausible to conclude that, if this program was not in existence, the participants would have gone to the library, sent out resumes on their own, or attended another job training program in the community and achieved the same results.

Having data only on program participants also does not demonstrate that the program is the reason for participants' success. Other intervening variables may be contributors to individual success. For example, ice cream sales and crime both increase in the summer. Knowing this does not allow us to draw the conclusion that selling ice cream increases crime. It would be ridiculous to create a policy to curb the sales of or ban ice cream in order to reduce crime. Warmer weather is the causal factor in both circumstances. Similar correlations may also be found impacting social service programs.

A system evaluation of youth child welfare outcomes found that delinquent youth also served by the child welfare system had more positive outcomes related to relatively short lengths of stay in environments that were not their homes. In addition, these children experienced placement stability compared to youth of similar ages not involved with the court system. Examining this data alone, it would appear that the programming for delinquent children caused the improved outcomes. In reality, the delinquent children were being ordered into the child welfare systems placement by a judge. In many cases, these youth were experiencing better outcomes not because the program worked better for them, but because they did not need these services.

If these delinquent youth had been referred to the child welfare agency without a court order, the child welfare agency typically would not take the case. These youth would not meet the agency's identified criteria for services. However, because the judge ordered placement, the agency was required to take them. The delinquent youth had better outcomes because of their level-of-care needs, not because of the programming. If the organization did not explore this relationship further, leaders could have made erroneous conclusions about their program and made changes that were unnecessary and impeded the success of the other children they served.

If social service organizations fail to explore the causation of program impacts, they risk spending time and money on programs whose success actually stems from factors beyond those programs. For example, a ten-week intensive new mother health initiative that includes group classes and home visits might appear to be successful at increasing infant health outcomes, reducing postpartum depression, and reducing referrals to child welfare. However, if this program conducted an evaluation and looked at causation, they might find that mothers from a similar socioeconomic status who did not enroll in the program but also elected to attend a social group for new mothers were just as successful.

This would lead to the conclusion that it is the social interaction among the mothers that was driving success more than the high-cost in-home visits of a nurse. Understanding the programming that is driving the desired outcomes can enable organizations to operate more effectively and, often, to identify ways to reduce program costs and eliminate unnecessary services. The expansion of services and increased intensity of programming is not always the optimal solution.

There are many different program evaluation and research designs an organization can consider. As this book is designed to be a practical guide for increasing data-driven strategies and using the results to produce more successful and impactful organizations, theory on research methods and designs will not be covered in detail. Instead, this chapter presents some of the concepts an organization should consider when seeking to enhance data and information about program impact and also to explore how, specifically, such data will enhance current knowledge about their impact. Note: the strategies listed in this chapter strengthen how an organization uses data and information, but they are not required for achieving a high-performance measurement culture.

The Shift Toward Evidenced-Based Cultures

Many federal, state, and larger foundation funders are making a move toward funding *what works*, so they prefer to fund organizations that embrace evidenced-based programming. Evidence-based programs have the backing of rigorous and randomized controlled studies with significant results to support the outcomes an organization desires to achieve.

Funders appreciate evidence-based practices (EBPs) because they increase the likelihood that the programs they fund will get positive results. These types of programs are attractive politically because government funding organizations, foundation leaders, and other grant makers can demonstrate that they are not wasting money on unproven programs. Many funders want programs that have already passed this test of rigor and prefer that programs adopt these evidence-based programs instead of using homegrown designs. The more programs become evidence-based, the more likely they are to receive serious consideration and funding from funding organizations.

Many fields contain EBP registries. For example, the U.S. Substance Abuse and Mental Health Services Administration (SAMHSA) maintains a list of more than 310 evidenced-based programs and practices in the National Registry of Evidence Based Practices and Programs (NREPP). To be included in this registry, intervention programs must demonstrate that they have produced statistically significant behavioral outcomes for participants in the areas of mental health or substance abuse. They must also demonstrate that these outcomes are sustained over a designated timeframe. These results need to come from a least one study using an evaluation design that includes at least one control group as well as pre- and post-test assessments. Programs must also show that results were published in a peer-reviewed journal or other professional publication.

The Model Programs Guide of the Office of Juvenile Justice and Delinquency Prevention (OJJDP, an office of the federal government) provides information about evidence-based juvenile justice and youth prevention, intervention, and reentry programs. This resource for practitioners and communities sets out what works, what is promising, and what does not work in juvenile justice, delinquency prevention, and child protection and safety.

To be included in this database, a program must target offenders or individuals at risk to become involved in the justice system. Programs must aim at one of two goals: (1) prevent or reduce crime and victimization or (2) improve justice systems and processes. These programs must also demonstrate that evaluation research has been conducted with at least one randomized field experiment or a quasi-experimental research design with a comparison group, which are described a little later in this chapter. In addition, the evaluation must be published in a peer-reviewed publication or a comprehensive evaluation after 1980.

Both the SAMHSA and OJJDP databases show that the definition of evidence-based varies slightly depending on the field. Terms like evidence-based, research-based, blueprint program, model program, proven practice, promising practice, best practice, and effective program are sometimes used interchangeably. Typically, when a funder indicates a desire to fund programs that are evidence-based, the funder intends to fund only those programs that have been studied using a randomized comparison group. Funders typically require that study results show a statistically significant improvement compared to that achieved by an alternative practice or to no intervention whatsoever. In addition, funders look for consistent evidence of success in at least two studies and want to know the program can be replicated in other environments.

The Gold Standard: Randomized Controlled Trial

If an organization does not want to adopt another organization's evidence-based practice and instead would like its service-delivery model to become a recognized evidence-based approach, then it is very likely that the organization will need to invest in a randomized controlled trial (RCT). The RCT is a research methodology that involves randomly selecting subjects from a larger test group to receive an experimental product or service. The benefit of this approach is that it is the most rigorous method to determine whether a cause-and-effect relationship exists between a given service and the desired outcome.

RCT provides the necessary structure to raise and sufficiently answer the question "What would have happened to the same individuals at the same time had the program not been implemented?" Of course, it is impossible to attain a complete answer this question, because it implies an alternate reality. Therefore, randomized controlled trials work by creating a group that can mimic alternatives.

An RCT randomizes the population group that receives a program, service, or intervention and a group that does not. The group that receives no intervention is designated as the control group. The trial study then compares outcomes between those two groups. This comparison reveals the impact of the program. RCTs do not necessarily require a "no treatment" control. Control groups can be composed of individuals randomized into different versions of the same program, different programs trying to tackle the same problem, or no intervention at all.

The important component in RTC is the completely random assignment of a participant to either the control group or the intervention group. Using a randomization approach requires the program implementer to identify a target population. Following this step, program access is randomized within that population.

For example, if we wanted to compare the impact of a new child welfare approach to standard treatment programs using an RTC, the organization would first need to decide the criteria to describe the target population for the treatment. Next, when individuals were referred to the agency, program leaders would randomly assign those who meet the identified qualifications to one of three groups: the standard treatment group, the group that will receive the new approach, or the control group, which will receive the existing approach. It is important that the two groups be as similar as possible in demographic characteristics, as this helps reduce intervening factors related to the individuals in the group outside of the intervention approach.

Instead of random assignments at the individual level, sometimes an RTC design will include random assignment at a larger unit level. This approach is best used if the control and treatment groups may have interactions with each other. For example, the Robert Wood Johnson Foundation (2013) supported a rigorous randomized controlled trial evaluation of Playworks, a nonprofit organization that places adults in full-time positions at low-income schools to provide opportunities for healthy play during recesses. Rather than randomly assigning students to participate with the Playworks coaches, the researchers randomly assigned twenty-nine schools interested in the Playworks program into either a treatment group, which included schools with Playworks, or a control group, which included similar schools without Playworks. Using this approach not only was perceived to be more fair to the children in the schools receiving the program but also prevented program effects on students who participated from affecting other students who were not exposed to the program. For example, if one group of students appeared to be enjoying increased physical activity and making healthier choices, even students not participating in the program might have engaged in this behavior due to peer pressure alone. Randomization at the school level prevented such a scenario and ensured greater accuracy in RCT findings.

Programs that know they have more demand for services than they can meet are good candidates for RCTs. In these cases, the organization accepts applicants into a program. Participants are then randomly assigned to the current class or put on a wait-list for the next available session—one that will begin after the study design is complete. A comparison of program outcomes is then prepared, comparing and contrasting those currently enrolled in the program and those individuals still waiting to enroll. Because both groups expressed interest in the program or course, it is likely that members of both groups are more similar than would be the case if program leaders had chosen an unrelated control group when looking at program outcomes.

The current interest in RCTs is an encouraging sign of the growing momentum for linking nonprofit and government funding to proven results and investing in what works. Although RCTs are considered the gold standard in determining causation, they should not be viewed as the only option organizations have to more completely understand the effectiveness of program offerings.

For a variety of reasons, RCTs are not the right approach for every program. A randomized trial requires the sustained commitment of an organization, including a financial investment and staff or outside consultants who can ensure that the trial is conducted correctly. As funding is one of the main challenges for social-sector organizations, it is unlikely that the majority of nonprofits are ready to conduct RCTs for their programs.

In addition, in order to obtain statistically significant results, programs need to be large enough to produce sample sizes that are big enough for significant testing. There are also often ethical concerns about denying individuals admission into a treatment program. Given these many concerns, if a RCT is not feasible for an organization, parts of the RCT or other similar activities can be implemented to obtain greater proof of impact.

Introducing a Control or Comparison Group

One strategy an organization can implement to demonstrate that program impacts would not have occurred if individuals did not participate in the program is to introduce a nonrandomized control or comparison group. As with an RCT, the goal with a control or comparison group is to find a group of people who are similar to program participants but who have not gone through the intervention.

The downside of not randomly assigning people to the control group is that you cannot prove that any changes that occurred in the participants were not a result of other factors. For example, if you compare individuals receiving unemployment benefits who are currently enrolled in a job training program to other individuals who are receiving unemployment benefits but who have not participated in the job training program, any differences found could be due to the impact of the program but could also be a result of individual differences between the two groups. The individuals who are participating in the job training program could be more motivated than those who did not participate. Because there are many potential causal factors for change, the organization may find it difficult to prove program effectiveness.

Despite these limitations, an evaluation design that contains a control group is always more powerful than one that does not.

Having a control group allows an organization to tell the story of how their participants' impact is differentiated from the impact others naturally experience. If less-than-desirable results come back, program leaders are armed with the information needed to improve the program so the impacts are greater.

Circle Round the Square: A Case Study

As further illustration of this point, we will examine the outcome data produced from an evaluation of Paper Circle's Circle Round the Square (Jones, VanDixhorn, and Lewis, 2013). Circle Round the Square is an intensive, five-week arts enrichment program that provides students of an Appalachian town with hands-on experiences each summer. The program provides a wide range of arts and wellness activities that are lacking in the local K–8 school curriculum.

One of the program's desired outcomes was to increase self-esteem. Participant data revealed that students experienced, on average, a 4-percent increase in self-esteem based on pre- and post-test self-esteem scores (see Table 10.1). These results reveal that self-esteem increased as a result of this program. However, it is difficult to determine if participant self-esteem was likely to increase regardless of his or her participation in the program.

Table 10.1. Self-Esteem Data for Circle Round the Square Participants and Controls

	Participant Pre		Participant Post		
Impact	**Mean**	**% Positive Self-esteem**	**Mean**	**% Positive Self-esteem**	**Effect Size (Cohen's d)***
Self-Esteem	3.04	57.8%	3.15	62%	.1911

*Cohen's d is a measure of effect size. It provides an indication of how big or small a significant difference is. Typically less than 0.2 is considered a small effect, 0.5 represents a medium effect, and 0.8 indicates a large effect.

The story becomes much more interesting when the control group is added. Students of the same age who attended the same school as the participants served as a control group in this evaluation design. The control students completed the same self-esteem questions before and after this summer program. The results revealed that control students experienced a 3-percent decline in self-esteem scores. Interestingly, the results suggest that students who did not participate had slightly higher levels of self-esteem at the start of the program. After the program, both groups had similar levels.

As shown in Figure 10.1, adding the control group confirms not only that the program increases the self-esteem of participants, but also shows that students who are otherwise similar to current participants saw a decrease in their levels of self-esteem over the summer when they did not participate in this program. In addition, program staff learned that program participants saw significant increases in creativity and wellness when compared to the control group. The story revealed by this data is much more compelling evidence of success and helps make the case for the unique impact of the program.

Figure 10.1. Impact on Self-Esteem

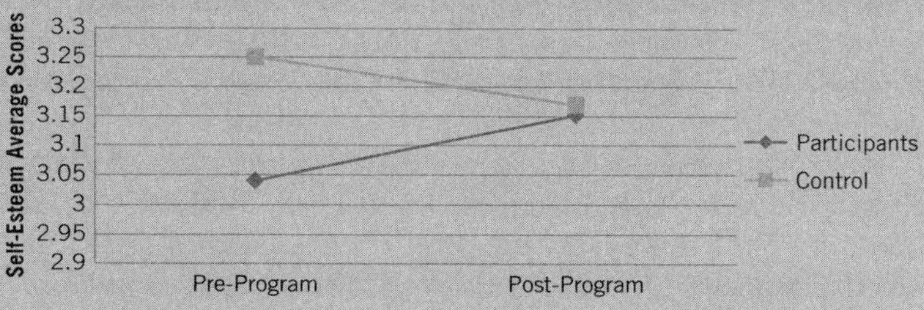

One limitation of these results is that students elected to participate in the summer arts program. Any child who signed up was enrolled. The control group was made of a random sample of students who are in the same age group and attended the same school as participants; however, it is unclear how students who elect to participate in a summer arts program differ from students who chose to participate in other activities or nothing over the summer.

What Circle Round the Square leaders can communicate clearly as a result of this study is the story of what happened that summer: program participants experienced significant increases in self-esteem while, over the same time period, similar but nonparticipating students experienced an almost equal decline in self-esteem. This information can be used to show funders how their investment benefited students. It addition, the evidence gathered can be used to request increased funding in order to expand the number of students this program is able to serve. As participation in this program grows, there may be a time when an ethical RCT could be conducted.

Programs that experience greater demand than availability are ideal candidates for RCTs because they can randomly assign students to participate in the program and designate others who will need to wait an additional year. This eliminates the issues of differences between students who elect to participate and those who do not, as the new study will compare only groups of students who have self-selected to participate.

External Benchmarks

Moving down the scale in rigor and control, but still a powerful method to help put organizational outcomes data into perspective, is the practice of using external benchmarks. External benchmarks are performance data used for comparative purposes. These can act like a type of control group by looking at the performance of the overall population or other groups in the field. Benchmarks can often be found in state or federal government websites and in existing research. For example, some indicators that are easy to access by the public and can be used as external benchmarks include graduation rates, health data, and unemployment data.

A program trying to improve the graduation rates of students, for example, knows that the district-wide graduation rate of the population they serve is 85 percent. Program staff members also know the graduation rate for the youth they serve is 95 percent. They can tell the story that program participants have a higher graduation rate than the overall district-wide population.

Again, one limitation of this approach is that it does not rule out other factors outside the program that may influence program participants and result in an increased likelihood that they will graduate. Despite this limitation, using external benchmarks is a powerful way for an organization to understand the extent to which their program is making a difference, compared to similar groups that are not experiencing the intervention.

A Word about Pre- and Post-Test Designs

Almost all funders who currently require organizations to communicate outcomes will at the very least expect to see a comparison between the conditions of the target population prior to the program and at the conclusion of the program, with or without a control group. In its most basic form, this design includes an assessment of participants' current state of outcomes—typically knowledge, skills, characteristics, or attitudes at the beginning of the program. This is often referred to as "baseline data." Funders look for such an assessment to be readministered at the conclusion of the program.

Baseline data include facts about the community or client group before a grant period or program begins. Program leaders use this baseline data to measure progress and determine a program's impact. Without baseline data, it is very difficult to know what change occurred in the participants while involved in the program. This design tells us how the program impacted the participants it served, but it cannot answer the question of whether such impacts would have occurred had the participants not gone through the program.

Because baseline data typically arrives later than is desirable, high-performance measurement cultures use logic models to decide on the categories of baseline data that are most important even before a grant opportunity arises. They see baseline data as the first step to tracking outcomes for grant reporting; it is also important information for setting organizational goals and objectives. Baseline data can come from agency records that track client performance. Such records may include census and local government data as it pertains to the target population or commonly administered pre-tests that gather critical information about participants prior to program engagement.

If a program decides to use local government or census data as a baseline, program managers and executive leadership should consider to what extent they believe the program serves clients within a certain period of time to impact the overall community indicator. If a community health center wants to reduce obesity rates in the community and uses community health data as the only baseline data, for example, unless they affect a large percentage of the population they may not see an impact.

Based on census data, if the center's target population consisted of low-income individuals who were uninsured and lived in a particular urban region, program staff might well identify approximately twenty-six thousand individuals in the region and find an estimated obesity rate of 79 percent. If this center served one thousand individuals in the course of one year and reduced the obesity rates of patients, twenty-five thousand individuals who are members of the total population living in poor census tracks would not be impacted by the organization.

If the center helped all the obese people in their care reduce their weight and the rest of the population stayed at the same weight, the obesity rate would drop to approximately 76 percent. Although this is a decent impact to the community, the more impressive story that the organization had 100-percent success would be buried by the larger sample. This example highlights how community indicators are great to track and cite as longer-term outcomes, but individual client data typically provides a more powerful way to capture and convey an organization's story of success.

Often, leaders of nonprofit and government organizations desire to understand a change in outcomes that are more difficult to measure or observe than those found in community data. Such results are often internal to participants and typically related to participants' knowledge, skills, attitudes, and perceptions. The only way to gather baseline data for these types of desired outcomes is to use an assessment administered directly by participants.

Examples of common constructs include self-esteem, depression, satisfaction, and other hard-to-observe behaviors. Even with a validated measurement tool, these assessments rely on the participants' perceptions of their individual outcomes instead of an objective measure such as weight, graduation, or unemployment.

A downside of using pre-test measures over a community indicator is that sometimes organizations find themselves needing to collect outcomes data after a program has already been initiated, making a pre-test model impossible. Also, depending on the subject, a pre-test might not yield accurate data, especially if the program is designed to change the participant's skill set or his or her knowledge of something that they have little knowledge of before they enter the program. This is particularly a concern when a program addresses complex subjects that are clarified over the course of the intervention (Howard and Dailey, 1979).

For example, a person entering a money management class may believe they understand the principles of money management simply because they understand checking accounts, interest rates, savings accounts, and CDs. However, once this student begins the course of study and learns that there are strategies such as mutual funds, money-market accounts, annuities, and life insurance that can also be considered in financial planning, the individual's starting score could be inaccurate and disrupt the overall effectiveness of pre- and post-test evaluation.

Retroactive Pre- and Post-Test Design

An alternative to the traditional pre-test/post-test design is to conduct a retroactive pre-test/post-test design (Pratt, McGuigan, and Katzev, 2000). In this method, an assessment is administered only once, at the end of the program, rather than twice, once at the beginning and once at the end. To assess change, this tool asks participants to refer back to a prior point in time, such as before the start of the program. Participants are then asked, following the conclusion of the program, to answer the same question, thinking about their feelings as they are after experiencing the program.

A retroactive pre-test/post-test design may be more appropriate for organizations with a very limited budget to conduct program assessment. These retroactive tests are more economical than traditionally designed tests, as they require only one administration, thereby saving printing costs and time spent in evaluation activities. This method will reduce a bias in the comparison data that might otherwise occur if participants are not present at the very beginning and also at the end of the program. This design has been shown to be more useful for documenting self-assessed changes, which often occur as a result of a particular intervention. This occurs in part because retrospective pre-test/post-test evaluations are more sensitive to respondent change than traditional pre-test/post-test evaluations.

Exhibit 10.1 provides an example of a retroactive pre-test/post-test assessment questions for a program designed to increase the evaluation capacity of an organization. Section 1 of this assessment asks participants to think about their knowledge of and familiarity with a concept prior to the training. Section 2 asks about the same concepts but instructs participants to answer the questions based on their current knowledge of the program. Program outcomes will be demonstrated by the change in scores in Section 1 and Section 2.

Section 3 provides statements of desired outcomes and asks participants to rate how much they agree that these things have occurred as a result of participating in the training. These types of questions give an organization insight into how much participants agree that desired outcomes have occurred. Although this method is not highly rigorous, it does provide leaders with important information of participant perceptions of the program. At the very least, mediocre to low scores on this type of assessment are an indicator that the program needs improvement. Higher, more positive scores are, at the very least, a first level of information to suggest program impact.

Exhibit 10.1. Sample Retroactive Pretest Format

Section 1

Please think about your knowledge and skill level prior to your participation in this program. How familiar were you with the following skills or concepts prior to participating in the training? Use the following rating scale: Unaware = 1, Somewhat Familiar = 2, Familiar = 3, Very Familiar = 4, Expert = 5.

1. Develop a program logic model.
2. Choose appropriate and relevant data-collection methods.
3. Importance of fidelity.

Section 2

How familiar are you now with the following skills or concepts? Use the following rating scale: Unaware = 1, Somewhat Familiar = 2, Familiar = 3, Very Familiar = 4, Expert = 5.

1. Develop a program logic model.
2. Choose appropriate and relevant data-collection methods.
3. Importance of fidelity.

Section 3

To what extent do you agree with the following statements with regard to your organization's participation with this training? Use the following rating scale: 1 = Strongly Disagree, 2 = Disagree, 3 = Neither Disagree Nor Agree, 4 = Agree, 5 = Strongly Agree.

1. I have better outcomes.
2. I have more confidence in my ability to determine program success.
3. I am more knowledgeable about program evaluation.
4. My organization has started to implement evaluation in other programs.

Isolating Intervention Effects

Social change is complex, and there are many contributing factors that impact a specific client outcome. Even when an organization compares its program outcomes with a control group, questions may linger: was it the program or some other factor that made the ultimate difference or influenced the desired change? For example, attendance and increased graduation rates may be influenced by activities conducted at the school level, the home level, or the community level.

A student who is at risk of dropping out of school may receive multiple interventions intended to keep him in attendance and on track to graduate from high school. His parents may intervene by spending more time with him working on homework and school projects. He may also be involved in an afterschool program, which gives him a mentor. Or he may have had previous involvement with the court and have an assigned probation officer. Finally, the school may be providing extra help. Given all these interventions in the student's life, how can the school know for certain that it was their program that impacted the student's attendance and graduation outcomes?

Unlike medical trials, in which doctors can control a single pill or dosage an individual receives to evaluate the effect of a health intervention, social program evaluation makes it nearly impossible and often undesirable to isolate the treatment group and ignore other interventions. After all, social programs are designed to work in the real world, not in a laboratory.

There is, however, a relatively easy and practical way to attempt to isolate a program or training effect by conducting a secondary evaluation. Once program staff knows the difference in the outcomes achieved, gathering data sets from both the control group and the treatment group, they can conduct a survey of key stakeholders to achieve a score that can help isolate the treatment effect. For the school program just highlighted, key stakeholders may be teachers, parents, and other individuals involved with the students in the school program. These people would be administered a short questionnaire that contains these three questions:

1. What percentage of the student's improvement can be attributed to the application of skills, techniques, and knowledge gained through this school program?

2. What confidence do you have in this estimate, expressed as a percentage?
3. What other factors contributed to this student's improvement in performance?

To examine how this impacts the interpretation of data, let us assume that once these surveys are collected from all stakeholders involved with the student, the average answer to the first question related to the percentage of student improvement attributed to the application of the skills learned in the program is 50 percent. We will also assume that the average answers to question two related to the rater's confidence in their estimate is 70 percent, meaning the stakeholders are 70-percent confident that the program contributed to about half of the student outcome success.

Other factors—such as parental involvement, court intervention, or church activities—may have been listed as the other factors that made up the additional 15 percent. The confidence percentage (70 percent) is then multiplied by the estimate (50 percent) to produce a usable intervention factor of 35 percent. This is then multiplied by the actual intervention results to isolate the effects of the program.

We will consider that this school program learned that only 55 percent of at-risk students who did not participate in the program graduated, compared to 85 percent who were involved in the program. Therefore, the comparison results would indicate that the program increased graduation rates by 30 percent. To estimate the program effects to allow for other outside factors that influenced the success of these participants, the intervention effect could be used to further reduce this number.

To achieve the isolated training effective, program leaders would multiple the .35 by the 30 percent. Therefore, program leaders could say that they believe the program accounts for at least a 10.5 percent increase in graduation rates. The additional 20 percent is influenced by the school's program as well as the other factors listed.

Isolating the training effects is a great way for organizations to demonstrate to funders that they recognize that they do not work in a vacuum, but they are interested in the unique impact that the organization contributes to participants' success.

It allows the organization to understand how stakeholders perceive the program. If participants experience desired outcomes, but stakeholders come back with low confidence that it was the program that contributed to the participants' success, then leaders know there are still things to work on. Also, the insight provided about the other factors that contributed to participant success can help the organization understand what groups or organizations they should be partnering with to provide an even stronger social return on investment.

Working with External Evaluators

As discussed in previous chapters, organizations often fall short of fully utilizing data, outcomes, and evaluation in their daily practice due to a lack of both evaluation expertise and trained staff. But there is a readily available solution.

Professional evaluators are trained to help nonprofit and government organizations design the best measures and evaluation plans. These individuals know how to conduct the appropriate statistical testing for credible and reliable impact results.

Leaders of high-performance measurement cultures know the value of having credible and reliable impact data. These leaders recognize that spending money on professional evaluation activities is an investment that will ultimately increase their competiveness and overall effectiveness. It is one of their secrets to success.

There are several reasons an organization would consider hiring an outside evaluation and outcomes consultant. The most common reason is that it is a requirement of the grant. Many grants call for an outside evaluator to ensure that proper research methods are employed and that there is a source of transparency in the finding. The good news is that when an outside evaluator is required, the grant typically allocates between 5 and 15 percent of the grant dollars to these activities.

If an organization is considering conducting a randomized controlled trial or other quasi-experimental design with control groups, an outside evaluator will save the organization much unneeded stress and potentially costly mistakes. An outside evaluator will have the skills and knowledge to guide organizational leaders toward the best model and sample size needed for a successful evaluation design. They also will have the skills and software to conduct the necessary statistical analysis.

An outside evaluator can add credibility to program results. This is especially true if a program is controversial or highly visible. Evaluators are objective observers of the program. The perceived independence of an experienced evaluator from outside the organization will help bring credibility to the organization's results.

In addition, independent evaluators are often able to gather program information that would be difficult for the organization to obtain on its own. For example, clients who are mandated to participate in a program may feel uneasy about giving their honest opinions to program staff. Yet an outside consultant, who can ensure confidentiality, may gain greater access and elicit truer responses from employees than program staff would.

If an organization does plan to use an outside evaluator, it is important that the consultant is engaged early in the process. This is especially true if the evaluation will be funded by external groups. Having an evaluation identified before submitting a grant application will demonstrate the organization's professionalism and commitment to data-driven strategies.

Among the many grant applications that funders receive, in many cases the evaluation section is the weakest component. Therefore working with an evaluation specialist early in the process will ensure that the organization has a well-organized and realistic plan for demonstrating impact. Again, this effort will increase the chances of winning more grant opportunities *in addition to* having reliable data that will allow the organization to achieve greater impact for those they serve.

External evaluators can be found in academic institutions as well as professional firms and independent consultants. Regardless of where the evaluator is found, it is essential that the person or persons who perform evaluation and outcomes measurement activities have the required knowledge, skills, and abilities to deliver high-quality and impactful evaluations. Too often organizations struggle with attempts to implement data-driven strategies, because they assign these tasks to a junior associate or an external evaluator who lacks the required skill set.

Hiring a mediocre evaluator may be worse than doing nothing, especially when an organization is new to evaluation and outcomes measurement. An unskilled evaluator may make the process more complicated than it needs to be, make inaccurate claims about what the findings say, or lack professionalism. This negative experience leaves everyone in the organization a little skeptical and distrusting of future evaluation activities and evaluators.

To make matters more complicated, there are no specific licenses or credentials required to become an evaluator. However, the American Evaluation Association (2004) has established a set of guiding principles for evaluators. These guidelines provide a number of key competencies and qualities organizational leaders should look for when selecting an evaluation specialist. A good evaluator will meet the following criteria:

- Understanding and practicing systematic inquiry
- Adhering to the highest level of integrity and honesty
- Showing respect for all people and situations
- Understanding responsibilities for the use and implementation of the data

Understanding and Practicing Systematic Inquiry

Systematic inquiry means that evaluators seek data-driven inquiry methods and adhere to the highest technical standards appropriate for the methods they use. A well-qualified evaluation professional will explore with the client the shortcomings and strengths of evaluation questions and approaches. He or she will effectively communicate these approaches in sufficient detail to allow others to understand, interpret, and critique their work.

A good evaluator will also be able to explain the ideal way to conduct a study. If the budget or circumstances do not allow the highest rigor possible, the evaluator should be able to propose an alternative way to stay within the budget constraints while at the same time being very clear regarding what will be lost by taking the alternative approach. Beware of an evaluator who advises or uses only one approach (qualitative research only or quantitative research only, for example) or one who does not fully understand the nature and goals of the program being evaluated.

Adhering to the Highest Level of Integrity and Honesty

Data has power and can easily be manipulated and misused. The organization must have complete trust in an evaluator for a successful and positive experience. A good evaluator should be able to provide examples of how he or she has worked to resolve any concerns related to procedures or activities likely to produce misleading evaluative information. If evaluators has not directly worked in the field, they should be able to discuss what they would do to resolve these conflicts. It is critical that evaluators can stand their ground to the client and report only the facts as found in the evaluation. Omitting data in order to make an organization look good is unethical, and evaluators with integrity and honesty will decline to engage in such a practice.

Showing Respect for All People and Situations

Effective evaluators will seek a comprehensive understanding of the contextual elements of the evaluation prior to suggesting any methods or approaches. They will ensure confidentiality or make it clear to participants when and if such confidentially cannot be guaranteed. Because evaluators are required to report justified negative or critical conclusions that result from the evaluation, they will propose approaches that maximize benefits and minimize any unnecessary harm to client and stakeholder interests. During the negotiation stage, good evaluators will consider whether the benefits of an evaluation or performing certain activities should be forgone because of the risks to the participants. They are interested in not wasting the organization's or the participants' time. The most-qualified evaluators keep evaluation tools as succinct as possible while optimizing tools for the most complete and representative results from the evaluation.

Understanding Responsibilities for the Use and Implementation of the Data

Although an evaluator may work for an organization, he or she has a responsibility to understand how their work and the outcomes of evaluation efforts can benefit all stakeholders and society as a whole. The evaluator will work toward the dissemination of evaluation results to a variety of stakeholders in understandable forms that respect all individuals involved and honor all promises of confidentiality.

It is important that the evaluator can communicate with individuals at all levels of the organization. If an evaluator uses only technical language and jargon, it may be hard for organizational staff to work with that evaluator, due to comprehension issues or potential intimidation. Evaluators should be able to turn complex, statistical evaluation results into easy-to-understand ideas that can be implemented throughout the organization.

One Step at a Time

The evaluation designs and methods described in this chapter are presented as strategies that organizations can employ once they have clarified their mission and identified important outcomes and impact measures. Before rushing into hiring an evaluator or trying to conduct experimental evaluation designs, organizations should focus on establishing the organizational culture and measures that will enable these higher-level and significantly more complex evaluation techniques. In addition, making the move toward optimal performance means starting from where the organization currently is and taking the first steps to move forward.

An organization's first step is to create a logic model and identify important outcomes measures. Prior to implementing any measurement, leaders should also determine how they will use this information to increase desirable organizational results, such as communicating to funders, preparing fundraising materials, and incorporating results into performance improvement. Once this has been determined, it may be helpful to test the measures to work out any flaws or issues with the measures.

When an organization feels comfortable with its selected measures, the leadership team can begin to track and compare internal results across a trial time period. If a program appears to be successful from an internal perspective, leaders may opt to establish a control group and explore the possibility of conducting a randomized controlled trial. But the most important step for leaders to take is making that initial commitment to move forward with data-driven strategies to help them better enhance the impact they deliver to those they serve.

Cook Inlet Tribal Council: A Case Study

Cook Inlet Tribal Council (CITC) stands for *people, partnership,* and *potential.* CITC is a tribal nonprofit organization helping Alaska Native and American Indian people residing in the Cook Inlet Region of south central Alaska to reach their full potential. One of CITC's flagship programs is the annual NYO Games, previously known as the Native Youth Olympics.

Each year, more than two thousand students from more than fifty communities across the state participate in the NYO and JNYO Games. Youth strive for their personal best while competing in traditional contests including the Alaskan High Kick, the Seal Hop, and many other games. Open to youth from all backgrounds, NYO fosters important values including teamwork, leadership, respect, and healthy lifestyles.

For many years, CITC did not have any data regarding the impact of their programs. Program leaders knew intuitively that the program was having a positive impact on students' lives, but they had never collected data to measure outcomes in a formal way. Development staff knew that having more data on the impacts of the program would help them better tell their story and recruit more sponsors and funders for the event.

CITC leaders decided to start where they were. They created a retroactive pre-test survey tool to assess student perceptions of the impact of their programs. This self-report measure was administered to male and female NYO Games athletes in grades seven through twelve upon completion of the games. Through this survey, they found that students reported many positive outcomes.

Students indicated that concepts such as teamwork, determination, sportsmanship, leadership, hard work, self-confidence, self-esteem, and cultural values improved through their participation in NYO Games. Seventy-two percent of athletes credited their participation in NYO Games with helping them to stay in school, and 75 percent said the Games helped improve their grades. The 2013 results were up from 67 percent and 66 percent in 2012, respectively (Cook Inlet Tribal Council, 2013).

Of course, there are limitations to this study, because it relies on self-reporting, and there is no control group to compare the NYO athletes to other students. But, at a minimum, this survey provides information that the students believe their participation in NYO games has a positive value in their lives. As a result of collecting this information, CITC has been successful in attracting new donors to invest in the games, and many existing donors have increased their level of support. In addition, conversations have been initiated with key partners on how to increase the scale and scope of NYO to be included in school district activities throughout the state, helping to further increase the organization's reach and overall impact.

It is likely this opportunity would not have arisen if the organization had delayed data collection because of limited resources or expertise. Because CITC program leaders did not wait to conduct a more rigorous evaluation, but started where they were, they now have compelling evidence of the program's reach and perceived success from the target population.

Next Steps

Regardless of the strategies employed to successfully capture impact, an organization must follow a clear plan to communicate results. The next chapter reveals key strategies for successful communication.

Impact & Excellence

Chapter Ten Discussion Questions

1. Identify the current state of the rigor of your organization's evaluation efforts:
   a. Don't conduct any studies or measure outcomes
   b. Established outcomes measures
   c. Have baseline data
   d. Pre- and post-test administration
   e. Control group
   f. Randomized controlled trial
2. What are the limitations of your current impact data?
3. Based on your current state of rigor, what steps could you take to increase the rigor of your evaluation results?

11

Communicate Value

The single biggest problem in communication is the illusion that it has taken place.
—GEORGE BERNARD SHAW

EVERY GOVERNMENT AND NONPROFIT ORGANIZATION that embraces a high-performance measurement culture adopts established measures to collect and evaluate quality information. When this information is communicated, it leads directly to greater impact and excellence. The measures themselves are not responsible for success. Rather, success is driven by a social sector leader's ability to accurately gather, interpret, and convey information, applying it across the organization, and drawing from it to tell the organization's story in a compelling manner.

Collecting information on important outcomes measures can catapult the social sector organization to a new level of success. Clearly communicated outcomes further enhance the potential these organizations have to attract new donors, increase public awareness, and shape positive attitudes toward their cause. Effective communication also improves the organization's capacity to form new partnerships and further engage the organization's board and staff.

In a high-performance measurement culture, leaders consistently communicate the value of their activities, programs, and services. They also remain receptive to new input, inviting opportunities to gather new information as they focus on key performance measures. The most successful leaders establish communication and feedback loops that build on their organization's impact and excellence.

This chapter's epigraph is a cogent observation from George Bernard Shaw: "The single biggest problem in communication is the illusion that it has taken place." Most social-sector organizations fail to extract nuggets of information and translate existing performance measures into the powerful communication tools they might become. In many government and nonprofit organizations, a grant writer or program officer is often responsible for producing a report for a funder or executive committee that then summarizes the results of program data. These costly reports are distributed to key stakeholders. They may even be presented at monthly or quarterly meetings. However, after an initial review, the information is filed away and typically forgotten until the next performance report is distributed.

High-performance organizations attract increased funding through grants, donor gifts, sponsorships, and government allocations. They experience increases in partnerships and positive press. They realize these results not because they have access to the data, but because they apply the data in ethical and strategic ways, thereby influencing stakeholders to take action.

The leaders of organizations with high-performance measurement cultures often choose to incorporate data in compelling communication strategies. They communicate fully and often. These organizations use data to powerfully illustrate the organization's authentic success and cast a compelling vision—one that inspires belief in the organization's ability to fulfill the promise of its stated mission.

High-impact organizations do not rely on a single type of communication. Instead, they strategically weave data into the fabric of an organization's key messages. Leaders of the most effective organizations share the story of the organization's impact and excellence in a variety of ways, embracing creative approaches and tapping various mediums for communicating with stakeholders. Unlike previous periods in history, the twenty-first century affords social-sector organizations an impressive array of alternative communication methods.

Options for Communicating Value and Impact

The following are just a few among the many opportunities for organizations to communicate unique value and impact to stakeholders:

- Grant applications
- Websites
- Annual reports
- Internal memos
- Presentations
- Speeches
- Videos
- TV commercials
- Online advertising
- White papers
- Casual conversation
- Billboards
- Social media

With such an overwhelming number of choices, the challenge for leaders is to discern which methods hold the greatest promise to communicate to a particular audience segment. Overreliance on too few communication channels will result in ineffective communication. Scattered communication through too many channels without a cohesive, clearly articulated, and concise messaging strategy will prove equally ineffective.

Before social-sector leaders are able to decide on the best communication strategy, they must identify the audience and know which channels that audience most frequently accesses. The Five Whys and the logic model discussed in Chapter Eight are optimal tools to help staff and executive leaders identify key audiences and those messages that are most relevant to a specific audience segment. Important stakeholders can be identified as organizational leaders examine the inputs and participant columns in the logic model.

Depending on whether the audience is composed of members who are stakeholders or participants, the next step is to identify the answers to the questions listed in the Five Whys exercise, listing the outcomes that each particular stakeholder group is most interested in understanding. Next, leaders can decide how to best communicate these outcomes with this audience segment and identify the actions the organization hopes this stakeholder group will take when it receives communication about those outcomes.

Table 11.1 presents an example of how a local nonprofit organization providing long-term care services and supports plans to communicate outcomes and performance measures. This organization's primary success measures include caregiver and client perception of outcomes. Those outcomes include satisfaction, increased quality of life, and the ability to live in their own home. Other measures include the percentage of clients referred from various outreach activities, average cost-per-consumer care plan, percentage of hospital readmissions, and percentage reduction of clients transferred to a nursing facility.

While all outcomes are important to staff, management, and the board of directors, this organization plans to use different outcomes in different applications, depending on the audience. For example, this organization recognized that it was necessary to communicate all internal success measures to donors and participants. Internally, organizational leaders plan to use outcomes to improve training, conduct performance improvement, and manage the budget.

Using the Five Whys exercise, leaders also identified what participants and donors were most interested in knowing: that clients were satisfied and able to increase their quality of life by participating in programs. Therefore the measures related to these outcomes are communicated to both participants and donors. In addition, this organization measures success in terms of fewer hospital readmissions among clients, a reduction in the number of clients who need to be moved to nursing facilities, and an increase in the number of clients who conveyed satisfaction with program services and an improved quality of life. The organization communicates outcomes in these identified areas to stakeholders through marketing materials, grant applications, and website updates.

The foundational belief behind such communication efforts is that if participants understand outcomes, they will continue to engage in the organization and refer friends and family members. Knowing these outcomes will inspire others to consider increased

Table 11.1. Outcomes Communication Strategy

Audiences	Outcomes	How to Communicate	Desired Actions Taken
Staff/ Management	Caregiver/client perception of outcomes Percentage of clients referred from outreach activities Average cost per consumer care plan Percentage of hospital readmissions Reduction in the percentage of nursing facility transfers	Meetings, e-mails, internal memos and reports, display outcomes on bulletin boards, annual reports, and grant applications	Utilization review Training Process/quality improvement Manage the budget Fee for services Design marketing materials
Board	Caregiver/client perception of outcomes Percentage of clients referred from outreach Percentage of hospital readmissions Average cost per consumer care plan Reduction in the percentage of nursing facility transfers	Meetings, emails, progress reports, annual reports	Manage the budget Educate and inform Determine fee for services Design marketing materials

Table 11.1. Outcomes Communication Strategy, (*continued*)

Audiences	Outcomes	How to Communicate	Desired Actions Taken
State Agency Funders	Caregiver/client perception of outcomes Percentage of clients referred from outreach activities Average cost per consumer care plan Percentage of hospital readmissions Reduction in the percentage of nursing facility transfers	Meetings, annual reports, grant applications	Fee for services Increase perception of effectiveness Strengthen partnerships Increase grant allocation
Partnering Hospitals	Caregiver/client perception of outcomes Percentage of hospital readmissions	Meetings E-mails	Strengthen partnerships Increase referrals
Other Donors/ Potential Donors	Caregiver/client perception of outcomes Percentage of hospital readmissions Reduction in the percentage of nursing facility transfers	Marketing materials, website, conversations, grant applications	Strengthen perception of effectiveness Increase grants
Participants	Caregiver/client perception of outcomes Percentage of hospital readmissions Reduction in the percentage of nursing facility transfers	Marketing materials, website, conversations, letters	Increase satisfaction with organization Increase new clients Increase engagement with the organization

funding, increased client referrals, and increased positive perception of the organization. These key communication activities are worthy endeavors that result in increased opportunities for impact and excellence.

Sticky Strategies

Nonprofit and government organizations with high-performance measurement cultures have an increased capacity to influence key stakeholders to take decisive action. These organizations combine data and outcomes measures with key communication strategies to bring about desired actions and behaviors, including favorable funding decisions, increased referrals, and elevated community support. Their goal is to present data in a compelling, ethical, and impactful manner that captures the unique impact the organization is making. However, many organizations make the mistake of presenting data in a manner that fails to inspire action. They either present too much information or present it in a fashion that is too complicated or too technical.

Dan and Chip Heath (2008) provide an easy framework organizations can use to ensure that key ideas stick in the minds of important stakeholders and lead to action. In their bestselling book, *Made to Stick: Why Some Ideas Survive and Others Don't,* they outline five elements that compel decision makers to act. The book suggests that communication should be unexpected, concrete, credible, emotional, and relevant. Organizations that consistently capture a variety of success measures are in the best position to easily incorporate these five elements into key communication strategies.

The Ohio Department of Aging's story is a great example of the powerful communication strategies that are possible for organizations that embrace a high-performance measurement culture focused on output and outcome measures. As detailed in the following case study, the department director was able to quickly use the organization's data to demonstrate how the organization's efforts saved the state $250 million in Medicaid expenditures. The organization developed compelling communication strategies to help restore program funding in a time of unprecedented budget cuts. This, in turn, allowed the department to eliminate waitlists and provide services to all Ohio seniors in need. Much of the organization's success occurred because staff members were able to combine outcome data with the five communication criteria proposed by the Heath brothers.

The communication of unexpected outcomes and output data provides a powerful way to capture an audience's attention, pique or renew interest in the organization, and follow the thread of its success in the community it serves. Typically, unexpected information strategies begin with "Did you know?" followed by a statement that is unknown to or counterintuitive for the intended audience.

The Ohio Department of Aging: A Case Study

The Ohio Department of Aging used output data such as cost per service, percentage of Ohioans served, and percentage of dollars spent to heighten awareness and pique interest. In 2008, Ohio spent $2.6 billion serving that state's aging residents who were over sixty years old and required long-term care, whether in nursing facilities, through in-home care, or in community-based settings (Jones, 2010).

Although on average the cost of home- and community-based care was approximately one-third that of nursing facility care, only 39 percent of clients were being served through the preferred home-based care and in community-based settings (Jones, 2010). Surprisingly, at that time the nationwide average of those age sixty and older receiving Medicaid-funded long-term care who were being served in home- and community-based settings was 50 percent.

The desired outcome was to bring Ohio up to the national average by diverting and transitioning individuals from the more expensive and less desirable nursing home setting to the less expensive and more desirable home and community-based setting. Recent funding decisions made the achievement of this goal difficult, because the Ohio legislature had reduced funding to the in-home and community-based waiver program and created waitlists to receive this type of care. The result was that many seniors requiring this care were forced to enter nursing facilities.

A Closer Look. It is important that information communicated to stakeholders is concrete and detailed, increasing the likelihood that it will be fully digested and remembered by those who consume it. The Ohio Department of Aging developed a compelling communications tool in the form of a Long-term Care Savings Calculator. This creative approach to communicating progress toward desired outcomes allowed the agency's data benchmarks to stand out in a crowded field of reports and information.

The Long-term Care Savings Calculator was a simple spreadsheet that allowed stakeholders to interact with the consequences of potential funding decisions. It showed clearly the number of individuals in Ohio needing Medicaid-funded long-term care and other supports. In addition, the savings calculator detailed the average cost to serve an individual in each of the possible settings. For example, the Long-term Care Savings Calculator demonstrated that, if Ohio moved to the national average by serving 50 percent of Ohio's seniors who required long-term care outside of nursing facilities, the state would save approximately $250 million in a single year (Jones, 2010).

In addition, the savings calculator showed that more than eight thousand of the nearly forty-six thousand Ohioans receiving nursing home care could be diverted to the lower-cost, more desirable setting of in-home and community-based care. The long-term care savings tool was distributed to the governor's office, key legislators, and the media, providing a powerful and specific example of how policy and budget decisions would impact not only Ohio's seniors but also the long-term state budget.

Credibility and Communication

If unexpected and concrete data and information sources are not credible, then they will do little to influence change. Organizations that successfully communicate key outcomes do everything possible to ensure that the information will be seen as credible so decision makers will believe it and act on it. The Ohio Department of Aging was able to ensure credibility by using data collected by several independent evaluators that reported findings similar to the data they had released. The organization's leadership extracted data from the Medicaid Information Management

System, from the Scripps Gerontology Center of Miami University of Ohio, and from national research conducted by the Lewin Group to validate and support the agency's findings.

Emotional and Relevant

Data alone can seem cold and impersonal. Effective communication strategies tap into the audience's desires, needs, and wants. Government and nonprofit organizations that realize the greatest success in communicating outcomes incorporate an emotional element alongside data. The Ohio Department of Aging was able to relate their unique story to data compiled by AARP of Ohio showing that more than 80 percent of AARP members agreed the state should make it a top priority to help people stay in their homes as long as possible.

Most Ohioans had a personal experience with the aging of a loved one. Nearly all those who encountered the statistics thought about their own desires for their senior years. The statistics and stories about older Ohioans being forced to move into nursing homes because there was a waitlist for in-home and community-based care was an issue that intersected with their desires.

Sharing stories as well as data allows decision makers to humanize the information, which may result in further engagement and action on the part of recipients. The Ohio Department of Aging did not rely on internal data alone. Instead, the agency partnered with their clients and the media to tell the story of what it meant for Ohioans to access the care they needed in their own homes. These stories highlighted how effective this program was at delivering high-quality, timely services that gave caregivers peace of mind and kept seniors healthier, increasing their quality of life.

The Ohio Department of Aging provides an excellent example of first understanding the audience, then using success measures combined with effective communication elements to achieve positive results. The agency did not simply focus on selfish interests such as increased funding of its programs and services that would keep operations running as usual. Instead, the organization's leaders collected outcome data on the specific ways programs and services served stakeholders. They were able to communicate how programs improved the quality of life for both

Ohio seniors and caregivers, saved taxpayer dollars, and helped the state more effectively manage its Medicaid spending. As a result of these communication efforts, the legislature decided to restore the program's funding, allowing the Ohio Department of Aging to continue to achieve positive outcomes for Ohio's seniors.

Turning Data into Dollars

Federal, state, or local legislatures, corporate and government grant makers, foundations, private donors, and customers must make sound decisions about the stewardship of funds. All funders are interested in investing their resources in services that do the most good and have the greatest impact on the things they value most.

Social service organizations that embrace a high-performance measurement culture and that intentionally and powerfully communicate their value consistently receive the funding they need to achieve their strategic vision. By communicating value to their stakeholders, these organizations differentiate themselves from those with parallel services who are competing for the same funds. Organizations with high-performance measurement cultures go beyond a simple restatement of outputs. They use measurement systems designed to quantify impact and close the loop by fully communicating the impact they achieve.

Consider these three program descriptions:

1. Program X provided recreational services to one hundred underprivileged youth.

2. Program Y provided recreational services to one hundred underprivileged youth. Our after-school program improved average reading comprehension by two grade levels and kept 99 percent of the at-risk youth we served in school and 100 percent of these youth out of the juvenile justice system.

3. Program Z provided recreational services to one hundred underprivileged youth. Our after-school program improved average reading comprehension by two grade levels, kept 99 percent of the at-risk youth served in school, and kept 100 percent of at-risk youth out of the juvenile justice system. For every $500 invested

in the program, the lifetime earning potential of one child is increased by $300,127, which represents a 62,200-percent return on your investment.

In this description, Program X is an example of an organization communicating the "what" and the "who" and is solely focused on outputs. This description lets a decision maker know what is being offered and who is being impacted.

Program Y not only communicates who or which particular subset of the population the program serves and what the organization actually does, but it also discusses outcomes. This description lets stakeholders know that the money they donate to the organization increases reading comprehension, keeps youth engaged in school, and reduces delinquent behaviors. The organization offers hard data to back up each of these specific impacts the program is achieving.

Program Z communicates everything that programs X and Y do, but this organization also communicates the social return on investment. Funders learn that for every $500 donated, the earning potential over the course of that youth's life increases by an astounding $300,000.

Organizations that translate outcomes into return on investment are the most attractive to funders because they communicate specifically what a donor's financial contribution provides. Assuming similar program results, Program Z is most likely to win the grant because funders understand how their money will have an impact on youth, families, and the community.

Many leaders dream about being able to make straightforward and factual impact and effectiveness claims such as those communicated by Program Z, but they believe the steps necessary to uncover such specific information is too complicated or would require the diversion of significant funds. This perception is a myth. If an organization is establishing the right outcomes, consistently collects data, and has an internet connection or access to a local library for research, discovering and communicating the organization's impact and return on investment is a relatively easy task.

Five Key Steps for Turning Data into Dollars. All programs should be designed with the overall mission or goal of the organization in mind. Each and every activity should have a purpose and be undertaken to solve a particular problem or improve a specific condition that supports the mission. Organizational leaders can use the logic model to ensure that program activities are linked to the program goals.

Drawing on academic research provides another avenue for making the funding case. As the organization communicates how program activities are likely to achieve program goals and enhance the overall mission, it can support its case with related research findings. We live in an age with easy access to an abundance of research. Even a quick database search will likely reveal articles and studies with research that can help an organization improve its program to achieve the desired success or better demonstrate value. Incorporating credible research helps persuade funders to respond favorably to the organization's request.

The second step to secure funding through data is to ensure that the right outcome measures are in place. In the preceding example, the outcomes measured for Program Z were the high school dropout rate, an increase or decrease in delinquent behaviors and court involvement, and change in reading comprehension.

The third step requires organizations to consider how they will establish change as part of their plan. For outcomes such as increased education or health, it is important to use validated, preestablished measures. A baseline number should be set prior to the start of programs and services. In the case of Program Z, leaders needed to show how they decreased the dropout rate and delinquency while simultaneously increasing reading comprehension.

The fourth step in determining return on investment involves outside research. Useful research includes studies focused on an organization's target population and research related to the problem the organization is attempting to solve. Program Z may have located the variance in average annual earnings between a high school graduate and a high school dropout within minutes with a simple online search. An abundance of credible data and information is available with a search engine query. Helpful information can also be found in online journals and at libraries.

The fifth and final step is to put all the pieces of information together. For this example, the organization needs to calculate the percentage of change in reading comprehension as well as the percentage of participants who achieved desired outcomes.

If the organization is tracking program outcomes throughout the duration of a youth's participation in the program, this step is relatively easy.

Combining output and outcomes measures with outside research and data will allow program leaders to calculate the social return on investment, using the following formula:

$$\text{Social Return on Investment} = \text{Net Program Benefits}/\text{Program Costs} \times 100$$

In Program Z's case, two measures were used to determine the return on investment: the average cost of services per successful youth (program costs) and the net estimated increase in lifetime earnings (program benefit). The average cost of services per successful youth is calculated by dividing the program's total budget by the number of successful students. For this example, the average cost per successful youth is $500. The greater the number of successful students the program serves, the lower the program cost per student.

For example, if Program Z successfully graduated ninety of one hundred youth from the program and the total program costs the agency $45,000 dollars, then total program costs divided by the ninety successful participants equals $500. If the organization graduated ninety-five of the students served, the average cost per successful student would decrease to $473.68. Therefore increasing program outcomes increases efficiency, and decreasing outcomes decreases efficiency.

The estimated increased lifetime earnings are calculated by taking the difference between annual average salaries of high school dropouts and the annual average salaries of high school graduates and multiplying that by thirty years (an estimated average). The U.S. Census Bureau (2012) reports that the average high school dropout has annual earnings of $20,242, which is $10,385 less than a high school graduate's annual earnings of $30,627. The average lifetime difference in earnings is calculated by multiplying the annual difference ($10,385) by thirty years, which comes to increased lifetime earnings of $311,550.

The net program benefit represents the difference between the estimated increased lifetime earnings and the program cost per successful student. To achieve the social return on investment, this net program benefit is divided by the initial investment to serve one participant. In this example, the difference between the initial investment to serve one youth and the lifetime earning potential is $311,000 ($311,550 less $500). This difference is then divided by the initial investment of $500. To convert this number into a percentage, it must be multiplied by 100, totaling 62,200. Another way to report this data is to communicate that the lifetime earnings for a single participant will equal more than 622 times the initial investment of $500.

Using the Isolated Intervention Effect to Calculate ROI

In Chapter Ten, the concept of the unique intervention factor was introduced as way to communicate a program's unique impact. Calculating this factor allows program leaders to isolate the unique effect of a program independent of other factors outside the program that may have impacted program success. This factor is also useful to use when communicating and calculating a program's ROI.

For example, imagine a small business training program that has been shown to increase small business sales by $7,000 a month compared to a control group of businesses who are waitlisted to participate in the program. If program leaders wants to communicate to stakeholders that they realize there may be other factors contributing to the success of these business, they may decided to conduct a survey of stakeholders to discover the intervention training factor by asking them how much they believe the increased sales were a direct impact of the training and how confident they are in their estimates.

With this information in hand, program leaders can now calculate a social return on investment that takes into consideration only the unique impact of the training. Before calculating the social return of investment, the program benefits can be reduced by the intervention factor. If the intervention factor is .35, for example, the adjusted program impact will be a $2,500 monthly sales increase instead of $7,000. This is calculated by multiplying the program benefit of $7,000 by the intervention factor of .35.

Now, $2,500 will be used as the program benefit rather than the original $7,000 program benefit, leading to a more representative capture of the training program's true impact. Although using the isolated training factor reduces the program return on investment calculated by the organization, the audience for the data is more likely to accept this result, because leaders have more accurately pinpointed the program impacts.

Friends of the Children: A Case Study

Friends of the Children is a nonprofit organization that provides an excellent example of how to use outcome and impact data to inform and inspire visitors for the organization's website (www.friendschildren.org). This organization demonstrates the five strategies of effective communication and also provides information on the organization's social return on investment.

Under the "How We Succeed" tab on its website (Friends of the Children, 2012), the organization provides six photos of children they serve. When a visitor clicks on a photo, she can read that child's story and learn about the program's specific impact in that child's life. The stories are written in the voice of the mentor. Each story explains the challenges this particular child faced before entering the program and conveys some of the successes the organization has seen in that particular child during the course of his or her participation. These stories are effective because they are both concrete and emotional.

In addition to these stories, Friends of Children also provides research and specific outcomes measures on its website. The information under the "Friends Works" tab highlights goals, success measures, and related research. Outcome measures are listed as follows:

- 85% of our program graduates earned a high school diploma or GED, compared with the national graduation rate of 69%.
- 97% of our adolescents who graduated also avoided involvement with the criminal justice system, despite at least 60% having one parent who has been incarcerated.
- 98% avoided early parenting, despite at least 60% having been born to a teen parent.

Source: http://www.friendschildren.org/friends-works/measure-of-success/

A Closer Look. The data shared on this organization's website clearly shows how the organization's mentoring services are effective at reaching the organization's stated goal of assisting disadvantaged youth to grow into strong, self-confident, contributing members of their communities. These data are unexpected, emotional, and inspiring. To demonstrate credibility, Friends of the Children also provides documents demonstrating the validity of research its programs are founded on and shares published data about its chosen model of care. The organization also includes the fact that the National Institutes of Health (NIH) is currently conducting a five-year impact study on the organization's programs.

In addition to sharing outcomes data and compelling stories, Friends of the Children provides a downloadable document that shows the organization's social return on investment (Chussi and Hamilton, 2011). The authors use the program's outcome data, including the percentages of students obtaining a GED, avoiding incarceration, and not becoming a parent before age eighteen.

The organization also communicates program costs, including costs for mentors, facilities and administrative overhead, and team leads. In addition, the model includes a comparison group of economically disadvantaged eighteen-year-olds living in Multnomah County, where 70 percent of residents are black and 30 percent are white. The results of the study demonstrated that program benefits stands at 7.2 times the cost of the program. In addition, results show that the lifetime average benefit is $898,697 per student.

Creating Internal Communication Systems

Successful communication strategies take time and careful planning. Organizations that excel at communicating performance measures take a proactive approach. They create strong internal communication systems that support external communication. They ask program officers to collect the required data in the specified time frames. They ensure that grant writers and development officers understand the outcome and program data needed to effectively share the organization's story.

The majority of funders, including both government programs and corporate or private foundations, now require organizations to submit, as part of all grant applications, their proposed outcomes and outcomes measures and demonstrated program impact. This shift in funding requirements means organizations need meaningful outcome data and measurement plans in place to ensure swift and effective grant applications.

Grant writing and development specialist Kerri Mollard of Mollard Consulting partnered with Measurement Resources for a two-day virtual Managing to Outcomes Bootcamp for nonprofit and government leaders. Mollard taught the importance of establishing a strategic plan for internal communication. Such a plan should combine the organization's key outcomes and performance measures with elements required by grant and development staff. For easy use of outcomes in reporting, Mollard further advises organizations to institute a final reports plan that ensures the avoidance of the all-too-common "I need data by tomorrow" practice. As an organization adopts a systematic plan to gather data and stories throughout a grant period, it simplifies the communication process (Mollard, 2012).

Grant Application Management

Mollard suggests that organizations adopt the following strategies to ensure successful management of grant deadlines:

- The grants calendar should be understood by development and grant writers as well as by the organization's program staff.
- Development and grants staff should invite program staff to a quarterly grants meeting to discuss the to-do list. Program staff should include development and grants staff in discussion about outcomes and data gathering.
- Development and grants staff should job shadow or volunteer in programs to witness the work and impact firsthand.
- The organization should create an index of stories, tied to outcomes and cross-listed with programs and audiences.
- When possible, staff should standardize data and outcomes reports needed for funders.

Getting Started with Communicating Outcomes

Great organizations reach their stated goals with confidence and communicate their value with honesty, integrity, and passion.

Their outcomes measures provide the quality information needed to make sound management decisions. Leaders use the information gathered internally to communicate the value of these measures to staff and to improve operations. They apply the data and communicate it externally to tell the organization's story. Yet establishing a well-organized data collection and communication systems at a social-sector organization does not happen overnight. It takes persistence, repetition, consistency, and building on past success.

Successful leaders consistently communicate the importance of measures to help overcome any fears or barriers to support on the part of staff. Such fears often stem from previous efforts that have failed. In the past, decision makers may have asked for information but failed to act on the information they gathered. In some cases, day-to-day operations get in the way, and outcome data and reports that demonstrate the organization's unique value and impact are never fully communicated. When this has been the typical experience, it is likely staff have concluded that program evaluation, surveys, and outcomes measures are a waste of their time or just another thing on their to-do lists.

An effective leader will move forward, using a balance of understanding, dialogue, and innovative communication strategies to establish a successful data-driven culture. Great leaders recognize that staff members' fear or uncertainty often originates with previous actions or inactions, which have taught staff that the data they so carefully collected has no real value. Thus staff members do not view measurement activities as a critical component of organizational growth and improvement. If this resistance is not addressed, efforts to implement a robust measurement program and communicate outcomes may be thwarted by lack of participation, waning enthusiasm, or poor data compliance by staff.

To break the cycle, decision makers need to begin with renewed vigor. Leaders must clearly communicate the purpose and value for the organization as a whole and for those who will invest their resources in data collection and evaluation. If organizational staff members have been less than diligent with inputting data, the worst thing a leader can do is to postpone administering the required surveys, stop using data-gathering tools, or cease the evaluation of results.

A common problem encountered by many organizations seeking to adopt a high-performance measurement culture is poor-quality data or missing data. Great leaders recognize the value and importance of communicating findings even if there is missing data. When one organization found that 70 percent of program data was missing, the director chose to hire an outside evaluator anyway. Though no clear conclusions could be drawn with full confidence because of this missing data, information was still presented to staff.

In this case, when staff members saw the types of information gathered and realized the questions that might have been fully answered had they gathered more complete data, they became much more interested. By proceeding with the evaluation despite missing data, organizational leaders showed staff that their data collection and evaluation efforts were important, had real value, and held the potential to improve their individual performance and clients' lives.

Once staff members begin to see the value and importance of measurement activities and to understand how noncompliance prevents the organization from making powerful decisions with confidence, data-collection compliance nearly always increases. Consistent communication will spur staff to greater action and support efforts required to collect better information for future decision making across all levels of the organization. In the preceding example, if results had not been shared, staff would have continued to believe that their efforts to measure outcomes were not important.

Another strategy to communicate the move toward a data-driven culture is to reward team members for data-collection compliance. Successful government and nonprofit organizations whose leaders have embraced a high-performance measurement culture avoid chastising staff about poor compliance in the early days of a measurement program. They do not rush the establishment of compliance and reporting systems.

Instead, these organizations set clear data-gathering compliance goals that communicate to staff that this practice matters and is important. An example of a clear goal might be, "By next quarter 95 percent of the data will be collected and shared by the stated deadline." Goals are consistently communicated to reinforce the importance of collecting data. The cycle is complete when leaders report back to staff what they are doing with the data collected through their diligent and sustained efforts.

Next Steps

High-performance organizations with a strong management foundation are able to use data to share a compelling story that ultimately allows them to service more clients, improve operations, increase revenues, and strengthen the attitudes, perceptions, and valuable partnerships with key stakeholders that keep the organizations strong and healthy. The next step is to build on these solid communication strategies. The organization must create plans to improve operations and celebrate the organization's success. This will be the focus of the next chapter.

Impact & Excellence

Chapter Eleven Discussion Questions

1. Look at your organization's current marketing materials, websites, reports, and other communication tools. How well is the organization incorporating outcomes and data in each? How might the organization improve current communication efforts?
2. Collect the organization's output, outcomes, and related program stories. Develop a pitch that includes the communication of outcomes that are unexpected, concrete, credible, emotional, and relevant.
3. What is the organization's social return on investment? If you have not yet established a social return on investment, what data and research would need to be available in order to calculate it? Create a plan to establish this measure.
4. Create a plan for continual communication of program outcomes and grant requirements by grant staff and program staff. Ensure open communication channels between these two groups.

12

Change and Celebrate

Insanity is doing the same thing over and over again expecting different results.
—ALBERT EINSTEIN

THE FIFTH ELEMENT ON THE PATH to easy and effective impact and excellence seems obvious, but it is frequently overlooked and often avoided in social-sector organizations. Nonprofit and government leaders are often hesitant to implement changes to programs and operations that disrupt the status quo, even when things are not going well for the organization.

Typically, leaders avoid change because they are afraid of failure or an adverse public reaction. The popular expression, "The devil you know is better than the devil you don't know," accurately describes why many leaders shy away from change and often go out of their way to avoid it. However, this reluctance to implement needed change is not found among social-sector leaders who embrace a high-performance measurement culture.

Why is this the case? Measuring and evaluating results allows these leaders to make decisions with confidence and leads them toward the success they most desire for their respective organizations. Organizations with high-performance measurement cultures have systems in place for using performance and outcomes measures to make positive programmatic and organizational changes. In addition, they have created formalized systems for celebrating their success, no matter how big or small.

Embracing Change Confidently

Many organizations make the mistake of rushing into change or avoiding risk altogether. Innovation is often squelched in the social sector because stakeholders perceive the consequences of failure to be too great. They fear the wrong decisions will result in bad press, loss of elections, reduction in funding, or negative consequences to clients. This fear perpetuates the status quo and results in stalled advances throughout the social sector. On the other end of the spectrum, some social sector leaders leap to decisions based on consensus or a best-guess approach without taking the time to evaluate the data and often implement change too quickly and haphazardly.

When social-sector organizations base decisions on outcomes from measures aligned with organizational mission and objectives, they naturally embrace change in a more confident manner. Access to the right data equips organizations that might otherwise be hampered by endless second-guessing or a shot-in-the-dark approach to move forward confidently. Solid data-collection efforts provide a natural safety net that empowers leaders to make innovative and sometimes even radical performance improvements that might otherwise seem foolhardy or ill-advised.

When interpreted and applied correctly, data functions as a figurative parachute, allowing the organization to effect change at a brisk but controlled pace. Organizations naturally become more innovative and steer clear of the adverse effects experienced when decisions are either avoided outright or made swiftly without the backing of such data. Confident that embracing change will not result in a devastating crash for the organization, leaders move forward knowing they have the ability to course correct as needed.

Based on solid organizational data, leaders can identify solutions to pressing problems and incorporate strategic changes with confidence. Successful leaders do not hesitate to make necessary changes, because they know they can justify decisions with high-quality, relevant data. Once the changes are made, the same measurement systems that provided key inputs will quickly inform these social-sector leaders of the degree to which the changes implemented have been successful.

If the change is successful, the leader can reinforce this success and implement it on a larger scale. If the change does not achieve the desired results, then the leader has newfound knowledge about what does not work. In addition, leaders have access to data that will allow the leadership team to institute a plan for improvement, eventually leading to stronger, more effective, and more efficient operations.

The most damaging thing an organizational leader can do is to design a well-crafted performance and outcomes system and communicate the results but fail to use the data to take corrective action. Such a practice leads the organization into a cycle that replicates what Albert Einstein defined as insanity: "doing the same thing over and over again and expecting different results."

Here are three reasons social-sector organizations should not invest time and resources in data collection if they are not committed to developing a plan for making meaningful changes using the data they collect:

1. **Inaction is a waste of time and resources**. There is no point to capturing, collecting, and analyzing data if it will sit unused in a database or be housed in a shelved report.

2. **Inaction breeds staff resentment and distrust**. Not using data that staff, clients, and stakeholders invest time in gathering, evaluating, and entering discourages participation in future data-collection compliance efforts. When data is not used, leaders send a message to staff that data has little or no value or impact on the organization's growth and success.

3. **Inaction produces the same results the next time**. This practice will keep an organization playing small and not reaching its highest possible level. Inaction hurts clients. Often an organization's staff and program directors have at their fingertips valuable information with the potential to greatly improve programs and client outcomes. Not implementing change based on this information keeps clients from receiving the best possible experience from the organization.

The Power of Using Data: A Case Study

An Ohio child welfare collaborative instituted performance measures to ensure that cases of abuse, neglect, and dependency were being processed in a timely manner and leading to optimal outcomes for families. By state law, child abuse, neglect, and dependency cases must be disposed of within ninety days of a finding of guilt in an adjudication hearing. If a dispositional hearing does not occur within that time frame, the court, on its own motion or on the motion of a party, may dismiss the case without prejudice (Ohio Revised Code, 2003).

This ninety-day rule led to many county court cases being dismissed prior to disposition and then refiled. Refiling resets the clock and causes a delay, which is generally not in the best interest of the child, as this further delays permanency and stability for the child. In addition, frequent use of the ninety-day rule violates the spirit of the state statute.

In this case, the group discovered that 23 percent of abuse, neglect, and dependency cases were being dismissed and refiled, following this ninety-day rule. This practice was having a negative impact on children by keeping them in temporary placement longer than necessary. In addition, it increased costs to the courts and clogged up dockets, leading to mismanagement of staff time and, often, to an increase in child welfare expenditures, which were necessary to cover placement for those children.

A statewide evaluation conducted by the Ohio Supreme Court examined the increase in dismissed and refiled cases. A collaborative committee was convened to conduct an internal evaluation. This committee identified several reasons for the high incidence of dismissed cases.

First, the committee found that the magistrates were not holding attorneys accountable for excessive requests for dismissals. The committee discovered other factors related to scheduling difficulties, for both magistrates and other affected parties. Based on these findings, the collaborative committee identified several key solutions. They agreed to implement the suggested changes and convene monthly to review the data on dismissals. Over the course of six months, the dismissal and refiling rate was reduced from 23 percent to 10 percent, a significant improvement.

The information the group used for evaluation and decision making included data they were already required to submit to the Supreme Court regularly. They had been submitting this data for years, yet prior to convening the collaborative committee, no action was being taken on this data. Unfortunately, it took a statewide evaluation conducted by a funder to spur the court to action on its data. Once the court convened the committee and took a strong, data-driven approach, using the available data to effect positive change, they saw swift results. The committee found a dramatic decrease in the percentage of dismissals and refiled cases system wide.

A Closer Look. This case study demonstrates the power of data-driven decisions, consistent communication, and the ability to effect change based on data. Unfortunately, a majority of government and nonprofit organizations are similar to the child welfare collaborative. They wait to take action on collected data and suffer the consequences of doing so. Only a handful of today's social-sector organizations have a proactive plan for taking action on the data they collect. Fewer still are committed to using collected data to implement lasting change.

I would estimate about 30 percent of organizations with well-aligned performance measures and measurement systems routinely and systematically make improvements based on data. The remaining 70 percent may intend to make changes based on their measures, but in most organizations, six months later no significant changes have been made. Furthermore, these social-sector organizations are often experiencing the same results. Typically, the organization has access to an abundance of relevant and useful data. Information is not the problem. True success is prevented because the organization fails to act or lacks a sustained commitment to implementing change.

Best Practices for Using Data to Implement Change

Successful organizations embrace a clear commitment to make data-driven decisions and implement change when the data suggests it is needed. Without a structured plan for using data, it is natural to put implementation on the back burner or to delay change management activities. Next, we will consider best practices for using data to implement change in the social-sector organization.

Tie Measures to Performance Goals

The more measures are tied to the day-to-day work of the organization and its staff, the more likely employees will be naturally motivated to make adjustments needed for the organization to achieve its desired outcomes. Both individual and group performance goals can be set based on results. When performance and outcome measures are relevant and aligned with the mission, this highly successful practice engages the staff and substantially improves the results realized in mission-driven organizations.

Convene a Data Review Committee

One barrier to making changes with data lies in securing buy-in from key stakeholders. One successful practice is assigning a standing committee primary responsibility for a monthly or quarterly review of progress on all performance and outcomes measures. Composed of seven to nine members who represent a diverse group of decision makers, this committee is tasked with making decisions based on data and evaluating progress toward the organization's desired outcomes. If the organization staff has fewer than seven people, the entire staff should meet as a data review committee.

It is important to select a mix of committee member types, including idea generators, strong strategic thinkers, those capable of systems thinking, and those who take a process-oriented approach. Such diversity maximizes the group's productivity and effectiveness. The outcome of this committee's work will be not only a plan for change but also the clear communication of the importance of embracing change. Such a group will naturally be motivated to implement a plan for positive progress.

Establish a Champion

On the committee, a champion should be assigned to each measure. One individual can be the permanent keeper of all activity surrounding a particular measure, or one champion can be assigned for all measures. The designated champion assumes responsibility for ensuring quality data-gathering compliance and reviews the assigned measure on a regular basis. A champion also ensures the full implementation of any action items aimed to increase a particular measure and evaluates and communicates the degree of success achieved.

Champions should be given the authority to give direction, coach others in the organization, and offer advice for that particular measure. Champions should be members of the data review committee, rather than other individuals within the organization. If there is more than one champion for the set of measures, the data review committee chair should provide oversight for implementation and changes instituted for all the measures.

Meet Regularly

The data review committee should adopt a schedule or regular committee meetings in conjunction with the organization's annual planning process, placing meeting dates on the calendar. It is best if members know that they will be meeting on a consistent schedule—the third Wednesday of every month, for example. If this meeting must be rescheduled, set a new date at the time of cancellation. A consistent meeting schedule underscores the value and importance of the committee's assigned responsibility both to those who serve on it and to others in the organization.

Use a Consistent Meeting Format

At meetings of the data review committee, a standardized format should be followed. Each meeting should include an examination of data trends for the past twelve to eighteen months. The committee should compare the results against any established benchmarks or performance goals. Then the team should discuss any changes that occurred in the past data review period (typically during the past month or preceding quarter). Table 12.1 displays a sample data review format a committee may follow. Such changes in the organization might influence performance measures either positively or negatively and therefore impact the success of a particular change.

The next step is to explore whether the data suggest that further action or changes are needed. It is important to consider

Table 12.1. Data Review Committee Meeting Template

Performance or Outcome Measure	12 Month Rolling Average	Current Quarter's Average	Performance Goal	Under / Over Goal	Past Changes that Impacted this Goal	Were Changes Successful?	What Future Efforts Will Increase Outcomes?	What Information is Needed?	Implementation Plan

whether and to what degree desired outcomes are occurring in the organization. If the data suggest that changes are required, the committee should identify what additional information is needed, outline proposed changes, and design a plan for implementation. Lastly, the group should discuss how the desired results will be communicated and celebrated.

Committee Success: A Case Study

A method similar to that described in this chapter to implement change was employed to help a committee considering strategies to improve outcomes for delinquent juveniles. The committee focused its discussion on best practices for alternatives to juvenile detention. Typically, the juvenile courts that implemented such best-practice strategies reduced costs and also saw a significant reduction of long-lasting negative consequences for public safety and youth development.

The committee selected specific practices designed to reduce unnecessary delays in case processing, which would result in shorter lengths of stay in detention for juveniles. The outcome for the court would be the efficient use of nonsecure alternatives and the reductions in failure-to-appear and rearrest rates.

This review committee used data to examine how effectively policy changes enabled the court to reach its desired outcomes. A detailed analysis had previously been conducted for the court and had provided the committee with information that showed that case process delays in the juvenile court system were related to increases in continuances and increased docket volume of school truancy filings.

To assess favorable progress toward their goals, the committee met to examine quarterly trends in the number of days juveniles were held in detention, the average days it took juvenile court cases to be processed, the number of formal school truancy filings in the system, and the length of stay for youth being held on transfers to adult court (called "bindovers," as the court binds over the youth for trial or further inquiry). Table 12.2 provides an example of this group's specific performance measures and quarterly trends over a fifteen-month period.

Table 12.2. Juvenile Detention Performance Measures

	2 Q 11	3 Q 11	4 Q 11	1 Q 12	2 Q 12	Avg	Goal
Average days held In juvenile detention	11.27	12.08	9.72	9.95	8.25	10.25	<7
Average number of days for a case to be processed	168.64	144.19	120.31	92.24	n/a	111.98	<90
Average number of continuances per case	0.90	0.87	0.80	0.66	0.32	0.71	0
Number of chronic school truancy cases filed	480	2	178	472	690	364	n/a

A Closer Look. The committee began its work with the careful examination of trends during the second quarter of 2011. They discovered that, during this period, youth were being held in detention an average of eleven days. During this three-month period, 480 truancies had been filed. The court took an average of 168 days, almost double the desired 90 days, to process cases. In addition, cases were likely to experience at least one continuance. The committee used this data to implement specific strategies, beginning with immediate shelter care hearings for youth being held unnecessarily in detention. In addition, they established new committees assigned to study school truancy issues and other issues related to case processing.

Most of these strategies were implemented in the first and second quarters of 2012. At the end of second quarter, the group reconvened to examine the progress and impacts of their efforts. They discovered that both the emergency shelter care practice and a focus on the reduction of detention lengths were having a positive impact. The average number of days youth were held in detention decreased from 11.27 to 8.5 days.

The committee also realized slight reductions in the average numbers of days to process cases, down from 168 to 92 during the second quarter. In addition, the data showed a significant reduction in continuances, from .90 per case to .32 per case. Reviewing the data was encouraging to the committee and suggested that their efforts and discussions in pursuit of these outcomes were working.

One measure that did not see improvements was the increase in chronic school truancies. There was a significant increase in filings compared to the previous year's filings over the same quarter. In fact, filings had increased from 480 to 690. Based on the data review, the committee decided to ramp up its previous implementation efforts while also exploring ways to work with schools and other community groups to reduce the number of school filings.

Implement Change

High-performance measurement cultures require leaders with the ability to successfully enable constructive change. Social-sector leaders achieve desired success by focusing on the problem at hand and also by anticipating and responding to stakeholders' fear of the unknown and their natural resistance to change. When measures are aligned with the true mission of the organization, it is much easier to overcome such resistance and to significantly reduce fear, if not eliminate it. This is especially true when the leader has done a good job of cultivating and communicating the vision of the organization.

Without the necessary data and information, effective change becomes almost impossible. Change is scary, and stakeholders and staff need to be both engaged and confident in the organization's leadership during times of change. Leaders that come to staff with data-informed decisions can obtain buy-in for proposed strategies and break through natural barriers to change.

The Measurement Culture Study revealed that 77 percent of organizations with a high-performance measurement culture were successful at using data to create organizational change. In contrast, none of the organizations with a moderate- or low-measurement culture achieved change. In other words, fear and resistance to change are seldom barriers to success for organizations with a high-performance measurement culture. Measures and data provide the solid foundation for organizations that successfully implement positive change.

Celebrate Success

Measurement results naturally lead to change in high-performance measurement cultures, and it is important for organizations to celebrate such change, whether great or small. Even when positive change occurs, it can prove stressful. Recognizing the progress the organization has accomplished motivates staff to move forward and gives them the confidence needed to continue building on their success into the future.

Studies have shown that in the public sector meaningful recognition is correlated with employee retention, good morale, loyalty, commitment, and satisfaction in the workplace. Yet one study of public sector employees revealed that, despite this demonstrated relationship, few organizations have effective reward systems in place (Saunderson, 2004). Most organizations are missing a huge opportunity to increase productivity and morale. Leaders of high-performance organizations understand that recognizing and rewarding success is the foundation of growth and continuous improvement.

Organizations with effective recognition programs have strong leadership participation and supportive cultures. These organizations increase job satisfaction and productivity by communicating and celebrating their staff's hard work. They provide linkages between employee efforts and the impact and outcomes the organization contributes to the community.

Communicating and sharing outcome measures provides a way to recognize, educate, and bond with stakeholders. When measures are used as positive internal management tools, they allow employees to know precisely how their contribution is making a difference and contributing to the vital mission of the organization. Such a practice may also inspire employees to see how they can increase the impact they are already making.

Studies indicate that social-sector employees highly value the celebration of success. Celebrations are the orchestrated experiences of linking relationships and value to the contributions made; the award is the icing on the cake (Saunderson, 2004). Rewarding employees for reaching outcome goals provides this linkage of relationships and value.

Effective recognition systems do not have to include large monetary rewards. As highlighted in Chapter Two, the administrator of the Dallas County Tax Office created an effective reward system with a series of reliable performance standards that measured important elements of the organization's mission. Instituting such rewards allowed the agency to operate with less staff, control budget growth, improve staff morale, and increase customer satisfaction, all while experiencing unprecedented demand for service.

Potlucks, pizza parties, an afternoon off, a day's vacation, and an organization-wide picnic are a few of the ways nonprofit and government organizations might choose to celebrate the impact that staff members are making for the organization and its mission. When presenting an award, high-performing organizations place an emphasis on how specifically the individual or team contributed to the increased outcome measures. Celebrating success leads to increased success in the future.

The reason that organizations with high-performance measurement cultures are significantly more successful than those with moderate- and low-measurement cultures boils down to how these different organizations use their data. The organizations that will continue to thrive, have the greatest impact, and make our world a better place are those that reward the dedicated work of staff and stakeholders. Such recognition motivates people to continue to give all they can and to strive for the next level of success. In addition, these organizations are not satisfied with the expectation of mediocre results. Rather, they consistently monitor outcomes and results and make the necessary adjustments and changes to achieve the highest success possible.

Next Steps

By following the Five C's of Easy and Effective Impact and Excellence shared in this book, leaders prepare nonprofit and government organizations for greater impact. In the next chapter, we will look at ways in which social-sector organizations can leverage a high-performance measurement culture and thrive in today's challenging environment.

Impact & Excellence

Chapter Twelve Discussion Questions

1. Develop a list of at least five things your organization is doing well. How could staff celebrate those successes?
2. How will you regularly celebrate success?
3. How does your organization currently use data for program improvement? What data does the organization already have that could be used for program improvement? Develop a plan to start reviewing and taking meaningful action on existing data.

13

Taking the First Step

Faith is taking the first step even when you can't see the whole staircase.
—MARTIN LUTHER KING, JR.

THE PROBLEMS THAT PLAGUE TODAY'S SOCIAL SECTOR do not begin with a failed mission. Nor do they stem from a lack of drive among government and the nonprofit organizations engaged in making our world a better place. The root of many failures in the sector can instead be traced to the failure on the part of many organizations to adopt and fully leverage the natural advantages of a high-performance measurement culture.

Social sector organizations continue to err on one side or the other of the measurement equation. Many leaders and funders make decisions from their hearts but miss the opportunity to align their heart-based decisions with the facts at their disposal. In contrast, well-meaning and practical-minded experts who sit on nonprofit boards often lean toward operating these organizations as business enterprises, advocating for key decisions to be based on revenues alone, rather than considering what impact the organization is making in the lives of its clients and the community it serves.

As we have seen, size and budget are not accurate predictors of an organization's ability to achieve impact and excellence. Success comes once the leader makes a commitment to model leadership, structures, practices, and measures that are supported by a high-performance measurement culture.

Five Keys to Impact & Excellence: A Review

Most organizations begin to address shifts in funding patterns in one of two ways: Either they engage a program evaluator to assist them in navigating change, or they simply implement the performance measures requested by the funder. Either action is an important step toward instituting a high-performance measurement culture, but these activities alone do not prepare the social-sector organization for optimal success.

True success comes when performance and outcomes measures are not viewed as another thing on the "to do" list but rather are incorporated into the fabric on the organization. Lasting change comes when an organization focuses on five key factors of impact and excellence. Here, again, are the Five C's—the essential steps that every social-sector organization must take:

1. Make the necessary changes to organizational *culture and leadership*.
2. *Clarify* the organization's mission.
3. *Capture* impact, measuring the right things.
4. *Communicate* results effectively.
5. Implement data-informed *changes* and *celebrate* success.

The Measurement Resources Survey shows that more than 73 percent of the organizations currently in the social sector need to make significant shifts in the way they think about and use current data if they wish to become high-performance organizations focused on managing to outcomes. As funders increase their expectations of an organization's ability to demonstrate unique impact and value, those organizations that are most serious about making this commitment are the ones that will thrive in the twenty-first century and beyond. These organizations will attract more grants and donors, develop a stronger base of loyal supporters, and cultivate a more engaged, motivated workforce as they share success stories.

The shift to a high-performance measurement culture does not happen in one day or as a result of a single meeting. It requires continuous and consistent effort, discussion, and planning. The good news: although much time must be invested, these shifts require minimal monetary resources in advance. The biggest challenge is overcoming the organization's current inertia and natural resistance to change.

Effective change is a function of three factors: dissatisfaction with the current state, a vision of what is possible, and the first concrete steps toward embracing a new vision (Beckhard, 1969). If positive results are to occur, all three ingredients must be present and must be strong enough to overcome the natural resistance to change.

Now is the time to embrace a new vision of what is possible for every social-sector organization. We have examined the reasons for organizations in the sector to be dissatisfied with the current state. Now leaders of organizations committed to establishing a high-performance measurement culture can choose from among the many recommended strategies and select the first concrete steps best suited to their particular situation.

To ensure an optimal outcome, actions need to be tailored to the individual organization's needs, desires, and mission. There is no prescribed or required set of actions that fits every organization; however, every organization can begin by adopting a successful action planning model.

An Impactful Action Planning Model

Regardless of the specific actions required to become a high-performance organization rooted in data-driven decision making, the following seven-step action planning model gives leaders the confidence to create a series of first steps that will quickly move the organization in the right direction. Measurement Resources has consistently used this model to help an organization's staff overcome the natural resistance to change and embrace a data-driven approach.

1. **Embrace Diversity**. The goal of action planning is change, so it is important that organizations involve key employees and other stakeholders to assist in implementing a desired change. An action planning committee should include individuals at various levels of the organization and those who represent different functional capacities. This diversity will lead to richer ideas and increases accountability, staff buy-in, and follow-through.

2. Dream Big. Successful plans are built on a clear picture of the future that generates excitement and anticipation. Sector leaders can use the information in this book and their answers to key questions at the close of each chapter to begin organization-wide discussions and the visioning process. Before moving to action, the group must first consider the desired vision.

Here are some questions to consider:

- What might our organization look like in its ideal state?
- How would that feel?
- Who does our organization truly serve?
- What outcomes might our organization achieve?
- What would staff and stakeholders be contributing?
- How would staff and stakeholders feel if our organization were thriving and fulfilling its mission?

In this vision process, it is critical that the group focus on its desire for the future rather than naming and listing current barriers to that vision. Organizations often get derailed at this step, because of the "Yes, buts." These statements typically sound like, "It would be awesome if we could achieve that, but our funders would never go for that." Or "It would be great to know if we were having that kind of impact, but that would be impossible to measure."

This type of language will keep any group stuck. This is especially true of visioning meetings. The goal of the visioning process is envision the future and, more importantly, to connect with the vision on an emotional level. Once this has been accomplished, it is much easier to overcome perceived barriers and do the hard work needed to achieve the vision.

3. Get Real. To get to where they want to go, leaders and staff must accept where they are right now. Prior to developing action items, organizations can take a data-driven approach to understanding the current reality. It is important to understand financial trends, staff strengths and weaknesses, current program success, and the needs and desires of all stakeholders, including customers.

In initial planning meetings, staff should take inventory of current measures and data, assess the organizational culture and examine leadership strengths and weaknesses. A self-assessment tool included in Appendix A will prove useful for this task. Other tools that help organizations understand the current state are available at the Measurement Resources website (www .measurementresourcesco.com).

At this stage, planning committees should consider how efforts that come from the planning process will be evaluated. Such a determination will provide baseline data against which to measure progress and determine future success. It is also the first step toward strengthening the organization's measurement culture.

A simple way to identify the best way to evaluate efforts is to add a question to the stakeholder survey, listing key elements of the organization's vision and asking respondents to rank those elements on a 1–10 scale, with 1 not at all aligned with that vision and 10 fully aligned with it. This helps the committee to assess where the organization currently stands and provides critical information about how much work lies ahead.

4. Deal with the Gaps. The next step is to identify the gaps between where the organization is currently and the desired future vision. These gaps are the basis of the planning process. Often organizations do not reach the highest level of success because they base their action plan on wants, failing to recognize those things that need to be in place before moving to action. Resist the temptation to discuss goals or strategies before these gaps are fully identified.

5. Set Short-, Medium-, and Long-Term Goals. Next, the committee should use the identified gaps to determine action planning goals. The group decides what they want to achieve in a month, three months, six months, and over the course of a year. With each goal, the planning committee should discuss how members will know once they have achieved success.

For example, a group may identify gaps in the organization's structures or a lack of systems for communicating performance measures. The committee may decide that in three months they would like to review all organizational policies and identify those that do not support a high-performance culture. They may choose to propose any changes to the policy within six months and implement these changes within twelve months.

In this example, organizational leaders would identify potential committee members and set up a performance measure review committee. Then, by six months, this new committee would conduct its review and determine an action structure. By twelve months, the committee would be fully operational. Success for the first two goals, with benchmarks at three and six months respectively, would be determined by whether or not the identified actions took place. The third goal, however, might be measured by determining whether the organization has made changes to its programs based on a review of all program data and measures.

6. Focus on the Now. This step invites the committee to decide which actions need to occur to achieve short-term goals. Groups should decide what, specifically, needs to be done this month or this quarter to reach term targets. It is important for the committee to be specific regarding who will do what by when. Dates for progress review and for a decision on next steps should be nonnegotiable.

It is not important to have the entire step-by-step action plan laid out at the beginning of the process. This can prove overwhelming and lead to failure. It is quite common for groups to start down a path but gather new information that may lead them to modify the actions required to achieve the next goal target. Working on one short-term goal at a time makes the plan much more manageable and is more likely to produce favorable results.

7. Repeat Step Six. Once the committee has achieved its identified short-term goals, it reconvenes to establish an action plan for the next set of goals—which in turn becomes the new short-term goals. This cycle continues until the desired future state is achieved.

This method allows the organization to work progressively on taking the steps that lead to its desired final destination, instead of becoming overwhelmed with the lengthy process they may see ahead. Regardless of the number of actions an organization must take to create a high-performance measurement culture, these seven steps put the organization in the best possible position to motivate staff and manage organizational change.

Although not necessary, it is often helpful to have an outside consultant assist with the action planning process. Consultants may be engaged to conduct an objective current state assessment and to help the planning committee ask the right questions and avoid getting stuck. Consultants often keep the organization focused on its goal and provide needed accountability. If an organization has a history of undergoing planning processes without the consistent follow-through needed to achieve desired outcomes, an outside consultant is highly recommended and can make a substantial difference.

Model of Success

A child service agency recently went through this proven twelve-month planning process. The director was new to the organization and wanted a plan to revolutionize the organization's culture and move toward becoming a high-performance organization. The planning committee was composed of the director, all department supervisors, and a few key line staff responsible for data collection, evaluation, and implementation.

The group arrived at the following vision to help guide the planning process:

- Respectful communication between families and staff and between all staff members
- New thoughts and ideas are able to be shared
- There is a feeling of trust and full disclosure
- Innovation is encouraged at all staff levels
- Staff feel they are able to put ideas in place
- A cohesive department

This description of the future vision focused on a collaborative, engaged, cohesive, and innovative department, which would lay the foundation for data-driven decision making. Prior to engaging in the planning process, the organization conducted an organization-wide survey focused on staff attitudes and perceptions of the current organizational culture and various organizational change processes currently in place. These results were examined as a part of early planning meetings so the committee could better understand the organization's current state. The group used these survey results to identify the gaps between the organization's future vision and its current state.

During the planning meetings, the committee arrived at the following three twelve-month strategic focus areas with goals and actions to support the overall vision of becoming a high-performance culture.

Strategic Focus: Education

Twelve-Month Goal: All staff will receive training in best practices, and we will have a system in place for ongoing and updated training and education around these and new practices.

Strategic Focus: Communication

Twelve-Month Goal: There is a system of diverse, consistent, and respectful communication methods that include small group meetings where two-way, data-driven communication is encouraged.

Strategic Focus: Culture and Engagement

Twelve-Month Goal: We are a cohesive and innovative department composed of members that understand, trust, and support each other.

Prior to the implementation of any action items, planning committee members were asked to reach a consensus on where they felt the organization was currently on each of the three strategic focus areas. They used the 10-point scale described in the seven action planning steps; in this case 1 represented nowhere close to the goal and 10 represented fully realized. The group rated increased education on best practices a 2.5, effective communication a 2, and engaged organizational culture a 1. These scores indicated that the group had a significant workload to deal with to reach their desired goals.

Next, the group turned its focus to creating action items, concentrating on the first quarter only. The first steps included activities that were easily achievable, such as the following:

- Train all staff on best practices.
- Hold a Q&A lunch following the overview training.

- Visits to each unit by the director to explain the vision and ask for feedback.
- Hold supervisors responsible for holding monthly unit meetings.
- Develop a shared drive that contains all best practices information and references.
- Hold one mandatory meeting with all staff.

The group met quarterly to discuss what worked and what didn't. From these findings, they developed a plan for the next quarter. Occasionally one action item would not be accomplished in the assigned quarter. In such a case, the committee would carry the action over to the next quarter to ensure it would be completed. The committee continued to meet for a full year.

Celebration of Success

At the conclusion of the twelve-month planning period, the committee turned to the data to measure its success. Specifically, committee members wanted to know whether their action items had led to increased education, communication, and engagement, as these were the three focus areas initially identified. To measure change, the committee administered a second organizational culture survey with the addition of items related to specific actions instituted by the committee during the course of the past year. The same vision questions were also administered anonymously to members of the planning community to measure their own evaluation of success.

The survey results revealed that the organization's efforts in increased training and communication had a significant and positive impact on attitudes and knowledge throughout the organization around best practices and positive culture changes. Increased education regarding the best practices moved from an average score of 2.5 to 7, while effective communication increased from an average score of a 2 to 7.8. The engagement in organizational culture moved from an average score of a 1 to 7. And the committee reported other successes:

- An external system offers ongoing training in best practices through regional training centers.

- Unit and staff meetings are held monthly.
- There is better acceptance and understanding of best practices.
- People are sharing new thoughts and ideas; innovation seems to be encouraged.
- The number of functional work teams and the work product coming out of those teams have increased.
- There is greater cohesion among at least some staff.

The staff survey also revealed significant gains in employee perception of department communication, feedback, and understanding one's particular impact on the department. This record of success allowed the client to go back to their staff and celebrate the specific ways in which their efforts paid off.

Taking the time to celebrate allowed the organization's leadership team and staff to reflect on how far they had come in such a short time before moving toward the next goal. They were also able to report back to their funder, demonstrating the clear results achieved with the dollars invested in the organization to date. This type of feedback is essential for continued success and attraction of continued and increased funding and support.

Moving Ahead

This organization not only offers a great example of how to use the planning process to achieve great results, but also demonstrates how this process becomes ingrained in the way the organization does business. Even when a grant to cover outside consulting services was concluded, this organization built on the momentum and continued to work toward goals.

After survey results were collected, this committee convened again, focusing on steps to accomplish even greater success in a second year. They did not abandon their goal to fully realize their vision of thriving success in these three strategic areas.

Taking the Leap Toward Impact & Excellence

In the photograph in Figure 13.1, it may appear that a large man is throwing a small child off the roof of a boathouse. They are my

Figure 13.1. Matt Jones Helps Our Son Leap

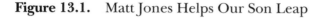

husband, Matt, and our son, and the real story is that our son, then nearly four years old, actually begged us to let him jump off the roof. He had seen many older children—who were undoubtedly more experienced swimmers—make such a jump, and he wanted to try. He was excited and enthusiastic about the desired activity.

After all our son's pleading and impassioned stating of his case, my husband and I agreed to allow him to jump. He knew how to swim, he had a life vest on, and he was clearly excited about the experience. Our only requirement was that he allow my husband to drop him from the roof, because we wanted to make sure he landed far enough out to clear the motor under the boat.

This leap is an apt analogy for how many government and nonprofit organizations currently view the shift to outcomes and measurement. They feel as if funders and stakeholders are throwing them into the deep waters of evaluation and outcomes, regardless of whether or not they are ready to take the plunge. Nonprofit and government leaders should be *excited* for the possibilities that come from creating a data-driven, high-performance measurement culture. What can the shift open up for organizations and their participants? It will almost certainly lead to increased funding, increased impact, and increased staff morale, and, ultimately, it will position organizations as leaders in their respective industry or sector.

There is no need to make excuses about why an organization cannot implement the required strategies. Just as my son had his life jacket and knew how to swim, organizations can turn to the tools provided in this book and other resources now available to help the social sector achieve their goals and reach their desired level of success. To solve the world's most complex problems, today's social-sector organizations must depend on leaders who are willing to step up and take a stand for impact and excellence. Nonprofit organizations and government agencies must embrace data-driven solutions that equip them to demonstrate successful outcomes. Embracing high-performance measurement culture provides a way forward.

Now is the time of opportunity for the sector. Communities, taxpayers, and funders are waiting. Will the sector as a whole navigate this shift? Time will tell. Change begins where you are.

Impact & Excellence

Chapter Thirteen Discussion Questions

1. Review your answers to the discussion questions posed at the conclusion of Chapters Eight through Twelve. What areas need to be strengthened to move toward a high-performance measurement culture?
2. Who should be involved in your organization's action planning committee? Establish a plan to convene this group and start taking action.
3. What could your organization accomplish by taking the leap toward a high-performance measurement culture?

Appendix A: Leadership and Culture Self-Assessment

On a scale from 1 to 5, how would you rate your senior leadership team's ability to perform the following activities?

Leadership Competencies	Poor	Fair	Average	Good	Excellent
Cultivating Organizational Vision and Purpose: Helps individuals and teams align their efforts with the mission of the organization	☐ 1	☐ 2	☐ 3	☐ 4	☐ 5
Building Partnerships and Alliances: Creates and fosters win-win and interdependent relationships that help individuals, teams, and organizations advance organizational goals	☐ 1	☐ 2	☐ 3	☐ 4	☐ 5
Directing and Measuring Work: Uses measures and milestones that support progress on daily work, long-term goals, and projects	☐ 1	☐ 2	☐ 3	☐ 4	☐ 5

Leadership Competencies	Poor	Fair	Average	Good	Excellent
Enabling Constructive Change: Redirects and mobilizes organizational energy in ways that enhance quality and improve effectiveness	☐ 1	☐ 2	☐ 3	☐ 4	☐ 5
Encouraging Dialogue: Creates a culture where members express their views and openly discuss differences	☐ 1	☐ 2	☐ 3	☐ 4	☐ 5

On a scale from 1 to 5, how would you rate your organization's practices and policies in the following important organizational areas?

Organizational Structures	Poor	Fair	Average	Good	Excellent
Autonomy	☐ 1	☐ 2	☐ 3	☐ 4	☐ 5
Training	☐ 1	☐ 2	☐ 3	☐ 4	☐ 5
Feedback	☐ 1	☐ 2	☐ 3	☐ 4	☐ 5
Upper Management Communication	☐ 1	☐ 2	☐ 3	☐ 4	☐ 5
Innovation	☐ 1	☐ 2	☐ 3	☐ 4	☐ 5

Appendix B: Measurement Resources' Measurement Culture Study Results

The Measurement Culture Survey Project was designed to examine the extent to which government and nonprofit organizations are embracing a measurement culture and to discover how such a culture impacts organizational outcomes. A strong measurement culture is defined by the extent to which an organization collects data *and* adopts a system for synthesizing, using, and communicating the collected data in daily management activities.

Two published articles influenced the design of the questions that appear on the final Measurement Culture Survey (Jo Ann Zimmerman and Bonnie Stevens, 2006, and Joanne Carman and Kimberly Fredericks, 2010). Items and questions gleaned from the results of these two studies helped create Measurement Resources' Measurement Culture Survey.

This survey measures the type of data organizations collect, determines how often they conducted evaluations, and identifies how they used collected data to effect change within the organization. The survey also assesses the extent to which organizations achieve successful organizational outcomes, such as increased revenues, strengthened organizational culture, improved change management, and increased external and internal relationships.

The survey captures the demographics of the organizations, including size, budget, and growth rate over a two-year period, and projected growth in the next two years. The survey collects information on the type of organization and the organization's focus and mission. Currently, 254 nonprofit and government organizations have participated in the survey. Of those organizations, there are valid and complete responses for 202 organizations. Of the total sample, nonprofit organizations make up 78 percent (157 surveys), government organizations represent 15 percent (33 surveys), and for-profit social service organizations represent 6 percent (12 surveys).

The Measurement Culture Benchmark Report was offered as a complimentary incentive for participation to each respondent who provides a validated organizational name, title, and e-mail address. This report compares the participant responses to the total survey population. The following contains the complete data from the survey and displayed in the Benchmark Reports.

Study Demographics

- Seventy-seven percent nonprofit agencies, 7 percent county and municipal government agencies, 10 percent state government agencies, 6 percent for-profit social service organizations
- Fifty-six percent annual budget < $2 million, 12 percent annual budget $2–5 million, and 32 percent > $5 million
- Total size (staff plus volunteers) ranged from none to 41,632, with a median size of 65

Figure B.1. Types of Organizations

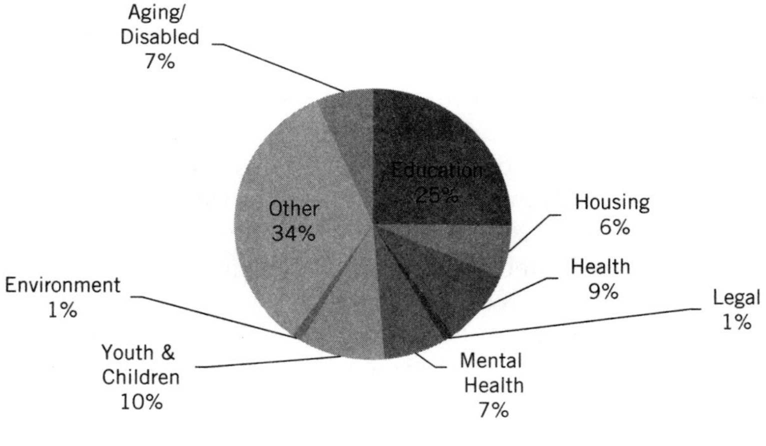

Figure B.2. Past Growth

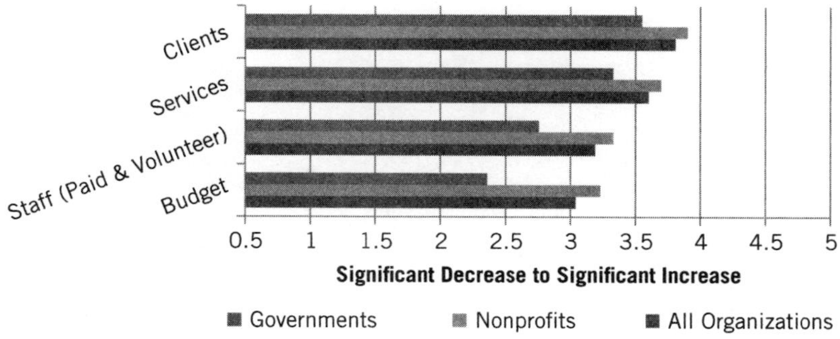

Figure B.3. Future Growth

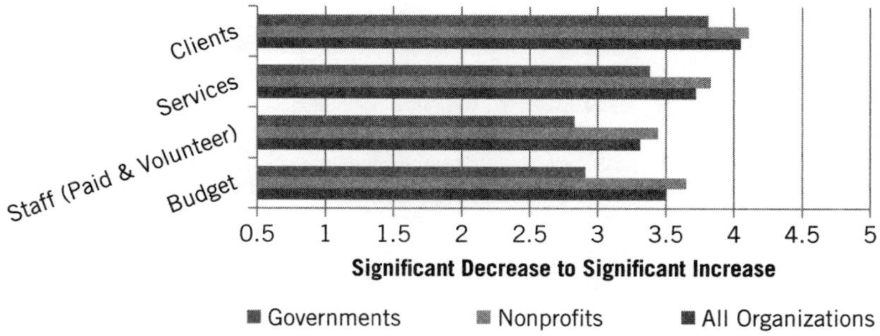

Figure B.4. Measurement and Evaluation Culture

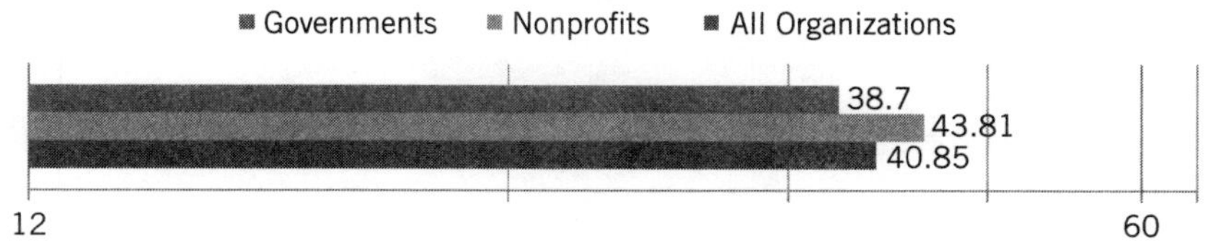

Organizations with a strong measurement and evaluation culture consistently use data-driven techniques to guide decision making. The results indicate that performance measurement and/or evaluation results are not consistently used in the participating organizations' decision-making processes.

Figure B.5. Measurement Utilization

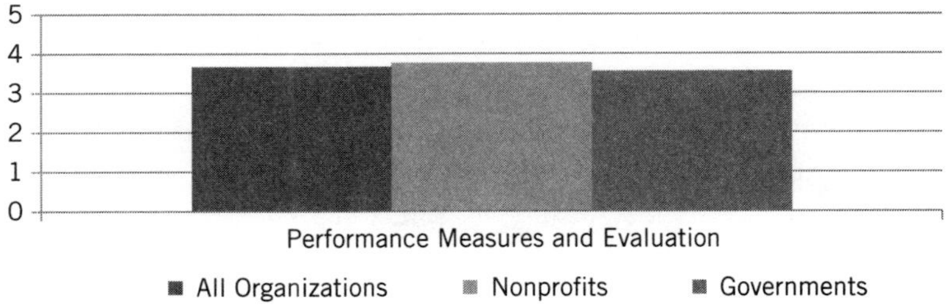

Figure B.6. Measurement Frequency for Types of Decision Making

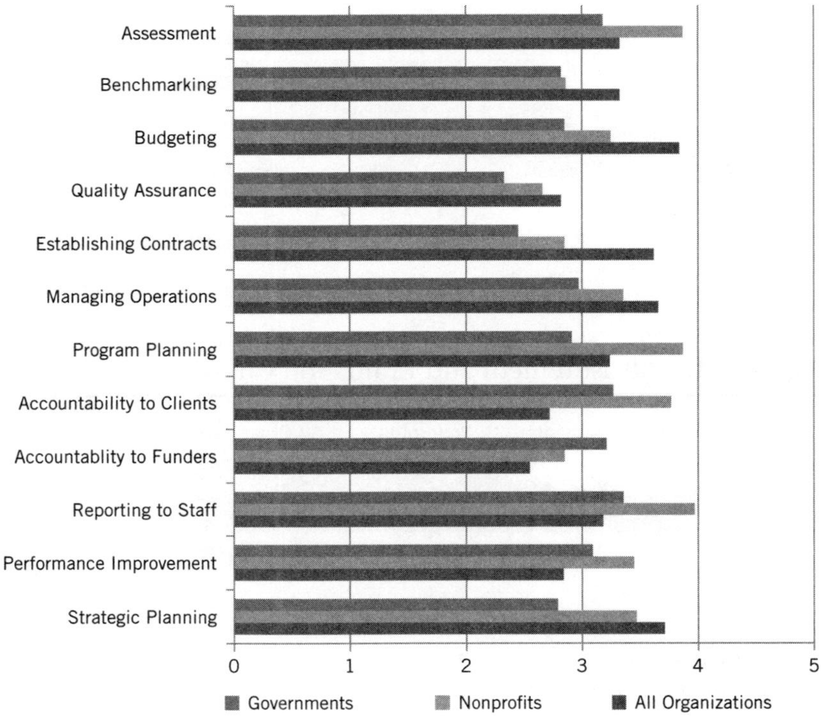

Measurement Effectiveness

Overall, participating organizations report measurement to be effective for numerous organizational management activities and outcomes. Government organizations report a lower degree of success with using data to improve all organizational outcomes compared to nonprofit participants.

The following defines each of the organizational outcomes as they were measured in this study.

- **Increasing Effectiveness:** Improve responsiveness to clients and increase the overall effectiveness of programs.
- **Improving External Relations/Communication:** Increase the communication regarding measurement with others and improve client satisfaction and communication with funders and stakeholders.
- **Improving Internal Relations/Communication:** Increase the communication and coordination between departments and programs and improve employee morale.

Figure B.7. Effectiveness of Measurement on Management Activities and Outcomes

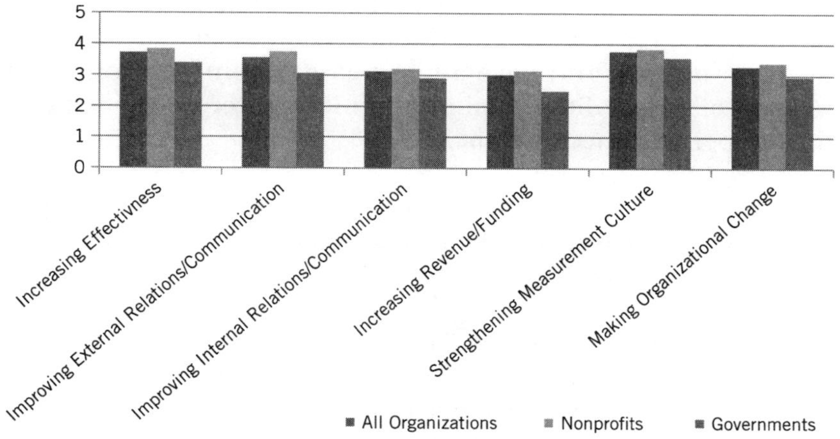

- **Increasing Revenue Funding:** Improve cost saving, change appropriation levels, and increase funding and sales.
- **Strengthening Measurement Culture:** Increase the focus and awareness of the results and factors that impact performance.
- **Making Organizational Change:** Change strategies to achieve desired results and reduce or eliminate ineffective services and programs and duplicate programs.

Measurement Culture and Effectiveness in Achieving Outcomes

- Twenty-three percent of the participants had a Culture score of 52 or higher, representing that they consistently use measurement in decision making and have a high-measurement culture. Twenty-seven percent of nonprofits and 18 percent of governments fell into the high-performance category.
- Sixty-four percent of the participants had a Culture score between 51 and 27, representing that they use measurement for some types of decision making and not for others and have a moderate-measurement culture. Sixty-five percent of nonprofits and 73 percent of governments fell into the moderate-performance category.
- Thirteen percent of the participants had a Culture score less than 26, representing that they rarely use measurement in decision making and have a low-measurement culture. Eight percent of nonprofits and nine percent of governments fell into the low-performance category.

The more frequent and consistent organizations were in using performance measures in their management decisions, the more effective they were in

- Increasing revenues ($r = .64$, $p < .01$)
- Improving external relations ($r = .63$, $p < .01$)
- Improving internal relations ($r = .624$, $p < .01$)
- Increased organizational efficiencies ($r = .62$, $p < .01$)

- Strengthening organizational culture ($r = .60, p < .01$)
- Implementing organizational change ($r = .61, p < .01$)

Comparison of Measurement Culture and Effective Accomplishment of Organizational Outcomes

Organizational Outcomes	% High Culture Reporting Effectiveness	% Moderate Culture Reporting Effectiveness	% Low Culture Reporting Effectiveness
Organizational Efficiencies	88%	50%	18%
External Relations	82%	48%	7%
Internal Relations	76%	23%	7%
Increased Revenues	66%	18%	4%
Strengthening Organizational Culture	98%	55%	26%
Successful Organizational Change	**72%**	**26%**	**11%**

Source: Measurement Resources Company Measurement Culture Survey Data

Organizational Development Measurement Tools

In addition to performance measures and evaluation techniques, survey participants also use a variety of other measurement-based management tools in their decision making. The majority of organizations reported conducting strategic planning, employee satisfaction surveys, and management training around performance measures and evaluation at least once in the past two years.

How often have the following interventions been conducted in the past two years?

	All Organizations	Nonprofits	Governments
Strategic planning	62% used 1–2 times	61% used 1–2 times	61% used 1–2 times
Employee satisfaction survey	51% never	50% never	61% never
Customer/ consumer satisfaction survey	41% 1–2 times	39% 1–2 times	42% 1–2 times
Management training in performance measures and/ or evaluation	46% 1–2 times	47% 1–2 times	42% 1–2 times
Line staff training in performance measures and/ or evaluation	46% never	44% never	50% never
Benchmarking against similar organizations	43% never	41% never	42% never

References

American Evaluation Association. *Guiding Principles for Evaluators.* July 2004. http://www.eval.org/p/cm/ld/fid=51

Anderson, A. *The Community Builder's Approach to Theory of Change: A Practical Guide to Theory Development.* Washington, DC: The Aspen Institute, 2005.

Beatty P. "The Dynamics of Cognitive Interviewing." In S. Presser, J. M. Rothgeb, M. P. Couper, et al. (Eds.), *Methods for Testing and Evaluating Survey Questionnaires.* Hoboken, NJ: Wiley, 2004.

Beckhard, R. *Organization Development: Strategies and Models.* Reading, MA: Addison-Wesley 1969.

Bill and Melinda Gates Foundation. *Who We Are Financials.* February 2014. http://www.gatesfoundation.org/Who-We-Are/General-Information/Financials

Blackwood, A., Roeger, K., and Pettijohn, S. *The Nonprofit Sector in Brief: Public Charities, Giving, and Volunteering, 2012.* Urban Institute, 2012.

Boris, E., Leon, E., Roeger, K., and Nikolova, M. *Human Service Nonprofits and Government Collaboration.* Washington, DC: Urban Institute, 2010.

Brock, A., Buteau, E., and Herring, A. "Room for Improvement." *Foundation Support of Nonprofit Performance Assessment.* The Center for Effective Philanthropy, 2012.

Brown, A., and others. JAI Market Segmentation Research. May 2011. http://www.jazzartsgroup.org/jai/jai-market-segmentation-research

Carman, J. G., and Fredericks, K. A. "Evaluation Capacity and Nonprofit Organizations." *American Journal of Evaluation, 31*(1) (2010): 84–104.

Childs, D. *Effective Performance Measures.* Presented at Public Performance Measurement and Report Network Annual Conference in Chattanooga, TN, March 2010.

Chussi, M., and Hamilton, B. *Return on Investment Fact Sheet.* Portland, OR: Friends of the Children, 2011. http://www.friendschildren.org/wp-content/uploads/2009/10/FOTC-ROI-model-fact-sheet-2011_national1.pdf

Collins, J. *Good to Great: Why Some Organizations Make the Leap and Other Don't.* New York: HarperCollins, 2001.

Communities in Schools. *Communities in Schools Theory of Change.* After the Leap Conference. Washington, DC: December 5, 2013.

Connell, J., and Klem, A. "You Can Get There from Here: Using a Theory of Change Approach to Plan Urban Education Reform." *Journal of Educational and Psychological Consultation, 11*(1) (2000): 93–120.

Cook Inlet Tribal Council. *2013 NYO Games Athlete Survey Results.* Anchorage, AK: Cook Inlet Tribal Council, 2013.

Drucker, P. "Planning for Uncertainty." *Wall Street Journal,* July 22, 1992, p. A12.

Edna McConnell Clark Foundation (EMCF). "Evidence." January 2013. http://www.emcf.org/our-strategy/our-selection-process/evidence

Federal Interagency Forum on Child and Family Statistics. *America's Children: Key National Indicators of Well-Being, 2013.* Washington, DC: U.S. Government Printing Office, 2013.

Friends of the Children. *How We Succeed.* 2012. http://www.friendschildren.org/lives-changed

Gillespie, R. *Manufacturing Knowledge: A History of the Hawthorne Experiments.* Cambridge: Cambridge University Press, 1991.

Hackman, J. R., and Oldham, G. R. "Motivation through the Design of Work: Test of a Theory." *Organizational Behavior and Human Performance,* 16 (1976):250–279.

Hall, P., and Burke, B. *Historical Statistics of the United States Chapter on Voluntary, Nonprofit, and Religious Entities and Activities: Underlying Concepts, Concerns, and Opportunities.* Working Paper #14. Harvard University, November 2002.

Heath, C., and Heath, D. *Made to Stick: Why Some Ideas Survive and Others Don't.* New York: Random House, 2008.

Howard, G., and Dailey, P. "Response-Shift Bias: A Source of Contamination of Self-Report Measures." *Journal of Applied Psychology, 64*(2) (1979): 144–150.

Hrywna, M. "Giving Beat GDP Before Inflation." *Nonprofit Times,* July 1, 2013, p. 3.

Jones, S. *Moving Beyond the Numbers: Lessons Learned from an Interactive Performance Measurement Tool.* Presented at Public Performance

Measurement and Report Network Annual Conference in Chattanooga, TN, March 2010.

Jones, S. *Measurement Resources' Achieving Excellence Member Survey.* Columbus, OH: Measurement Resources Company, 2013.

Jones, S., VanDixhorn, K., and Lewis, T. *Circle Round the Square 2013 Evaluation Report.* Columbus, OH: Measurement Resources Company, 2013.

W.K. Kellogg Foundation. Using Logic Models to Bring Together Planning, Evaluation, and Action. Logic Model Development Guide. Battle Creek, MI, 2014. http://www.wkkf.org/knowledge-center/resources/2006/02/WK-Kellogg-Foundation-Logic-Model-Development-Guide.aspx

Knowlton, L., and Phillips, C. *The Logic Model Guidebook: Better Strategies for Great Results.* Thousand Oaks, CA: Sage, 2009.

Leonard. K., and Loew, L. *Leadership Development Factbook 2012:* Benchmarks and Trends in U.S. Leadership Development. Deloitte, 2012.

Levi, J., and others. *F as in Fat: How Obesity Threatens America's Future.* Robert Wood Johnson Foundation, 2013.

Likert, R. "A Technique for the Measurement of Attitudes." *Archives of Psychology, 22*(140) (1932): 1–55.

Lowery, A. "Homeless Rates in U.S. Held Level Amid Recession, Study Says, But Big Gains Are Elusive." *New York Times,* December 10, 2012. http://www.nytimes.com/2012/12/10/us/homeless-rates-steady-despite-recession-hud-says.html?_r=1&

McShane, S., and Von Glinow, M. *Organizational Behavior: Emerging Knowledge and Practice for the Real World.* New York: McGraw-Hill, 2010.

Miller, B. (Director). *Moneyball.* DVD. United States: Sony Pictures, 2011.

Mollard, K. *Outcomes and Grants.* Presented at Measurement Resources Company Managing to Outcomes Bootcamp, September 13, 2012.

Morino, M. *Leap of Reason: Managing to Outcomes in an Era of Scarcity.* Washington, DC: Venture Philanthropy Partners, 2011.

Morino, M. *Why We Need a Mass "Missouri" Movement.* July 2012. http://www.vppartners.org/learning/chairmans-corner/why-we-need-mass-missouri-movement

National Center for Charitable Statistics. Business Master File. December 2013. http://nccs.urban.org/database/overview.cfm#BMF

National Center for Chronic Disease Prevention and Health Promotion. Health-Related Quality of Life Nationwide Trend. January 2012. http://apps.nccd.cdc.gov/HRQOL/TrendV.asp?State=1&Category=1&Measure=5

Ohio Revised Code. Title 21 Ch. 51 §35. Procedures for Hearings in Juvenile Court. April 2003.

Pew Research Center. *Public Trust in the Government.* October 2013. http://www.people-press.org/2013/10/18/trust-in-government-interactive

PNC Financial Services Group. *About* PNC *Grow Up Great.* February 2014. http://www.pncgrowupgreat.com/about/index.html

Pratt, C., McGuigan, W., and Katzev, A. "Measuring Program Outcomes: Using Retrospective Pretest Methodology." *American Journal of Evaluation, 21*(3) (2000): 341–349.

Results for America. *Moneyball for Government. Moneyball Principles.* December 2013. http://moneyballforgov.com/moneyball-principles

Robert Wood Johnson Foundation. *Does Recess Equal a Better School Day?* May 2013. http://www.rwjf.org/content/dam/farm/reports/issue_briefs/2013/rwjf406050

Roeger, K., Blackwood, A., and Pettijohn, S. *The Nonprofit Almanac 2012.* Urban Institute, 2012.

Saunderson, R. "Survey Findings of the Effectiveness of Employee Recognition in the Public Sector." *Public Personnel Management, 33*(3) (2004): 255–275.

Sinex, Simon. *Start with Why: How Great Leaders Inspire Everyone to Take Action.* New York: Penguin Group, 2009.

State of Ohio. *State of Ohio Combined Charitable Campaign 2012 Resource Guide.* 2012. http://das.ohio.gov/LinkClick.aspx?fileticket=Fymwg2wVUxY%3d&tabid=585

Turock, A. *Getting Physical: How to Stick to Your Education Program.* New York: Doubleday, 1988.

U.S. Office of Management and Budget. M-13-17 Memorandum to the Heads of Departments and Agencies. July 26, 2013a.

U.S. Office of Management and Budget. Table 15.5, Total Government Expenditures by Major Category of Expenditure as Percentages of GDP: 1948–201. December 2013b. http://www.whitehouse.gov/omb/budget/Historicals

United States Census Bureau. Table 231. Educational Attainment by Selected Characteristics: 2010. *Statistical Abstract of the United States: 2012* (p. 152). Washington, DC: United States Census Bureau, 2012.

United States Constitution. Preamble. 1787.

Weiss, C. H. "Nothing as Practical as Good Theory: Exploring Theory-Based Evaluation for Comprehensive Community Initiatives for Children and Families." In J. P. Connell, A. C. Kubisch, L. B. Schorr, & C. H. Weiss (Eds.), *New Approaches to Evaluating Community Initiatives: Concepts, Methods, and Contexts* (pp. 65–92). Washington, DC: The Aspen Institute, 1995.

Willis, G. *Cognitive Interviewing: A How to Guide.* Research Triangle Institute, December 2013. http://www.hkr.se/PageFiles/35002/GordonWillis.pdf

Yost, D. *Statewide Audit of Student Attendance Data and the Accountability System.* Columbus, OH: Auditor of the State of Ohio, 2013.

Zimmermann, J., and Stevens, B. "The Use of Performance Measurement in South Carolina Nonprofits." *Nonprofit Management and Leadership, 16*(3), 2006.

Acknowledgments

There are so many people to thank in addition to the Source of all wisdom and vision, my Heavenly Father. Let me start by thanking Mario Morino for writing the book *Leap of Reason.* His message and boldness inspired me to continue the conversation on the importance of data-driven decision making in the social sector. Thank you to my mentors and cheerleaders during this process: Sara Acocks, Sandy Rees, Linda Hyden, David Sapper, David Childs, Nancy Stoll, Christy Farnbauch, Kerri Mollard, Bev Seffrin, my Leverage Mastermind members, and my Beechwold Christian Church family. Your love and support are unparalleled.

Thank you to all of my past coworkers and wonderful clients. Your dedication for impact and excellence inspires me daily. Particularly, I want to thank Barbara Riley for providing me with an example of what excellence in public sector leadership looks like. Thank you to Phyllis Panzano for taking a chance on me and introducing me to the social sector. Thanks to my team at Measurement Resources, Tiffany Lewis and Katie Van Dixhorn. This book would not have been possible if not for the work that you are doing.

This book rests on the incredible love, sacrifice, and encouragement of my husband, Matt, our four children, and our parents, Dave and Linette Chaney, and Bob and Janet Jones. You helped make the impossible possible. I am forever indebted for your service and support.

Thank you to Dawn Richerson for your beautiful words and contribution to shaping this manuscript. There are no words to express my gratitude. And finally, thanks to Alison Hankey, Rob Brandt, Mark Karmendy, Kristi Hein, and others at John Wiley & Sons for making my vision for this book a reality.

About the Author

Sheri Chaney Jones has been helping government and nonprofit organizations save money, achieve performance goals, and operate more efficiently through performance management, evaluation, and organizational development for more than fifteen years. Sheri's passion for using data to uncover each organization's unique story has saved her clients hundreds of thousands of dollars, including strategic support that helped one government organization save $250 million annually in state Medicaid spending.

Sheri has educated nonprofit and government leaders, inspiring them to take their organizations to the next level by increasing the capacity for data-driven decision making. She conducts in-person and online workshops and presentations nationally and locally. She is an instructor at Franklin University and teaches Creating Measurement Cultures at the Ohio State University John Glenn School of Public Affairs as part of the Certified Public Manager's Program.

Sheri is the president and founder of Measurement Resources Company. Previously, Sheri served as the performance center manager for the Ohio Department of Aging and the deputy director of performance evaluation for the Franklin County Domestic Relations and Juvenile Court. Sheri earned her master's degree in industrial and organizational psychology from Central Michigan University and a bachelor of science with distinction in psychology from the Ohio State University. She is a member of the American Evaluation Association and the Ohio Program Evaluators Group.

Index